The Least
You Need to Know
About DOS

The Least
You Need to Know
About DOS

Patrick Bultema

Mike Murach & Associates, Inc.

4697 West Jacquelyn Avenue
Fresno, California 93722
(209) 275-3335

Editor

Cris Allen

Graphics designer

Steve Ehlers

Other books for PC users

The Only DOS Book You'll Ever Need by Patrick Bultema and Doug Lowe

Get More from Word by Using Style Sheets by Tim Schaldach

The PC Mailing List Book: Everything you need to know to set up, use, and maintain your mailing lists on a PC by Patrick Bultema

Write Better with a PC: A publisher's guide to business and technical writing by Mike Murach

20 19 18 17 16 15 14 13 12 11 10 9 8 7 6 5 4 3 2

ISBN: 0-911625-61-5

Library of Congress Cataloging-in-Publication Data

Bultema, Patrick, 1959-
    The least you need to know about DOS/ Patrick Bultema.
      p. cm.
    Includes index.
    ISBN 0-911625-61-5 (alk. paper) :
    1. Operating systems (Computers) 2. PC-DOS (Computer file) 3. MS
-DOS (Computer file)   I. Title.
QA76.76063B854 1991
005.4'46--dc20   91-34346
                                                                CIP

Contents

VI

Preface

If you use a PC, you need to know something about DOS. Why? Because some PC functions *must* be done in DOS. Some functions can be done more efficiently in DOS. And most PC problems have to be solved in DOS.

But that doesn't mean you have to be a DOS expert to use a PC. You just need a minimum set of DOS skills. For example, you need to know how to refer to DOS directories and files from your application programs; how to start your application programs from DOS or a shell, no matter who was using the PC last; how to manage your directories and files, so you can always find the file you're looking for; how to transfer data from one PC to another using diskettes; and how to back up the hard disk data on your PC. We call this book *The Least You Need to Know about DOS* because it will teach you that minimum set of skills as quickly and easily as possible.

When you finish this book, you'll be a competent, self-sufficient PC user. You'll know how to perform the essential DOS functions as efficiently as possible. You'll know when to use DOS and when to use your application programs for everyday PC functions. Most important, you'll understand how your system works so you'll be able to solve most of your problems by yourself. As a result, you'll rarely have to get help from the PC support group, the "help desk," an 800 number, a colleague, a friend, or your spouse.

Who this book is for

When I started writing this book, I pictured readers who had little or no experience with PCs. But as I worked on the manuscript, I continued to get calls for help from experienced PC users. To my surprise, most of their questions were answered in the first eight chapters of this book. In fact, if they all had copies of this book, I could have directed them to the chapters and illustrations that answered their questions.

That's when I realized that many experienced PC users don't have the skills presented in this book. That's why they need to ask for help so often. And that's one reason why they make only minor improvements in productivity when they switch from manual methods to PCs.

With that in mind, I recommend this book for anyone who isn't comfortable with DOS. That includes people with little or no PC experience. But it also includes the tens of thousands of PC users who don't get the most from their PCs because they don't know as much about DOS as they ought to know.

In terms of hardware and software, this book is for anyone who uses DOS on a PC with a hard disk. When I refer to *DOS*, I mean any version from DOS 2.0 through DOS 5.0. When I refer to *PCs*, I mean any IBM PC, XT, AT, or PS/2, including IBM compatibles and clones. And when I say this book is for hard disk users, I mean that it focuses on hard disk PCs from page 1, so you won't have to switch your thinking from a diskette system halfway through (as you do with so many other DOS books).

What this book teaches

If you look at the table of contents, you'll see that this book is divided into five sections. The first three sections contain the eight chapters that teach the essential concepts, terms, and DOS skills all PC users must know. That's just 175 pages of information that you can read and master in a few hours.

In section 4, you can learn how to use the *shell program* that comes with DOS 5.0. If you have DOS 5.0 on your PC, you should definitely read the four chapters in this section because this shell can help you work more quickly and easily. If you don't have DOS 5.0 on your PC, you can skip this section unless you want to learn more about shell programs and DOS 5.0.

In section 5, you can learn about two special DOS files called the AUTOEXEC.BAT and CONFIG.SYS files. These files affect the way your PC starts up and operates. If your PC is already working the way you want it to, you can skip the two chapters in this section unless you want to understand more about the way your PC works.

How to use the illustrations

To help you learn more easily, this book is packed with illustrations. It has dozens of examples of DOS commands along with the DOS output from the commands. It also has dozens of screen images that show you how to use the DOS shell. Illustrations like these make it easy for you to envision how a command or function works, so you can use this book for training even if you're not at your PC.

But the illustrations are more than just learning aids. They're also the best reference materials currently available. If, for example, you want to rename a directory, figure 6-15 shows you how to do it. If you want to copy files from a hard disk to a diskette, figure 7-7 shows you how to do it. And if you want to back up the files on your hard disk, figure 9-3 shows you how to do it. Normally, when you use one of the illustrations in this book for reference, you don't even have to read the related text because the illustration tells you everything you need to know to perform the function.

In appendix A, you'll find a quick summary of the commands presented in this book. But no reference summary at the back of any book is as thorough or as effective as the illustrations that are used throughout this book. That's why the summary in appendix A refers you to the figures used in the chapters.

What if you want to know more about DOS

As I wrote this book, I assumed that your PC would be set up for you and that help would be available to you for the technical functions that are rarely needed. As a result, this book doesn't teach you how to install DOS on your system. Or how to partition and format a hard disk. Or how to prevent and detect hard disk problems. Or how to improve the performance of your PC. For most PC users, those aren't essential skills.

But if your PC hasn't been set up for you or if you just want to know more about DOS, we offer an expanded version of this book called *The Only DOS Book You'll Ever Need*. We believe that it is the ideal book for people who provide support to less technical PC users. As a result, we recommend it for every corporate help desk, for every PC support person, and for the lead technical person in every user department. If you're interested in it, you can find complete ordering information at the back of this book.

Conclusion

In the last ten years, more than 200 books have been written about DOS. But they haven't worked. If they had, the average PC user wouldn't still be struggling with DOS. Even today, the introductory DOS books are so superficial that they don't teach you what you need to know. And the "fat" DOS books are so impractical that they teach you more than you *want* to know, but less than you *need* to know.

That, of course, is why I wrote this book. I wrote it because I've watched too many smart people get frustrated by DOS and by books on DOS. I wrote it because DOS just isn't that difficult. Above all, I wrote it because I believe you can learn the essential DOS skills in just a few hours so you can use your PC without frustration forever after.

If you have any comments, questions, or criticisms, I would enjoy hearing from you. That's why there's a postage-paid comment form at the back of the book. I thank you for reading this book. And I'm confident it will help you become a more competent, self-sufficient PC user.

Patrick Bultema
Fresno, California
September, 1991

PC concepts and terms for every DOS user

Before you can use DOS effectively, you need to understand the concepts and terms that apply to the PC you're using. That's why the two chapters in this section present those concepts and terms. In chapter 1, you'll learn the *hardware* concepts and terms that every PC user should know. In chapter 2, you'll learn the *software* concepts and terms that every DOS user should know.

If you're already familiar with PC hardware, you can probably skip chapter 1. But you ought to at least skim the chapter to make sure you know the concepts and terms it presents. On the other hand, you should probably read chapter 2 even if you are familiar with PC software. This chapter presents some concepts that will make it easier for you to learn how to use DOS. It also presents some terms that will help direct you to other chapters in this book.

Chapter 1

Hardware concepts and terms for every PC user

Do you know the difference between disk storage and internal memory? Do you know the difference between standard capacity and high capacity diskettes? Do you know why you usually lose your work when a power failure takes place while you're using an application program? Are you familiar with the terms listed in the first group at the end of this chapter?

If you've answered "yes" to all of those questions, you can probably just skim this chapter to make sure you know all the information it presents. But if you've answered "no" to any of them, you should read this chapter carefully. To use a PC effectively, you need to have a basic understanding of the equipment, or *hardware*, you're using. That's why this chapter presents the hardware concepts and terms every PC user should know.

To start, you'll be introduced to the types of PCs in use today. Next, you'll learn the critical concepts and terms that apply to the external and internal components of a PC. When you complete this chapter, you'll be able to use the terms you learned to describe the components of your own PC. And you'll have the hardware background you need for learning how to make effective use of your PC's software.

An introduction to PCs, XTs, ATs, PS/2s, and IBM compatibles

In 1981, IBM introduced a microcomputer called the IBM Personal Computer, or *PC*. This system came with two diskette drives but no hard disk. Then, in 1983, IBM introduced a hard-disk PC known as the *PC/XT*, which most people refer to as just an *XT*. And in 1984, IBM introduced an improved PC known as the *PC/AT*, which most people refer to as just an *AT*. Today, all three types of personal computers can be referred to as PCs, but if you want to be more specific, you can refer to your system as an XT or an AT.

You can also use the term PC to refer to systems that aren't manufactured by IBM. These machines are referred to as *IBM compatibles* or *IBM clones*. PC compatibles are popular because they are either more powerful or less expensive than comparable systems made by IBM.

In 1987, IBM introduced a new type of personal computer called the *PS/2*. The PS/2 is available in several models that cover a wide range of cost and performance. However, all of the PS/2 models can be referred to as PCs because they too are compatible with the PC. Because other manufacturers had difficulty copying the PS/2s, PS/2 compatibles didn't start to appear until early 1990.

As I explained in the preface, this book is designed for people who use PCs that have hard disks. But it doesn't matter whether you have an XT, an AT, a PS/2, or an IBM compatible. Although one PC may be faster than another, the same basic principles apply.

The physical components of a typical PC

Figure 1-1 shows a typical PC. As you can see, it consists of five physical components: a printer, a monitor, a keyboard, a mouse, and a systems unit. In a laptop PC, the monitor, keyboard, and systems unit are combined into a single carrying case, but on most other systems these units are separate and can be purchased separately. Because you're probably familiar with these five units already, I'll just describe them briefly.

The systems unit   The *systems unit* is the unit that the other physical components are connected to. This unit can also be referred to as the *electronics*

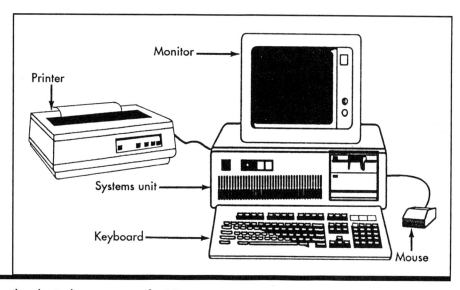

Figure 1-1   The physical components of a PC

unit or the *systems chassis*, but I'll refer to it as the *systems unit* throughout this book. As you will soon learn, this unit contains the processor that controls the operations of the PC. In contrast, the four other physical units are input and output devices.

The monitor   The *monitor* is an output device that can also be referred to as a *display*, a *screen*, or a *CRT. Monochrome monitors* can display only one color, which is usually green or amber on a dark background, but *color monitors* can display a variety of colors. Although most AT class and PS/2 systems are sold with color monitors today, there are still many XT class systems in use with monochrome monitors.

Like a television set, a monitor uses dot patterns to display characters and images. The more dots a monitor can display, the higher its *resolution* and the sharper its image. Not surprisingly, high-resolution monitors cost more than low-resolution monitors, just as color monitors cost more than monochrome monitors.

When a monitor is in operation, its images are controlled by an electronic circuit card within the systems unit. This circuit card is called a *display adapter*. If you buy a complete PC, the display adapter that goes with

Acronym	Adapter name	Standard resolution	Standard number of colors on screen
MDA	Monochrome Display	720x348	N/A
CGA	Color Graphics	640x200	4 of 16 available
EGA	Enhanced Graphics	640x350	16 of 64 available
VGA	Video Graphics Array	640x480	16 of 256 available
XGA	Extended Graphics Array	1,024x768	256 available

Figure 1-2   A summary of display adapter characteristics

the monitor is usually installed for you, so you aren't aware of it. But if you buy a replacement monitor for your system, you get the monitor and the display adapter as separate components.

Today, display adapters for PCs are available in the five standard forms summarized in figure 1-2. The *MDA* is the basic monochrome display. The other four display adapters provide progressively better color graphics. *CGA* was IBM's first color display adapter. Then, IBM introduced the *EGA* adapter. Because the EGA provided higher resolution and more colors than CGA, it quickly became the standard color display adapter. When *VGA* was introduced, it provided even higher resolution and more colors than previous adapters. As a result, most video adapters sold today are VGA-compatible. The next development was *XGA*. At the time this book was written, XGA was available only for high-end PS/2 systems. In the next two years, we'll find out if the XGA becomes the standard monitor that's sold with new PCs.

The keyboard   The *keyboard* is the main input device of a PC. Although it resembles the keyboard of a typewriter, a PC keyboard has more keys. For instance, figure 1-3 shows the two most common keyboard arrangements for PCs. Although the 84-key keyboard was the original keyboard for the AT, the 101-key keyboard is now a standard component of all PS/2s and most other PCs.

If you study the keyboards in figure 1-3, you can see that they include several types of keys. First, the keyboards include a full set of typewriter keys. Second, they include a numeric pad on the right side of the keyboard in the same arrangement as the ten keys on a calculator, plus a decimal point key. Third, both keyboards include ten Function keys numbered from F1 through F10, and the 101-key keyboard includes two additional Function keys numbered F11 and F12. Last, the keyboards include some special control keys such as the Escape key (Esc), the Control key (Ctrl), the Alternate key (Alt), the Page-up and the Page-down keys, and so on.

The Arrow keys move the *cursor* on the screen of a monitor. The cursor is the underline or highlight that identifies a specific character or area of a screen. As a result, the Arrow keys are often called *cursor control keys*.

If you have an 84-key keyboard on your PC, you have to know how the Num-Lock key works on it. Within the ten-key numeric pad of that keyboard, every key but the 5-key has a control function. For instance, the 7-key is also the Home key; the 8-key is also the Up arrow (↑) key; and the 9-key is also the Page-up (Pg-up) key. Then, if the Num-Lock light is on, each of the keys represents its decimal value or the decimal point. If the Num-Lock light is off, each of the keys represents its control function. To turn the Num-Lock light on or off, you press the Num-Lock key.

Because this doubling up of keyboard meanings can cause some entry errors, many people prefer the 101-key keyboard shown in figure 1-3. Here, the control functions of the ten-key pad are duplicated on control keys that are located between the typewriter keys and the numeric pad. Then, if you keep the Num-Lock light lit, you can use the control pad for control functions and the numeric pad for numeric entries.

If you've been using a word processing program, a spreadsheet program, or some other application program, you should already know how the function and control keys apply to that program. Then, in chapter 4 of this book, you'll learn how a few of these keys apply to DOS.

The mouse   A *mouse* is a small hand-held input device that was popularized by Apple's *Macintosh* computer. Although the original PC was not designed for the use of a mouse, mice have become more common on PCs in recent years. Today, most mice come with two buttons you can press, but there are also three-button mice.

The 84-key IBM-AT keyboard

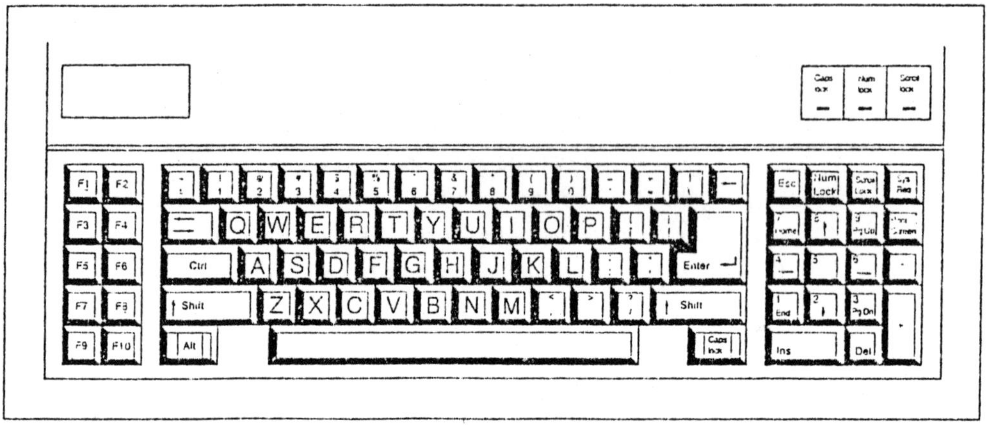

The enchanced 101-key keyboard

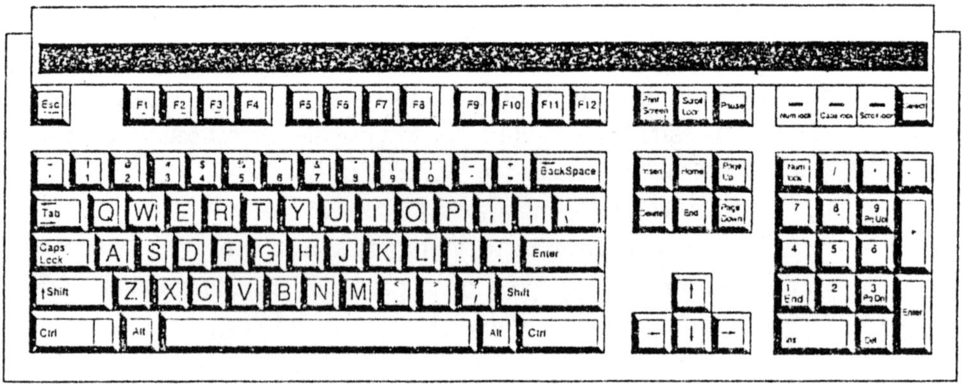

Figure 1-3   The two most common types of PC keyboards

If you've ever used a mouse or seen one used, you know that it's just a pointing device. When you move the mouse across a table top (or across a *mouse pad* on the table top), a pointer on the monitor moves in the same direction. This pointer on the monitor is called the *mouse cursor*. With a little practice, you can easily and quickly move the mouse cursor anywhere on the screen. Then, you can click the buttons on top of the mouse to perform various actions.

Exactly how you use a mouse, though, depends on the software you're using. And if your software doesn't support the use of a mouse, you can't use a mouse at all. Although many recent releases of software packages are designed to support a mouse, many programs still don't support one. That's why mice are just becoming popular on PCs.

The printer   The *printer* of a PC is an output device. Although many different kinds of printers have been developed, the most widely used printers today are dot-matrix printers and laser printers. Figure 1-4 illustrates some printing that has been done by these two types of printers.

Dot-matrix printers work by striking small pins against an inked ribbon. The resulting dots form images or characters on the paper. For instance, a 9-pin printer uses nine pins to print each character of data, while a 24-pin printer uses twenty-four pins to print each character. Because a 24-pin printer uses many more pins for each character than a 9-pin printer, its characters are sharper than those of a 9-pin printer. Today, most dot-matrix printers are either 9-pin or 24-pin printers.

When dot-matrix printers print text, they can do so in two different *print modes*: *draft mode* and *text mode*. For a 9-pin dot-matrix printer, the text mode is called *near letter quality mode*, and for 24-pin printers the text mode is called *letter quality mode*. When a printer can print in two modes, it prints more quickly in draft mode. For instance, my 24-pin printer prints at only 72 cps (characters per second) in letter quality mode, but it prints at 216 cps in draft mode. However, if you look at figure 1-4, you can see that the print quality of text mode is far superior to that of draft mode.

Today, dot-matrix printers can print text characters in more than one size and more than one typeface (or *font*), as shown in figure 1-4. They can print type styles such as italics and boldface. They can print graphics such as charts and diagrams. And they can handle cut forms as well as continuous

---

Printing done by a 24-Pin Matrix Printer

This is a sample of *draft mode* printing at 10 characters
per inch.
This is a sample of *draft mode* printing at 12 characters per
inch.

This is a sample of *text mode* printing in the Roman font
at 10 characters per inch.
This is a sample of *text mode* printing in the Roman font at 12
characters per inch.

This is a sample of *text mode* printing in the Sans Serif
font at 10 characters per inch.
This is a sample of *text mode* printing in the Sans Serif font
at 12 characters per inch.

Printing done by a Laser Printer

This sample shows why a laser printer is preferred for *desktop publishing applications.*
Because of its higher resolution, laser printing is easier to read than dot matrix printing.
In fact, most people can't distinguish text printed on a high-resolution laser printer (1,000
dots per inch or more) from text printed by a typesetter. In addition, laser printers offer a
wider variety of text fonts than dot matrix printers, which makes them even more useful
for desktop publishing applications.

Figure 1-4   Printing samples from two types of PC printers

forms. In general, the more you pay for a dot-matrix printer, the faster it
prints and the more features it comes with.

In contrast to dot-matrix printers, *laser printers* work on the same princi-
ple as photocopiers. The laser in a laser printer never actually touches the
paper. Instead, it flashes patterns of dots onto a rotating drum, which picks
up ink powder and deposits it on the page. Today, most laser printers print
with 300 dpi (dots per inch), but 1200-dpi printers are also available. Natu-
rally, the print quality (or resolution) of a laser printer depends on the
number of dots it prints per inch, and high-resolution printers are more expensive than low-resolution printers.

For graphics, laser printing is usually far superior to dot-matrix printing. For text, laser printers provide more type fonts and sizes than dot-matrix printers. And for both graphics and text, a laser printer is usually faster. That's why laser printers are commonly used for desktop publishing and graphics applications.

The primary components of the systems unit

If you've ever opened up the systems unit of a PC, you know it's full of electronic components. These components are attached to electronic cards that are inserted into the unit. Although you don't have to understand how any of these components work, you should have a conceptual idea of what the primary components of the systems unit are and what those components do.

Figure 1-5 is a conceptual drawing of the components of a typical PC. Within the systems unit, you can see four primary components: the diskette drive or drives, the hard disk, internal memory, and the processor.

The diskette drive or drives   You're probably familiar with diskettes and diskette drives already. The *diskette* is the recording medium on which data is stored, and the *diskette drive* is the device that writes data on the diskette and reads data from the diskette. Diskettes are also called *floppy disks*, but I'll refer to them as *diskettes* throughout this book.

You can see the front of a diskette drive on the front of the systems unit shown in figure 1-1. To use a diskette, you insert the diskette into the slot on the diskette drive and close the drive's latch (assuming the drive has a latch, not all do). If a PC has two diskette drives, they can be in a left and right arrangement, or they can be in a top and bottom arrangement.

Figure 1-6 shows the two sizes of diskettes that can be used with PCs. Originally, all PCs, XTs, and ATs used 5-1/4 inch diskettes, and all PS/2s used the newer 3-1/2 inch diskettes. Today, however, you can install a diskette drive for either type of diskette on an XT, an AT, or a PS/2.

To complicate matters, both types of diskettes come in two storage capacities: *standard capacity* and *high capacity*. These capacities are measured in *bytes* of data. For practical purposes, you can think of one byte of data as one character of data, and you can think of a character as a letter, a number, or a special character such as #, %, or &. Thus, ten bytes of diskette

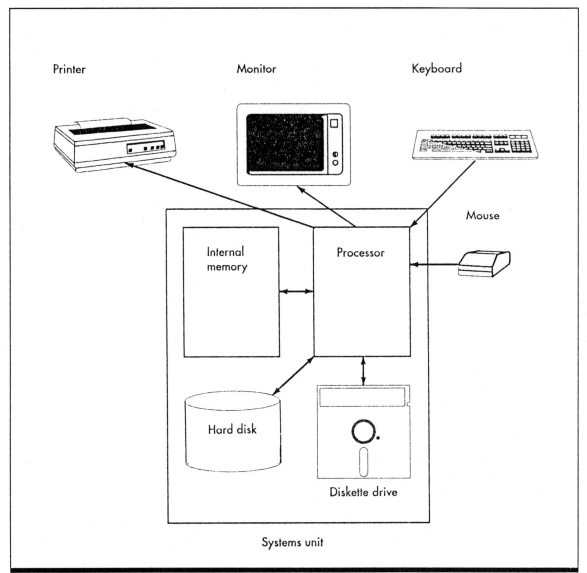

Figure 1-5   The internal components of the systems unit

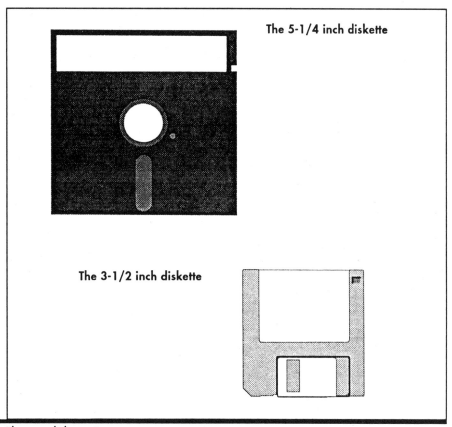

The 5-1/4 inch diskette

The 3-1/2 inch diskette

Figure 1-6   The two diskette sizes

storage are required to store the word *impossible*; four bytes are required to store the number *4188*; and two bytes are required to store *$9*.

For 5-1/4 inch diskettes, the standard capacity is 360,000 bytes, or 360KB (*K* stands for 1,000, *B* stands for bytes, and *KB* stands for *kilobyte*, which is approximately one thousand bytes). In contrast, the high capacity is 1,200KB, or 1.2MB (*M* stands for 1,000,000, *B* stands for byte, and *MB* stands for *megabyte*, which is approximately one million bytes). For 3-1/2 inch diskettes, the standard capacity is 720KB, and the high capacity is 1.44MB.

Figure 1-7 summarizes the diskette sizes and capacities. Because the labelling for diskettes is often confusing, this figure also lists the common

Size	Capacity	Common labelling notation
5-1/4"	360KB	5-1/4" Double-Sided Double-Density 5-1/4" DSDD
5-1/4"	1.2MB	5-1/4" Double-Sided High-Density 5-1/4" DSHD
3-1/2"	720KB	3-1/2" Double-Sided Double-Density 3-1/2" 2DD 3-1/2" 1.0M formatted capacity
3-1/2"	1.44MB	3-1/2" Double-Sided High-Density 3-1/2" 2HD 3-1/2" 2.0M formatted capacity

Figure 1-7   A summary of diskette characteristics

labelling designations for each type of diskette. Notice, for example, that the standard capacity diskettes are called *double density* diskettes, and the high capacity diskettes are called *high density* diskettes.

When you use a diskette to transfer data from one system to another, you must make sure you're using a diskette that is the right size and capacity for the system you're transferring the data to. In general, a 5-1/4 inch diskette drive on an XT can only read and write standard capacity diskettes. However, a 5-1/4 inch drive on an AT can read and write diskettes in either standard or high capacity. As a result, you must use standard capacity diskettes to transfer data between an XT and an AT. Similarly, a standard capacity 3-1/2 inch drive can only read and write standard capacity diskettes, but a high capacity drive can read and write diskettes in either standard or high capacity. So you must use a standard capacity 3-1/2 inch diskette to transfer data between a standard and a high capacity drive.

Today, a PC usually has one or two diskette drives even if it has a hard disk. Although you probably won't use diskettes much on a hard-disk system for running programs, they are commonly used for backing up the data on the hard disk. They are also used for transferring data from one PC to another.

For maximum compatibility between systems, some PCs have both a 3-1/2 inch drive and a 5-1/4 inch drive.

The hard disk   Like a diskette drive, a *hard disk* stores data on a disk, and it uses the same basic storage technology. However, unlike a diskette drive, the recording medium and the drive are sealed together in a single unit within the systems unit. As a result, a hard disk can't be removed from a PC the way a diskette can be removed. That's why hard disks can also be called *fixed disks*. In this book, though, I'll only use the term *hard disk*.

Today, most hard disks have a capacity of 20MB or more, and you can buy hard disks with capacities of 320MB or more. To put that into perspective, consider that one megabyte of disk storage can hold about 350 pages of word processing text. So a 30MB hard disk can hold about 10,000 pages of text. In contrast, a 360KB diskette can hold only about 125 pages. To look at it another way, a 40MB disk can store the equivalent of about 110 diskettes that have a capacity of 360KB.

To give you some idea of how a hard disk works, figure 1-8 provides a drawing of a typical hard disk after the protective cover has been removed. This device records data on both sides of three disk platters that are stacked on a spindle. The data is recorded on the disk surfaces in a series of concentric circles called *tracks*.

As shown in figure 1-9, each track on each disk surface is divided into a fixed number of *sectors*. In general, each sector of a hard disk can store 512 bytes of data, and most disks have 17 sectors per track. At 820 tracks per surface, that's 13,940 sectors per surface. Then, if the hard disk has three platters and six recording surfaces, the entire disk has 83,640 sectors. At 512 bytes per sector, that's more than 40MB of data.

To write data on a disk durface or to read data from it, the access mechanism of a disk drive has one *read/write head* (or just *head*) for each surface. Then, when the access mechanism is moved to a track, all of the heads are moved at once. If, for example, a disk drive has three platters and six disk surfaces, it has six read/write heads that access six tracks. These six tracks can be referred to as one *cylinder* of data. If, for example, the access mechanism is moved to the 75th track, all six tracks in the 75th cylinder can be read or written without moving the access mechanism again.

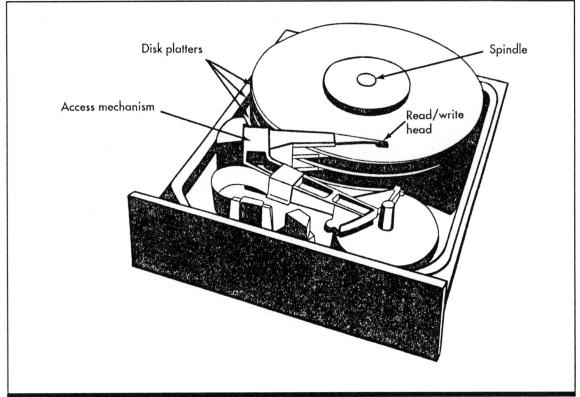

Figure 1-8   The physical components of a hard disk

Today, *access speeds* for hard disks are typically from 19 to 65 *milli-seconds* (thousandths of a second). That means it takes less than one-tenth of a second to move the access mechanism to the track that contains the data that needs to be accessed. Once a sector has been accessed, it can be read or written by the hard disk.

If this sounds like more than you need to know about hard disks, it probably is. I present this information because you will encounter terms like *track, sector, head,* and *cylinder* when you use DOS to perform disk operations. That doesn't mean, however, that you need to understand how a disk drive works. You just need to be familiar with these terms.

Now that you're familiar with hard disks, you should realize that the same basic concepts and terms apply to diskettes and diskette drives. Both

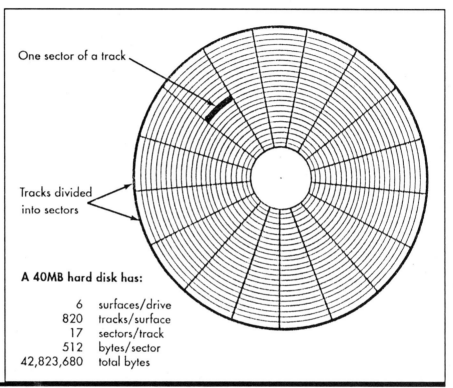

One sector of a track

Tracks divided into sectors

A 40MB hard disk has:

6	surfaces/drive
820	tracks/surface
17	sectors/track
512	bytes/sector
42,823,680	total bytes

Figure 1-9   Tracks and sectors on one surface of a hard disk

the 5-1/4 inch and 3-1/2 inch diskettes have a single disk platter, and data can be recorded on both sides of the diskette. Both types of diskettes have tracks on each surface, and the tracks are divided into sectors. However, the diskettes have many fewer sectors and tracks than a hard disk, so the capacity of a diskette is only a fraction of the capacity of a hard disk. Similarly, because a diskette drive stops between operations and a hard disk keeps rotating, the access speed of a hard disk drive is hundreds of times faster than that of a diskette drive. In practice, this means you are rarely delayed for more than a second or two by the operations of a hard disk, but diskette operations are often so slow that they're frustrating.

Because you can store so much data on a hard disk, you have to manage a hard disk more carefully than you manage diskettes. In particular, you have to use directories to organize the data on a hard disk. And you have to back up the hard-disk data so you won't lose it in the event of a hardware or software problem. As you read this book, you'll realize that one of its major purposes is to teach you skills that help you get the most from your hard disk.

Internal memory   Before your PC can operate on the data that is stored on a diskette or a hard disk, the data must be read into the *internal memory* of the system. This memory is made up of electronic components that are mounted in the systems unit. This memory can also be called *internal storage* or *RAM* (for *Random Access Memory*), but I'll refer to it as *internal memory* throughout this book.

Like diskette or hard disk storage, internal memory is measured in kilobytes or megabytes. Although the original PC was typically sold with either 64KB, 128KB, or 256KB of memory, an XT or an AT today is normally sold with 512KB or 640KB of internal memory. And some of the newer, more powerful PCs are sold with 1MB, 2MB, or 4MB of internal memory.

In contrast to the access speeds for hard disks, which are measured in milliseconds (thousandths of a second), the access speeds for internal memory are measured in *nanoseconds* (billionths of a second). This means data can be accessed thousands of times faster in internal memory than it can be in hard-disk storage. From a practical point of view, this means operations that take place in internal memory happen so fast that you're not aware of them. In contrast, you're often aware of hard-disk operations and you're usually aware of diskette operations.

Because a program must be stored in internal memory before it can be used, each program requires a specific amount of internal memory. For instance, *WordPerfect 5.0* requires a PC with at least 384KB of internal memory, and version 2.2 of *Lotus 1-2-3* requires at least 512KB of internal memory. However, because the PC was originally designed for a maximum of 640KB, only a few programs take advantage of memory that exceeds 640KB.

When you're using a PC, your current work is stored in the internal memory of the PC. However, the data stored in internal memory is erased when the power for the PC is turned off, either deliberately or due to power failure. That's why you must store your work to diskette or hard disk storage before you turn your PC off. Otherwise, your work is lost. In contrast to internal memory, diskettes and hard disks retain the data that has been stored on them whether or not the power is on.

The processor   If you look back to figure 1-5, you can see that all of the components I've described so far are connected to the *processor*. When a program is in operation, the processor controls all of the other components of the PC by executing the instructions of the program. Other terms for a processor are *microprocessor*, *central processing unit*, or *CPU*, but I'll use the term *processor* throughout this book.

The basic function of the processor is to execute any of the 100 or so instructions a PC is designed to perform. Some of these instructions perform arithmetic calculations like adding or multiplying. Other instructions make decisions by comparing two values and acting on the result of the comparison. Still other instructions communicate with devices like the keyboard, monitor, or hard disk.

Today, PC processors are identified by the *microprocessor chip* they're based upon. In an IBM PC or PC compatible, all of the processors are based on microprocessor chips that were originally manufactured by Intel with names like the 8086, the 8088, the 80286, the 80386, and the 80486 chip. The shortened versions of the last three chip names are the 286, the 386, and the 486.

Because the processor controls all of the operations of a PC, the speed of the processor can have an important effect on the speed of your PC. One measure of processor speed is *clock speed*. The clock in your computer is an electronic circuit that generates electronic pulses used to synchronize the operation of the computer's circuits. In general, the faster those pulses are generated, the faster the computer operates. The clock speed of the original IBM PC was 4.77 million cycles per second, or 4.77 Mhz (*Mhz* stands for *Megahertz*). Today, the clock speed for most 8088-based systems is from 8 to 10Mhz. The clock speed for most 286-based systems is from 10 to 20Mhz. And the clock speed for most 386-based systems is from 16 to 33Mhz. As I write this, the fastest 486-based systems have clock speeds of 50Mhz.

You should realize, though, that clock speed isn't the only factor that influences your processor's speed. Which processor chip your system is based on makes a big difference too. For example, the 80286 is inherently faster then the 8088. Thus, an 80286-based system running at a clock speed of 8Mhz is about twice as fast as an 8088-based system running at the same clock speed. Similarly, an 80386-based system running at 20Mhz is about twice as fast as an 80286-based system running at the same speed.

Although this simplified explanation of processor speed is probably more than you want to know, you should realize that the subject is far more complicated than I've indicated. Also, whenever you consider processor speed, you should realize that it is only one measure of the speed of your PC. When it comes to getting work done, the speed of your hard disk is often more important than the speed of your processor.

Other components of the systems unit

The components I just presented are the primary ones of a systems unit. However, a typical systems unit also contains dozens of other components. In this book, I won't try to describe all of them because you don't need to know what they do. You should, however, be familiar with conventional memory, extended memory, expanded memory, and the real-time clock.

Conventional, extended, and expanded memory   The first 640KB of internal memory can be referred to as *conventional memory*. If your PC doesn't have a full 640KB of conventional memory, and one of your programs requires more memory than your PC has, you can add memory to your system. On some PCs, you can add memory by installing memory chips into the main electrical board (the *motherboard*) of your systems unit. For others, you can add memory by installing a memory expansion card into an *expansion slot* in the systems unit.

Since the original PC was designed for a maximum memory of 640K, most programs aren't designed to use more memory than that. But some are. These programs use either *extended memory* or *expanded memory*. For instance, version 2 of *Lotus 1-2-3* can take advantage of expanded memory, while version 3 can take advantage of extended or expanded memory. You should realize, though, that there is a difference between extended and expanded memory. So before you add memory, you must make sure it's the right kind for the program that will use it and the right kind for your PC.

Then, to complicate matters further, there are two kinds of expanded memory: *EMS*, or *Expanded Memory Support*; and *EEMS*, or *Enhanced Expanded Memory Support*. Here again, before you buy a card for expanded memory, you must make sure it's the right kind of expanded memory card for the program and the right kind for your PC.

The real-time clock   On the older PCs, you usually have to enter the current date and time when you start the system. Today, however, most PCs include a battery powered clock that keeps track of the current date and time. So the date and time stay current even when the PC is shut off. Although there isn't any standard name for this clock, you'll often hear it referred to as a *real-time clock*.

The evolution of PC hardware

To give you some idea of how the PC has evolved, figure 1-10 summarizes some of the major PC developments of the 1980s. As you can see, we've gone from 8088 processors that run at 4.77Mhz to 486s that run at 50Mhz. This is an improvement in processing power of several hundred times. Similarly, the capacity of today's hard disk is almost one thousand times greater than the dual diskette capacity of the original PC. Along with greater disk capacity has come greater access speed. The latest class of PC can access the hard disk almost ten times faster than the original XT.

We've also gone from low-resolution, monochrome monitors to high-resolution, color monitors. From cumbersome 84-key keyboards to enhanced 101-key keyboards. From slow, single-font, dot-matrix printers to fast, multi-font, dot-matrix printers, and to laser printers. We've also seen the development of a faster cursor control device: the mouse.

Since the PS/2 with its several models was announced in 1987, it has become less common to refer to a PC as an XT, an AT, or a PS/2. Instead, a PC is likely to be identified by the processor chip it uses. These days, a PC is often referred to as a 286, a 386SX, or a 386 system. To fully describe a system, you often need to specify the processor, the type of monitor, the capacity of the hard disk, and maybe even the type of printer you're using.

Some perspective on hardware

Throughout this chapter, I've tried to simplify the concepts and to keep the number of new terms to a minimum. I've tried to present only those hardware concepts you need to know in order to use your software effectively.

Class	First Year	Processor Chip	Processor Speed	Hard Disk Access Speed
PC	1981	8088	4.77Mhz	Dual diskette
XT	1983	8088	4.77-10Mhz	65-100ms
Compaq Deskpro	1983	8086	4.77-10Mhz	65-100ms
AT	1984	80286	6-20Mhz	28-65ms
386	1986	80386	16-33Mhz	As low as 9ms
PS/2 Model 30	1987	8086	8-10Mhz	Dual diskette
PS/2 Model 50	1987	80286	8-20Mhz	20-80ms
PS/2 Model 80	1987	80386	16-20Mhz	20-40ms
386SX	1988	80386	16-20Mhz	20-40ms
486	1989	80486	25-33Mhz	As low as 9ms
486	1991	80486	50Mhz	Lower than 9ms

Figure 1-10   The evolution of the PC

I've also tried to present only those terms that you're most likely to encounter in PC magazines and manuals.

If you've ever talked with a computer salesperson, you probably realize that you need to know all these terms and more to discuss hardware features. You also need to know all these terms and more to read many of the articles and advertisements in PC magazines. Once you master the concepts and terms presented in this chapter, though, most of what you hear or read should make sense to you. And you should feel confident enough to ask questions about any terms you don't understand.

On the other hand, this chapter presents more than you need to know if all you want to do is use your PC effectively. That's why I've divided the terms listed at the end of this chapter into two groups. If you're familiar with the terms in the first group and you can identify and describe the nine PC components shown in figure 1-5, you're ready to go on to the next chapter. There, you'll learn the software concepts and terms that every DOS user needs to know.

Terms you should be familiar with before you continue

PC
XT
AT
PS/2
systems unit
monitor
keyboard
cursor
cursor control key
mouse
mouse cursor
printer
dot-matrix printer
laser printer
diskette
diskette drive
standard capacity diskette
high capacity diskette
byte
kilobyte (KB)
megabyte (MB)
hard disk
track
sector
read/write head

head
cylinder
internal memory
processor
conventional memory
extended memory
expanded memory
real-time clock

Other terms presented in this chapter

hardware
PC/XT
PC/AT
IBM compatible
IBM clone
electronics unit
systems chassis
display
screen
CRT
monochrome monitor
color monitor
resolution
display adapter
MDA
CGA
EGA
VGA
XGA
mouse pad
print mode
draft mode
text mode
near letter quality mode
letter quality mode
font
floppy disk
double density diskette
high density diskette
fixed disk
access speed
millisecond (ms)
internal storage

RAM
Random Access Memory
nanosecond (ns)
microprocessor
central processing unit
CPU
microprocessor chip
clock speed
Megahertz (Mhz)
motherboard
expansion slot
EMS
Extended Memory Support
EEMS
Enhanced Extended Memory Support

Chapter 2

Software concepts and terms for every DOS user

Do you know the difference between an application program and an operating system program? Do you know what the primary functions of DOS are? Do you know what happens when you use the DOS command processor to start an application program? Do you know you can buy utility programs that will help you perform some functions more quickly and easily than you can with DOS?

Unless you can answer an unqualified "yes" to those questions, you should read this chapter before you go on to the next one. To use a PC effectively, you must have a basic understanding of PC software. That's why this chapter presents the software concepts and terms every DOS user should know.

The term *software* refers to the *programs* that direct the operations of the hardware. This chapter starts by introducing you to the two primary types of PC programs. Next, you'll learn what DOS is and what its primary functions are. Then, you'll learn how DOS has evolved since 1981, and you'll get some perspective on the utility programs that improve upon DOS. When you complete this chapter, you'll have the background you need for learning the specific DOS skills that are taught in the rest of this book.

The two types of programs that every PC requires

In broad terms, PC programs can be divided into two types: *application programs* and *operating system programs*. To do work on your PC, you need both types of programs. In case you're not already familiar with both types, here's more information about each.

Application programs   An *application program* is a program you use to do your work. It lets you *apply* your PC to tasks like writing letters or preparing profit-and-loss statements. Today, thousands of application programs are available for PCs, so you can find one that's appropriate for just about any job you want to do.

Figure 2-1 lists three of the most popular types of application programs: word processing, spreadsheet, and database programs. This figure also lists some of the most popular programs of each type. If you've used a PC at all, you've probably used one or more of these programs.

When you use a *word processing program*, you prepare *documents* like letters, memos, or reports. When you use a *spreadsheet program*, you prepare *spreadsheets* like budgets or profit projections. And when you use a *database program*, you create and maintain a *database* like an employee, customer, or vendor database. Once you establish a database, you can extract information from it in the form of reports and other documents.

Word processing, spreadsheet, and database programs are considered to be *general-purpose programs* because you can use them for so many different jobs. But many other kinds of general-purpose programs are also available. For instance, *graphics programs* let you create charts, diagrams, and other graphic presentations. *Desktop publishing programs* let you create documents with published quality. And *integrated programs* combine the features of several different types of general-purpose programs. *Microsoft Works*, for example, provides word processing, spreadsheet, database, graphics, and communications features, all in one program.

In contrast to general-purpose programs, some programs are designed for special, narrowly-defined purposes. For example, you can buy a program that will help you manage rental properties, a program that will help you manage accounts receivables for a retail business, and a program that will analyze the

Program type	Examples	Operates upon
Word processing	*WordPerfect* *Microsoft Word*	Documents
Spreadsheet	*Lotus 1-2-3* *Quattro Pro*	Spreadsheets
Database	*dBase IV* *Paradox* *Q&A*	Records within a database

Figure 2-1   Three of the most popular types of application programs

quality of your writing. In fact, so many application programs are available today, it's difficult to categorize them.

Operating system programs   An *operating system* is a program that lets your application programs run on your PC. For instance, an operating system lets you load an application program into internal memory so you can use that application program. An operating system also provides functions that let your application programs access the data on a disk drive, print on a printer, and so on.

The concept of an operating system is elusive because much of what the operating system does goes on without you knowing about it. When you save a word processing document on a hard disk, for example, it's the operating system, not the application program, that writes the document on the disk. In other words, your application program communicates with the operating system without you knowing about it. Without the operating system, your application program wouldn't work.

Figure 2-2 presents the two main operating systems you can use on a single-user PC today: *DOS* and *OS/2*. If you review the characteristics listed for each, you'll soon realize that OS/2 is the more advanced operating system. It can use more of a PC's internal memory; it can run several application pro-

Operating system	Characteristics	Special requirements
DOS	640KB memory limit One application at a time Simple user interface called the command prompt	None
OS/2	16MB memory limit Multi-tasking capabilities Graphical user interface called the *Presentation Manager*	80286 processor 2MB of internal memory Programs written just for OS/2

Figure 2-2   The primary operating systems for single-user PCs

grams at once; and it provides a graphical user interface called the *Presentation Manager*. In contrast, DOS can use a maximum of just 640KB of internal memory; it can run just one application program at a time; and it has a simple user interface that consists of a command prompt.

On the other hand, OS/2 requires a 80286 processor or better, 2MB or more of internal memory, and application programs that are written specifically for OS/2. Furthermore, most PC users don't need the additional capabilities OS/2 provides. And, for those users who do, a Microsoft product called *Windows* adds most of the capabilities of OS/2 to PCs that run under DOS. In fact, the capabilities that DOS provides are more than adequate for most PC users. That's why DOS is used on the vast majority of PCs in use today. And that's why most people believe that DOS will continue to be the dominant operating system for several years to come.

DOS (pronounced *doss*) is short for *Disk Operating System*. This operating system is called *MS-DOS* when it's sold by the Microsoft Corporation, and it's called *PC-DOS* when it's sold by the IBM Corporation. To complicate matters, companies like Compaq Corporation and WYSE have their own versions of DOS. Fortunately, all of the DOS versions are essentially the same, so this book will teach you how to use DOS no matter whose version you're using. From this point on, I'll use the term *DOS* to refer to all versions of DOS.

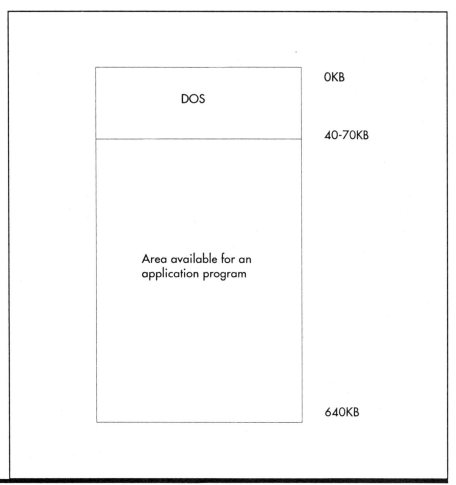

Figure 2-3   The contents of internal memory after DOS has been loaded into it

What DOS provides

When you turn on a hard disk PC, it starts by loading a portion of DOS from the hard disk into internal memory. This portion of DOS occupies from 40 to 70KB bytes of internal memory, as shown in the schematic drawing in figure 2-3. Because this portion of DOS remains in internal memory until you turn the PC off, DOS functions are available to you and your application programs whenever your PC is running.

```
c:\>
```

Figure 2-4   A typical DOS command prompt

In general terms, DOS provides three types of functions: command processing, DOS services, and DOS commands. Since all three are critical to the operation of your PC, I'll introduce you to each of them now.

Command processing   The DOS *command processor* is loaded into internal memory when you start your PC. When the command processor is in control of the system, it displays a *command prompt* like the one shown in figure 2-4. Often, this command prompt is displayed after your PC finishes its start-up procedure.

When the command prompt is displayed, the command processor is waiting for you to enter a *command*. For instance, you normally enter the letters *wp* to start *WordPerfect* and the numbers *123* to start *Lotus 1-2-3*. You can also start DOS commands from the command prompt, as you will learn in a moment.

Figure 2-5 illustrates how DOS uses the command processor to switch from one application program to another. When you start your PC, the DOS command processor is loaded into the internal memory of your system along with some other parts of DOS. This portion of DOS is referred to as the *resident* portion of DOS, or *resident DOS*, because it resides in internal memory whenever the PC is in operation. This is indicated by the contents of internal memory in step 1 of the figure.

When you enter *wp* at the command prompt, as shown in step 1 of figure 2-5, the command processor loads *WordPerfect* from the hard disk into internal memory, as shown in step 2. This is called *loading a program*. Then, the command processor passes control of the PC to the first instruction of the *WordPerfect* program. When you instruct *WordPerfect* to retrieve a document, it copies the document file from the disk into internal memory. This is called *loading a file*. When you finish your word processing activities and exit the *WordPerfect* program, control is passed back to the command processor, as shown in step 3. Then, the memory used by *WordPerfect* and the document is released, and the command processor waits for another command from the PC user.

When you enter *123* at the command prompt as shown in step 4 of figure 2-5, the command processor loads *Lotus 1-2-3* into internal memory as shown in step 5. Then, the command processor passes control to the first instruction of the application program. When you finish your spreadsheet work and exit the *Lotus* program, control is passed back to the command processor as shown in step 6. Then, the command processor waits for your next command. In this way, the command processor lets you switch from one program to the next.

DOS services   When an application program is running, DOS provides *DOS services* to the program. Some of the most important of these services are called *input/output services*, or *I/O services*. These services make it possible for the application program to receive input from the input devices of the PC and to give output through the output devices of the PC.

Figure 2-6 shows how DOS provides I/O services when an application program wants to retrieve data from a hard disk. Here, you can see that an application program doesn't access disk data directly. Instead, it requests DOS to do the work for it. In step 1, the application program asks DOS to retrieve data from the disk. In step 2, DOS directs the disk device to read the requested data. In step 3, the disk device reads the data and sends it back to

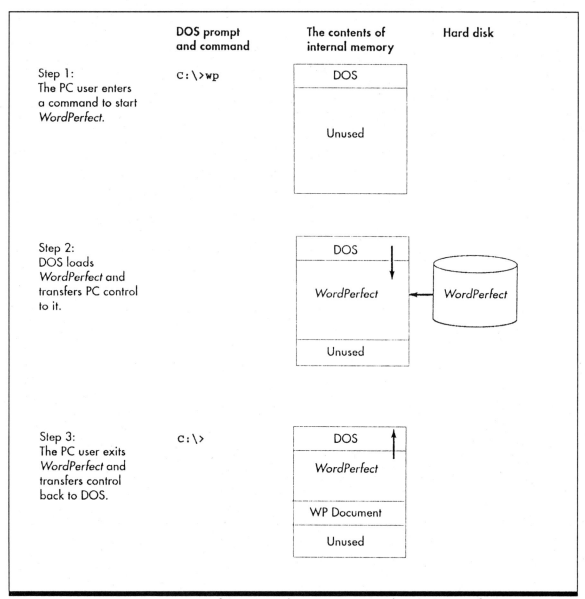

Figure 2-5   How DOS goes from one application program to the next (part 1 of 2)

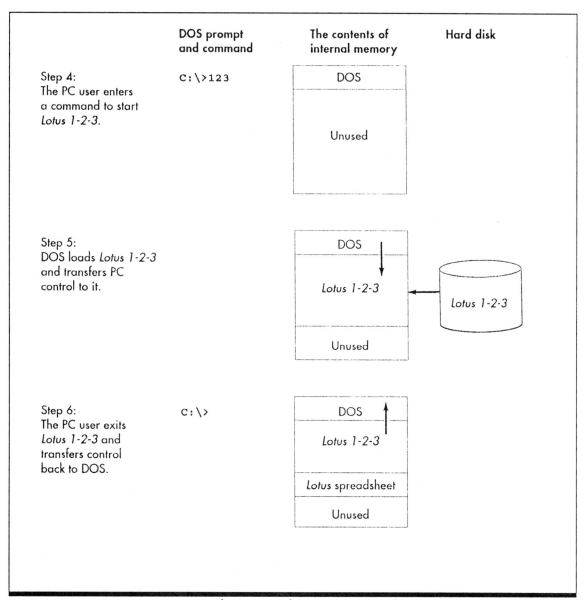

	DOS prompt and command	The contents of internal memory	Hard disk

Step 4:
The PC user enters a command to start *Lotus 1-2-3.*

Step 5:
DOS loads *Lotus 1-2-3* and transfers PC control to it.

Step 6:
The PC user exits *Lotus 1-2-3* and transfers control back to DOS.

Figure 2-5 How DOS goes from one application program to the next (part 2 of 2)

DOS. Finally, in step 4, DOS returns the requested data to the application program.

Actually, this process is much more complicated than figure 2-6 indicates. For example, DOS must be able to retrieve data from any type of disk drive, whether it's a 5-1/4 inch or 3-1/2 inch diskette drive, a 30MB hard disk, or a 300MB hard disk. In addition, DOS must be able to handle a variety of error conditions that might be encountered. For example, what if the data can't be found? Or what if a hardware failure occurs? By handling these kinds of details, DOS can insure that all application programs handle disk access in a consistent manner.

As part of its services, DOS also manages all of the files that are stored on a hard disk or diskette. In DOS terms, each document, spreadsheet, database, or program on a hard disk or diskette is called a *file*. To be more specific, you can think of a file as a document file, a spreadsheet file, a database file, or a program file, but DOS makes no distinction between them. It manages all of the files in the same way.

To keep track of the files, DOS requires that they be organized into *directories*. Then, in the directory entry for each file, DOS records the file name, the disk location, the file size in bytes, the date the file was last changed, and the time the file was last changed. As a result, an application program doesn't have to know these details when it requests an input or output operation for a disk file. Instead, the application program has to supply just the name of the file and the name of the directory that contains the file. In chapter 3, you'll learn how to refer to the files and directories you use on a DOS system.

Because you only use DOS services through your application programs, you don't have to be concerned about them. Most of the time, in fact, you won't even be aware that the services have been provided for you. When something goes wrong with a service request, though, you sometimes get a message directly from DOS. Then, it's obvious that the DOS services are in use.

DOS commands   In addition to the DOS services that you use indirectly through an application program, DOS provides commands you can use directly from the command prompt. Most of them let you manage the files and directories on a disk. But some perform other types of functions.

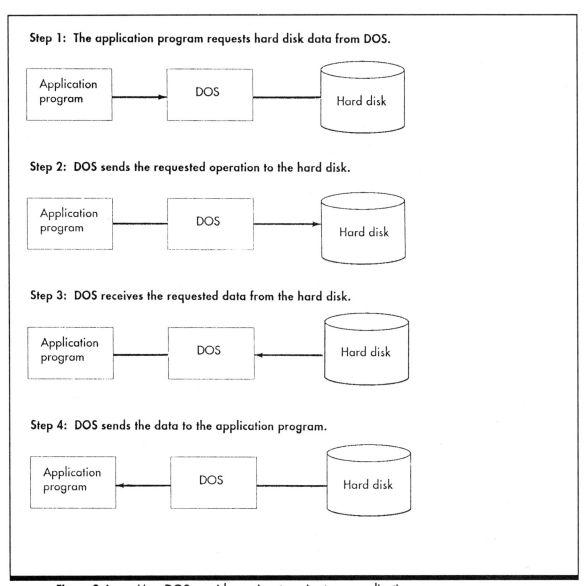

Figure 2-6   How DOS provides an input service to an application program

Figure 2-7 presents twelve typical *DOS commands*. Here, the commands are organized by type. The first group, for example, provides functions you can use to manage the files on a disk. These commands let you delete, rename, or copy one or more files. The other commands provide functions for managing directories, backing up the files on a hard disk, and so on.

In sections 2 and 3 of this book, you'll learn how to use these and other DOS commands. You'll also learn when and how to use them for maximum efficiency.

How DOS has evolved

Over the years, DOS has changed substantially, as summarized in figure 2-8. The original version of DOS was a modest operating system that was designed for diskette systems. Each subsequent version of DOS provided one or more improvements to the previous version.

In figure 2-8, you can see that each new version of DOS is given a number like 2.0 or 3.3. In general, a change in the first digit of a version number means a major revision of the program. However, a change in the digits to the right of the decimal point means a minor revision. This is true for application programs as well as for DOS. If you want to find out what version of DOS you have on your system, just type VER at the command prompt and press the Enter key.

As you can see in figure 2-8, both DOS 4.0 and DOS 5.0 provide a feature called the *DOS shell*. One of the purposes of this feature is to make it easier for you to use DOS. When you use the DOS shell, you can set up your system so a screen like one of the ones in figure 2-9 is displayed whenever you start your PC. Then, you can use the modules of the DOS shell to manage files and directories, to execute DOS commands, and to start your application programs without entering the commands at the command prompt.

Because the DOS 5.0 shell is a major improvement over the DOS 4.0 shell, this book only teaches you how to use the 5.0 shell. If you're currently using an earlier version of DOS on your PC, you can decide whether you want to upgrade to DOS 5.0 after you learn how its shell works in section 4 of this book. If you don't already have a shell program on your system or if you're using the DOS 4.0 shell, it's probably worth the time and expense to

Command type	Command	Function
File management	DEL	Deletes one or more files from disk storage
	REN	Renames one or more files in disk storage
	COPY	Copies one or more files from one disk location to another
Directory management	MD	Makes a new directory
	RD	Removes an empty directory
Backup	BACKUP	Copies the files and directories on a hard disk to a series of diskettes
	RESTORE	Copies the backup files and directories on a series of diskettes to a hard disk
Setup	DATE	Requests the current date and sets the internal clock using this information
	TIME	Requests the current time and sets the internal clock using this information
Error checking and recovery	CHKDSK	Checks a disk for errors and attempts to correct the errors
Information display	VER	Displays the version of DOS in use
	DIR	Displays the files and directories on a disk drive

Figure 2-7   Twelve typical DOS commands

upgrade your operating system to DOS 5.0 because the software is inexpensive and the installation process is relatively easy.

Although the DOS 5.0 shell makes it easier for you to use DOS, you still have to know how DOS commands work. So you should read sections 2 and 3 of this book before you read section 4. To make the most efficient use of

Version	Memory required	Major improvements
1.0	8KB	
2.0	24KB	Support for hard disks Directories
3.0	37KB	Support for 1.2MB diskette drives
3.1	39KB	Support for networks
3.2	46KB	Support for 3-1/2 inch diskette drives
3.3	55KB	Multiple logical drives on a hard disk New commands
4.0	70KB	Support for hard disk drives of more than 32MB Extended memory support DOS shell
5.0	60KB 18 KB*	Less conventional memory required Improved use of extended memory Task switching Full-screen editor New DOS shell and other utility programs

*When extended memory is used

Figure 2-8   The evolution of DOS

DOS, you'll use DOS commands entered at the command prompt for some functions even though you have the DOS shell.

Although you can use this book with any version of DOS that's 2.0 or later, you probably are using a version of DOS that's 3.0 or later. If you aren't, you probably should install a more recent version of DOS. Nevertheless, I'll let you know whenever I present a DOS feature that requires a version more recent than 2.0.

The first screen of the
DOS 4.0 shell

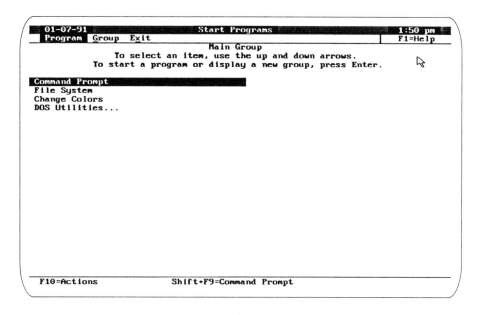

The first screen of the
DOS 5.0 shell

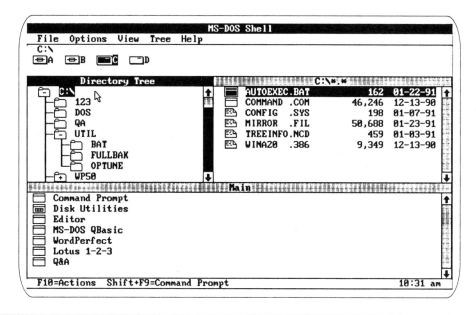

Figure 2-9 The opening screens of the DOS 4.0 and 5.0 shells

Utilities that improve upon DOS

From its beginning in 1981, DOS has never been all that people have wanted it to be. As a result, many *utility programs* (or just *utilities*) have been developed to improve upon DOS. Some of these utilities provide functions that DOS doesn't provide. And some perform functions better than DOS performs them.

Figure 2-10 summarizes five of the most common types of utilities. If you're like most PC users, one or more of these utilities can help you use your PC more effectively. Some of these programs are available commercially from the same distributors that sell application programs. Some are available at no charge or at just a nominal charge. And some that weren't available with earlier versions of DOS now come with DOS 5.0.

Two of the most popular types of commercial utilities are shell utilities and backup utilities. As a result, you're likely to find one or both of these utilities installed on a typical PC in business. Although this book doesn't present any of the commercial utilities in figure 2-10, you should at least know what these two types of utilities can do. Then, if you want more information about utilities, you'll find a full section devoted to them in *The Only DOS Book You'll Ever Need.*

Shell utilities   If your system starts with the command prompt, you probably don't have a *shell utility* (or *shell program*) installed on it. But if your system starts with a screen that is similar to one of the ones in figure 2-9, you probably do. A shell utility makes it easier for you to use DOS by providing an interface between you and the command prompt just as the DOS 4.0 and 5.0 shells make DOS easier to use.

If you're using DOS 3.3 or an earlier version of DOS, one way to get a shell program on your system is to buy a utility. The other way is to install DOS 5.0. But if you're already using DOS 5.0, you probably don't need a commercial shell because the DOS 5.0 shell is as good as most of them. In contrast, the DOS 4.0 has many weaknesses so 4.0 users should consider an upgrade to DOS 5.0.

Backup utilities   A *backup utility* (or *backup program*) is designed to back up the data on your hard disk faster and more easily than the commands

Type	Primary purposes	Typical programs
Shell	To make it easier to manage directories and files, to use DOS commands, and to start application programs	*PC Tools Deluxe* *Pathminder* *Norton Commander*
Backup	To backup and restore files more efficiently than the DOS Backup and Restore commands	*PC Tools Deluxe* *Fastback Plus* *PC Fullback*
Advanced disk	To prevent disk files from being lost due to hardware or software problems, and to recover files that have been lost or accidentally deleted	*PC Tools Deluxe* *Mace Utilities* *Norton Utilities*
Special-purpose	To provide a function that works better than the comparable DOS function, or to provide a useful function that isn't provided by DOS	*Cruise Control* *PrintQ* *Software Carousel*
Public domain and shareware	To provide utilities at no charge or at just a nominal charge to the PC user	

Figure 2-10   A summary of the most common types of utilities

DOS provides. A typical backup utility, for example, can back up 10MB of hard-disk data in about five minutes on a 286 system. In contrast, the DOS Backup command takes over 17 minutes to do the same job.

In chapter 8, you'll learn how to use the DOS commands for the backup and recovery of hard-disk data. If you have limited backup requirements, those commands may be all that you'll need for your backup functions. As you'll learn in chapter 8, though, most DOS users can benefit from the use of a backup utility.

Some perspective on software

The evolution of PC software since 1981 has been as impressive as the evolution of PC hardware. During that time, we've gone from small application programs that performed a limited number of functions to large programs that perform more functions than the average user knows what to do with. We've gone from programs that worked only in text mode on monochrome monitors to programs that use both text and graphic modes on color monitors. And we've gone from programs that printed text in only one font to programs that can print complex graphics as well as text in many fonts.

Although application programs have gotten easier to use, DOS hasn't. As a result, most PC users still have a difficult time using DOS effectively, just as they did back in the early 1980s. In fact, most PC users seem to avoid DOS whenever they can. They have to learn how to start their application programs, of course, but that's all many of them want to know about DOS.

Unfortunately, you need to know more than that if you want to get the maximum benefit from your PC. If you don't know how to use DOS, you won't be able to manage your files and directories as effectively as you should so they'll eventually get out of control. You won't back up your files as efficiently or as frequently as you should so you won't be protected from a hard disk disaster. If someone changes the way your PC is set up, you may not even be able to start your application programs. And whenever something goes wrong, you'll be at the mercy of someone who does know DOS.

That's why the next two sections in this book will teach you the essential DOS skills for all PC users. In section 2, you'll learn the DOS skills you need for working with your application programs. In section 3, you'll learn the DOS skills you need for managing your files and directories. Once you learn these skills, you'll be able to use your PC effectively.

Terms you should be familiar with before you continue

software
program
application program
operating system program

word processing program
document
spreadsheet program
spreadsheet

database program
database
operating system
DOS
command processor
command prompt
command
resident DOS
loading a program
loading a file
file
directory
DOS command
DOS shell
utility program
utility
shell utility
shell program
backup utility
backup program

Other terms presented in this chapter

general-purpose program
graphics program
desktop publishing program
integrated program
OS/2
Disk Operating System
MS-DOS
PC-DOS
DOS service
input/output service
I/O service

Section 2

The least you need to know about DOS to use your application programs

When you use application programs on a PC, you need to know something about DOS. At the least, you need to know how to identify DOS drives, directories, and files so you can save and retrieve your work files from your application programs. But you should also know how to start your application programs from the DOS command prompt with either DOS commands or batch files. So these are the skills you'll learn in this section.

When you finish this section, your PC and its software will be less mysterious to you. You'll understand how to use directories and files as you save your work on a hard disk. You'll know how to use 12 DOS commands from the command prompt that will help you use your application programs. And you'll always be able to start your application programs, no matter who used the PC last or for what purpose.

Even if you use a shell utility to start your programs, you need to master the skills in this section. Otherwise, you will always be dependent on others when you want to put new programs on your PC. Once you understand the commands presented in this section, though, you'll be able to handle the installation of all new programs by yourself. You'll also be able to use your shell more effectively.

Chapter 3

How to identify DOS drives, directories, and files in your application programs

Although most application programs today try to shield you from the intricacies of DOS, all of them use DOS specifications for files. As a result, you should know how to refer to DOS disk drives, directories, and files, whether or not you ever use DOS itself. In this chapter, you'll learn how to refer to any file on a DOS system by specifying its drive, directory, and file name.

To start, you'll learn how to give a complete file specification for any file on a DOS system. Then, you'll learn what the default drive and current directory are and how they affect your file specifications. Last, you'll learn how to use DOS file specifications within your application programs.

How to specify the drive, path, and file name for any DOS file

Whenever you use an application program or DOS to access a file, you have to specify what file you want to access and where the file is located. You supply this information using a *file specification*. A complete file specification consists of three parts: a drive, a path, and a file name. Figure 3-1 shows complete specifications for a file on a diskette and for a file on a hard disk. Now, I'll explain what each part of a file specification is.

Example 1: A typical drive, path, and file name for a document file on a diskette

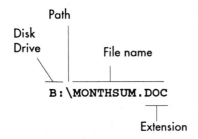

Example 2: A typical drive, path, and file name for a spreadsheet file on a hard disk

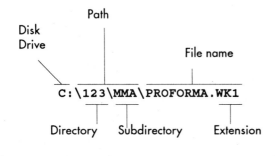

Figure 3-1   Typical drives, paths, and file names for word processing and spreadsheet files

The drive   DOS identifies the hard disk drive and diskette drives by letters. For instance, the first diskette drive on every system is always drive A, and the second diskette drive is always drive B. If a system has two diskette drives with one drive on the left and the other on the right, the one on the left is usually the A drive. If a system has two diskettes with one on top of the other, the one on the top is usually the A drive.

The hard disk, or at least the first portion of it, is always identified as drive C. However, one hard disk can be divided into more than one drive, as shown in figure 3-2. Then, the first drive is drive C; the second is drive D;

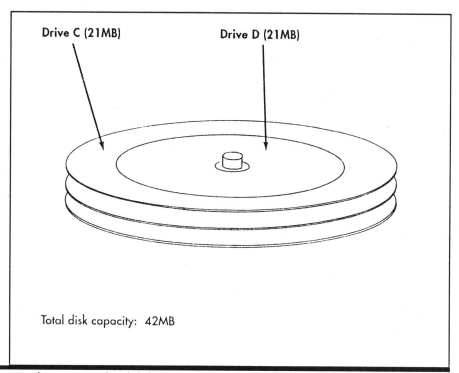

Drive C (21MB)   Drive D (21MB)

Total disk capacity: 42MB

Figure 3-2   Two drives on one hard disk

and so on. Today, a 40MB drive is likely to be divided into drives C and D, while a 120MB drive is likely to be divided into drives C, D, E, and F.

This division of a hard disk into more than one drive originally started because DOS was unable to manage hard disks that had capacities larger than 32MB. As a result, a 40MB hard disk had to be divided into two drives. DOS 3.3 was the first version of DOS to allow this division. Before DOS 3.3, you had to use non-standard software to divide a drive larger than 32MB into smaller, usable drives. Today, DOS 4.0 and 5.0 can treat an entire 40MB disk as the C drive, but it is still common to divide a large hard disk into smaller, more manageable drives.

In PC and DOS literature, the drives are often referred to as *logical drives* to distinguish them from the hard disk, or physical disk drive. Thus, one physical drive is divided into two or more logical drives. From a practical point of view, however, you can think of each logical drive as a physical drive. As a result, I won't distinguish between the two in the remainder of this book. I'll simply refer to disk drives by letter as in "the C drive" or "the D drive."

In this book, I assume that your hard disk has already been set up for you. At the least, then, you know that your PC has a C drive. In the next chapter, I'll show you how to find out whether your PC has other drives, and I'll show you how to find out the capacity of each drive.

To specify the disk drive in a file specification, you always give the drive letter followed by a colon. In figure 3-1, you can see that example 1 specifies the B drive, which is the second diskette drive of a PC. Example 2 specifies the C drive.

The path   In chapter 2, I mentioned that DOS lets you organize or group files into *directories*. The 1,368 files on my system, for example, are organized into 39 different directories. These directories are just a special type of file that DOS uses to keep track of the names and locations of the files that are stored on a disk. On a DOS system, every file must be stored in a directory.

Figure 3-3 illustrates a typical directory structure for a hard disk. For each hard disk or diskette, the top-level directory is always called the *root directory*. In this figure, the root directory contains references to five other directories named DOS, UTIL, WP50, 123, and QA. These directories contain the files for DOS, for some utility programs, for *WordPerfect*, for *Lotus 1-2-3*, and for *Q&A*.

Because one directory can contain entries for other directories, the subordinate directories can be referred to as *subdirectories*. In figure 3-3, for instance, the WP50 directory has two subdirectories named MMA and PROJ1, and the 123 directory has two subdirectories named MMA and DOUG. These subdirectories are just like any other directory; they're just subordinate to a higher-level directory. As a result, subdirectories can also be referred to as directories.

The *path* of a file specification identifies the directory for the file. More specifically, the path tells DOS how to get from the root directory to the directory that contains the entry for the file you want. In the directory structure in figure 3-3, the shaded path goes from the root directory to the WP50 directory to the PROJ1 directory.

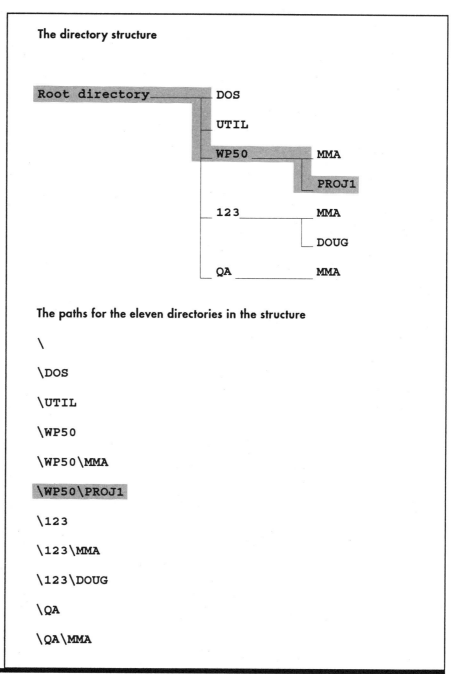

Figure 3-3 The paths for the directories of a hard disk

Below the directory structure in figure 3-3, you can see the specifications for the paths of the eleven directories shown in the structure. The first back-slash (\ ) represents the root directory. The level-1 directories are identified by the backslash followed by the directory name as in \DOS, \UTIL, \WP50, \123, and \QA. And the level-2 directories, or subdirectories, are identified by the backslash, the level-1 directory name, another backslash, and the level-2 directory name as in \WP50\MMA and \WP50\PROJ1.

Note in figure 3-3 that \PROJ1 isn't a valid path. To be valid, it must be preceded by its directory as in this path: \WP50\PROJ1. Note also that the same subdirectory name can be used within more than one directory. Thus, an MMA directory is subordinate to the WP50 directory, the 123 directory, and the QA directory. For DOS to tell these three directories apart, they must be referred to as \WP50\MMA, \123\MMA, and \QA\MMA.

If you refer back to figure 3-1, you can see that the path in the first example is just the root directory. The path in the second example, however, is the MMA subdirectory within the 123 directory within the root directory.

The file name   Whenever you save a new file on a hard disk or a diskette, whether you use DOS or an application program, you need to be able to create a valid *file name*. If you refer back to figure 3-1, you can see that a file name can be separated into two parts by a period. The part that comes before the period is required. I'll refer to this as the *name* portion of the file name. The part after the period is optional and is called the *extension*.

Figure 3-4 gives the rules for forming valid file names. If you use just letters and numbers in your names, you don't have to worry about the special characters listed in rule 3. Then, you just have to make sure that the name before the period is from one to eight characters and that the extension is from one to three characters. However, you may find that you can benefit from using characters like the dash (-) in file names. So don't completely rule out these other characters. Note also in rule 4 that DOS doesn't care whether you use uppercase or lowercase letters when you specify a file name. Both are treated the same. As you can see in the last two examples of a valid file name, you can omit the period if you don't specify an extension.

Although extensions are optional, many programs use them. For instance, version 2.2 of *Lotus 1-2-3* uses WK1 as the extension for the spreadsheet files you create, and *Microsoft Word* uses DOC as the extension for the

The rules for forming file names

1. The name must consist of from one to eight characters.

2. The extension is optional. If you have one, it must be from one to three characters, and it must be separated from the name by a period as in this example:

   `MONTHSUM.JAN`

3. You can use any character in the name or the extension except for the space and any of these characters:

   `. , < > ? / : ; " ' [ ] | \ + = *`

4. You can use either lowercase or uppercase letters in the name or the extension of a file name, but they are treated the same. As a result, the two names that follow are the same:

   `MONTHSUM.JAN`   and   `monthsum.jan`

Valid file names

`JAN90.WK1`

`letter.doc`

`5-16-90.doc`

`FEB90RPT`

`ltr10-21`

Invalid file names

`JANUARY90.WK1`   (The name is more than 8 characters.)

`JAN:90.WK1`   (The colon is an invalid character.)

`JAN90.TEXT`   (The extension is more than 3 characters.)

Figure 3-4   The rules for forming file names

document files you create. When you use these programs, though, you don't have to include the extension when your create a file name because the application program adds it automatically.

How the default drive and current directory affect a file specification

Whenever your PC is running, one and only one drive is the DOS *default drive*. In fact, DOS displays the default drive as part of its command prompt. Similarly, one directory is identified as the *current directory* for each drive. When you use DOS, you don't have to specify the drive and path in a file specification if the file is in the current directory on the default drive.

Some application programs work that way too. They assume that the DOS default drive and current directory are intended whenever the drive and path are omitted from a file specification. That can simplify your file specifications considerably because it often means that you only have to specify the file name. *WordPerfect*, for example, looks for a file in the current directory on the default drive whenever the drive and path are omitted from a file specification.

In contrast, some application programs have their own default drives and directories. When you use one of these programs to save or access files, the DOS default drive and current directory don't matter. Instead, the program looks for a file in its own default directory on its own default drive. For example, *Lotus 1-2-3* and *Q&A* are programs that keep track of their own default directories and drives. Then, when the file you want is in the program's default directory on the default drive, you can omit the drive and path from the file specification.

You should also realize that the current directory can affect how DOS interprets the path you use in a file specification. If you begin the path with a backslash, the directory path begins with the root directory. In this case, the current directory has no effect on the path. However, if you do not begin the path with a backslash, the path begins at the current directory rather than the root directory. In that case, you can omit the current directory from the path.

To illustrate, suppose you want to access a file named JAN90.WK1 in the 123\MMA directory. If you use a complete path, like this:

`\123\MMA\JAN90.WK1`

the path will access the file no matter which directory is current. However, if the 123 directory is current, you can start the path like this:

`MMA\JAN90.WK1`

Because the first backslash is omitted, DOS looks for the MMA subdirectory in the current directory (123) rather than in the root directory.

Although omitting the current directory information from the path can sometimes save you a few keystrokes, it can also create problems. For example, suppose you believe the 123 directory is current, but in reality the current directory is WP. Then, when you save a file using the path MMA\JAN90.WK1, the JAN90.WK1 file will be saved in the WP\MMA directory, not in 123\MMA. As a result, you should give the complete directory path whenever you aren't certain what the current directory is.

How to use file specifications in application programs

Once you understand DOS file specifications, you shouldn't have any trouble using them in your application programs. With some programs, the file specifications appear as complete specifications so you can see the drive and path for each file you save or retrieve. Figure 3-5, for example, shows the screen *Lotus 1-2-3* displays when you save or retrieve a file. As you can see, *Lotus* displays the complete drive and path it uses for the file. Then, if the drive and directory are set to the ones you want to use, all you have to do is enter a file name to retrieve or save a file. If the drive and directory aren't the ones you want, you can set them the way you want them before you retrieve or save a file.

Other programs, however, don't always display complete specifications. When you use the Save or Retrieve commands in *WordPerfect*, for example, you get the prompts shown in figure 3-6. But these prompts don't tell you what the drive and path are. Then, if you enter just the file name for a Save command, that file will be saved in the current directory on the default drive.

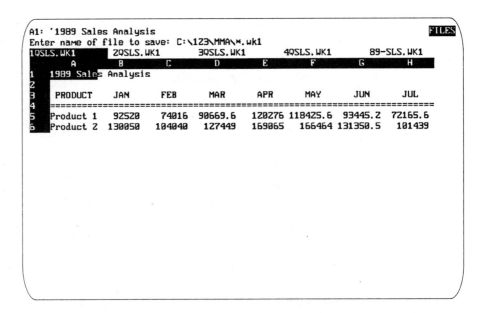

```
A1: '1989 Sales Analysis                                                  FILES
Enter name of file to save: C:\123\MMA\*.wk1
1QSLS.WK1       2QSLS.WK1       3QSLS.WK1       4QSLS.WK1       89-SLS.WK1
       A           B        C        D        E        F        G        H
1  1989 Sales Analysis
2
3  PRODUCT     JAN      FEB      MAR      APR      MAY      JUN      JUL
4  ===============================================================================
5  Product 1   92520    74016    90669.6  120276  118425.6  93445.2  72165.6
6  Product 2   130050   104040   127449   169065  166464 131350.5  101439
```

Figure 3-5   The drive and directory information that *Lotus 1-2-3* displays when you save or
retrieve a file

The prompt for the Save command

        Document to be saved:

The prompt for the Retrieve command

        Document to be retrieved:

Figure 3-6   The *WordPerfect* prompts for the Save and Retrieve commands

But if the default drive and directory are not the ones you think they are, you won't know where your file is getting stored.

To avoid problems, you should make sure you know what the defaults are whenever you give an incomplete file specification. If you don't know, you should give the complete specification, which includes the drive and path. Then, the file will always be stored on the drive and directory given by the complete file specification, no matter what the default drive and directory are.

How to use the * wildcard in the file specification for an application program

If you look closely at the file specification in the second line of figure 3-5, you'll see that it contains an asterisk:

```
C:\123\MMA\*.WK1
```

This * is one of the two types of *wildcards* that DOS provides. It is called the *** wildcard*, and it represents one or more characters of any kind. As a result, this *Lotus* command displays only the files that have an extension of WK1. Since all *Lotus* spreadsheets have this extension, this command displays only the spreadsheets in the directory, not any other kinds of files.

Some common forms of file names that contain wildcards are illustrated in figure 3-7. As you can see, *.* refers to files with any name before the period and any extension; *.WK1 refers to files with an extension of WK1; *.DOC refers to files with an extension of DOC; and *. refers to files that don't have an extension. Many application programs use simple wildcard specifications like these.

In chapter 6, you'll learn how to use wildcards in DOS commands. There, you'll learn how to use the * wildcard in more complex forms, and you'll learn how to use the ? wildcard. In the meantime, you don't have to use * wildcards at all. You just have to understand what they mean in the specifications displayed by your programs.

If you do change a wildcard specification that is displayed by an application program, you should realize that the function that is going to be performed will be changed accordingly. If, for example, you change the *.*

Wildcard examples	Meaning
`*.*`	All files (any name, any extension)
`*.WK1`	All files with an extension of WK1
`*.DOC`	All files with an extension of DOC
`*.`	All files without any extension

Figure 3-7 Some common forms of file specifications that contain * wildcards

specification to *.DOC when you're using *WordPerfect*'s List-files command, it will only list the files that have an extension of DOC, not all the files in the directory. Sometimes, it makes sense to change a specification in this way so the application program does its function on just those files you specify.

Some perspective on DOS drives, paths, and file names

In the next chapter, you'll see how drives, paths, and file names are used in DOS commands. You'll also realize that a typical DOS system has to keep track of hundreds of files stored in a dozen or more directories. Because directories and files can easily get out of control, chapter 6 will show you how to manage the directories and files on your system.

Terms

file specification	file name
logical drive	extension
directory	default drive
root directory	current directory
subdirectory	wildcard
path	* wildcard

Chapter 4

How to use DOS commands to start your application programs

In this chapter, you'll learn how to use DOS commands to start your application programs from the command prompt. If you've been using a shell utility or a menu to start your programs, you may never have done this before. But you need to know how to do this if you want to understand how DOS works. Later on, this understanding will help you start your programs more efficiently whether you do it from the command prompt or from a shell utility.

This chapter starts by showing you how to enter a DOS command. Next, you'll learn how to use four DOS commands to start your application programs. Then, you'll learn how to use eight other DOS commands that can help you use your PC. When you complete this chapter, you'll have a better understanding of how DOS works and why you need to know how to use it.

As you read this chapter, you can try the DOS commands on your own PC right after you read about them. Or you can read the entire chapter first and then try the DOS commands using the figures as guidelines. If you would like more direction as you experiment with the commands, you can do the exercises at the end of the chapter.

Because these chapters are heavily illustrated, you'll be able to see how the commands work before you actually try them. But to master the use of the DOS commands, you need to try them on your own PC. As you do, you'll see how your system varies from the system used for the examples in this book.

What DOS does when you start your PC

If your PC has a hard disk, DOS is stored on it. So to start your system, all you have to do is turn on the monitor and the systems unit. If all of the components of your PC are connected to a surge protector or some other single power source, all you have to do is throw the switch on that unit.

Before you turn the systems unit on, though, you must make sure that you don't have a diskette in drive A and that the door of drive A is open. If drive A contains a diskette, your PC looks for DOS on the diskette instead of the hard disk. Then, if the diskette doesn't have DOS on it, your PC will display an error message. At that time, you can take the diskette out of drive A and restart your systems unit.

When you start your PC, it automatically performs two functions. First, it checks itself to make sure it's working properly. This is called the *self-test*, or *POST (Power-On-Self-Test) routine*. If anything goes wrong during this test, the PC displays an error message. On most PCs, the self test takes just a few seconds. On others, it takes minutes. During this time, your monitor may look as though nothing is happening. But since you can't do any work on your PC until the self-test is over, you just have to wait.

Second, the PC loads the resident portion of DOS from the root directory of the C drive of the hard disk. This is called *booting the system*, which comes from the expression "pulling yourself up by your own bootstraps." When this process is complete, the hardware transfers control of the system to DOS.

The DOS command prompt   As DOS takes control of the system, it may display several messages on the monitor. It may also ask you to enter the date and time. Eventually, though, DOS should display either the *command prompt* or a DOS shell. If the DOS shell appears, you can press the F3 key to get to the prompt. If some other program appears, exit from it and get to the prompt. You have to be at the DOS prompt before you can try out the commands presented in this chapter.

In its standard form, the prompt looks like this:

`C>`

This prompt displays just the default drive. However, some PCs are set up so the prompt displays the current directory along with the default drive in this form:

`C:\123\MMA>`

No matter what the prompt looks like, though, it means that the DOS command processor is waiting for your command.

In a moment, you'll learn how to use the DOS Prompt command to change your prompt so it displays the current directory as well as the default drive. Then, in the next chapter, you'll learn how to set up your PC so the prompt is always displayed in that form.

How to enter and correct a DOS command

To enter a DOS command, you type in the command at the command prompt and press the Enter key. That's all there is to it. On some keyboards, the Enter key is called the Return key. And on other keyboards, the Enter key is marked only with this symbol: (↵). Throughout this book, though, I'll refer to this key as the Enter key, no matter how it's marked on your keyboard.

Although you always have to press the Enter key to enter a command, I won't indicate that in the examples in this book. Instead, I'll just assume you know that you have to press the Enter key after each command. I'll also assume you know that the command always comes right after the (>) symbol in the command prompt. As a result, this example:

`C>dir a:`

means to type *dir a:* and press the Enter key.

With few exceptions, DOS doesn't care whether you use uppercase or lowercase letters in commands. So whenever possible, I'll use lowercase letters for them. This will help you tell the commands from the DOS prompts and messages, which are displayed in uppercase letters.

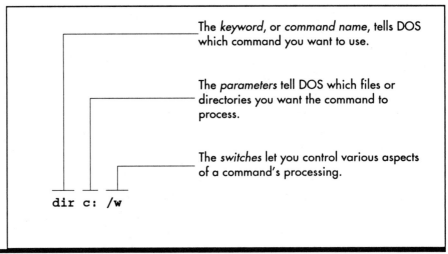

The *keyword*, or *command name*, tells DOS which command you want to use.

The *parameters* tell DOS which files or directories you want the command to process.

The *switches* let you control various aspects of a command's processing.

```
dir c: /w
```

Figure 4-1   The basic format of a DOS command

The basic format of a DOS command   Figure 4-1 gives the basic format for any DOS command. As you can see, a command can consist of three parts. The first part is the *keyword*. Since it identifies the command, it can also be called the *command name*. The second part is one or more *parameters*; they tell DOS what drives, directories, or files the command should work on. The third part is one or more *switches*; they tell DOS which variations of the command you want.

As you will see in a moment, some command formats consist of a keyword only; some consist of a keyword and parameters; and some consist of a keyword, parameters, and switches. You'll also see that the parameters and switches are often optional. In figure 4-1, for example, the Directory command contains a keyword (dir), one parameter (c:), and one switch (/w). But Directory commands can also be used without parameters and without switches.

When you enter a command at the command prompt, you must separate the parts of a command so DOS can tell what they are. Normally, you do this by typing in one or more spaces between the parts. So if a command consists of the keyword, a parameter, and a switch, you normally enter it like this:

```
C>dir \dos /w
```

Here, the keyword is *dir*; the parameter is *\dos*; and the switch is */w*.

Keystrokes	Function
F3	Retypes all of the characters from the last command you entered.
Ctrl+Pause or Ctrl+C	Interrupts the execution of the command and cancels it.

Figure 4-2 Keystrokes that help you correct, repeat, or cancel a command

For the examples in this book, the parts of a command are always separated by one or more spaces. You should realize, though, that DOS also recognizes the backslash and the slash as separators. As a result, DOS interprets this command:

```
dir\dos/w
```

as though it were written as:

```
dir \dos /w
```

Nevertheless, it's usually best to separate the parts of a command with spaces. That way, the commands are easier to read, and you can be sure that DOS is going to interpret them the way you mean them.

How to correct, repeat, or cancel a command   If you make a mistake entering a command, but you notice it before you press the Enter key, you can just backspace and correct it. If you press the Enter key before you realize you made a mistake, DOS will display an error message that indicates something is wrong with your command. One way to correct it is to enter the entire command again in its corrected form.

However, you can also use the Function key shown in figure 4-2 to help you correct a command. If a command is lengthy, using the F3 key is usually more efficient than entering the entire command again. If, for example, you press the F3 key after you get an error message from DOS, all of the characters from the last command that you entered appear at the new prompt. Then, you can backspace and make the required corrections. You can also use this key if you want to repeat the execution of a command.

Figure 4-2 also shows the keystroke combinations you can use if you want to cancel a command. First, you can cancel a command by holding down the Ctrl key while you press the Pause, or Break, key. Second, if your keyboard doesn't have a Pause key, you can cancel the command by holding down the Ctrl key while you press the letter *c*.

Two types of DOS commands

When you use DOS, you should realize that there are two types of commands: internal commands and external commands. Although DOS is always able to find and execute its internal commands, you sometimes need to tell DOS where to find its external commands.

Internal commands   As I explained in chapter 2, part of DOS stays in the internal memory of your systems unit whenever your PC is turned on. This portion of DOS is called *resident DOS*. It includes the command processor, and it also includes many of the DOS commands.

The commands that are a part of resident DOS are known as *internal commands*. Because they are always in internal memory, DOS always knows where to find them. Also, it doesn't have to load them from disk storage into internal memory before it can execute them. To use one of these commands, all you ever have to do is enter the command name at the command prompt.

External commands   If a command isn't in resident DOS, it's called an *external command*. Each of these commands is stored in a disk file called a *command file*. On a DOS system, the names of command files always have an extension of COM or EXE. Usually, these command files are stored in the DOS directory on one of the drives of your PC, but not all systems are set up that way. On some systems, for example, you find the DOS files in the root directory of the C drive.

Before DOS can execute an external command, it must find the command file for the command and load the command into internal memory. But not all systems are set up so DOS is able to find its external commands. If yours isn't, you should set the current directory to the one that contains the

Name	Format	Function
Prompt	PROMPT pg	Changes the format of the command prompt so it shows the default drive and current directory.
Change drive	Drive-spec	Changes the default drive to the drive specified.
Directory	DIR [file-spec] [/p] [/w]	Displays a directory listing for the specified files. The switches let you control how the command displays the listing.
Change directory	CD [directory-spec]	Changes the current directory. If the parameter is omitted, this command displays the path of the current directory.

Figure 4-3   Four DOS commands that will help you start your programs

external command files before you try to execute one of them. You'll learn how to do that in a moment. Then, because DOS always looks in the current directory for the requested command file, it will be able to find and execute the external commands.

On the other hand, some systems are set up so DOS can always find its external command files. Then, you can execute an external command the same way you execute an internal command. You just enter it at the command prompt. In the next chapter, you'll learn how to set up your system so DOS always knows where to find its external command files.

How to use four DOS commands that can help you start your application programs

Figure 4-3 gives the formats and functions for four DOS commands. Using just these commands, you'll be able to start all your application programs from the command prompt. Although you won't use the Prompt command much, it will help you use the other three commands. And you'll use the other three commands frequently.

In the formats in figure 4-3, I've used uppercase letters for the keyword for each command, and I've used lowercase letters for the parameters and switches. If the parameters or switches are optional, I've enclosed them in brackets [ ]. I've also used the abbreviation *spec* for the word *specification*. This is the notation that's used in most DOS manuals, and it's the one that's used throughout this book.

To use the commands in figure 4-3, you start by entering the keyword. Next, if the command requires parameters or switches, you enter them making sure that you use one or more spaces to separate the parts of the command. Then, when you've got the command the way you want it, press the Enter key so DOS will execute it.

When you enter a command, I recommend that you use lowercase for all its parts. Because DOS treats uppercase and lowercase letters as equals, this won't affect your commands in any way. But it will make it easier for you to enter commands.

The Prompt command   When the command prompt is in its standard form (C>), it tells you what the default drive is, but it doesn't tell you what the current directory is. To change the form of the prompt so it does tell you what the current directory is, you use the Prompt command with the parameter shown in figure 4-3.

The use of this command is illustrated in figure 4-4. After the command is executed, the prompt is changed to show that the current directory for the C drive is the root directory (C:\>). Now, if you changed the current directory to the DOS directory, the prompt would look like this:

```
c:\DOS>
```

This enhanced form of the prompt stays in effect until you turn your PC off.

Because a prompt that tells the current directory makes it easier to use the other DOS commands, you should always set your prompt to this form. However, you don't have to do this each time you start your PC. Instead, you can put a Prompt command in an AUTOEXEC.BAT file, as I'll explain in the next chapter.

The Change-drive command   To use the Change-drive command, you just type the letter of the drive that you want as the default drive followed by

```
C>prompt $p$g

C:\>a:

A:\>b:

B:\>d:

D:\>e:
Invalid drive specification

D:\>
```

Figure 4-4   The Prompt command and four examples of how to use the Change-drive command

a colon. When you press the Enter key, DOS changes the default drive and displays the new default drive in the command prompt. To illustrate, the first three Change-drive commands in figure 4-4 change the drive from C to A, from A to B, and from B to D.

To find out how many drives your hard disk is divided into, you can issue the Change-drive command to change from the C drive to the D drive. If DOS doesn't display a message that tells you there is no D drive, you can continue with the E, F, and G drives until you get a message that says there's no such drive. In figure 4-4, the last Change-drive command tries to change the default drive to the E drive, but DOS displays an error message that says that the drive doesn't exist. As a result, you know that the C and D drives are the only valid drives for the hard disk.

The Directory command   The Directory command displays a directory listing. If you don't specify any parameters in this command, DOS displays the current directory on the default drive. As a result, the Directory command in figure 4-5 displays the root directory for the C drive. This directory listing consists of five entries for each file. From left to right, they are the name of the file, the file extension, the size of the file in bytes, the date the file was last changed, and the time the file was last changed.

```
c:\>dir

 Volume in drive C is DISK1-VOL1
 Directory of C:\


 123          <DIR>        9-06-90    2:34p
 DOS          <DIR>        8-01-90    4:46p
 QA           <DIR>        8-01-90    4:46p
 UTIL         <DIR>        8-01-90    4:48p
 WP50         <DIR>        8-01-90    4:56p
 AUTOEXEC BAT        80    8-02-90    9:56a
 COMMAND  COM     25276    7-24-87   12:00a
 CONFIG   SYS        22    6-07-90   11:03a
         8 File(s)    6242304 bytes free

c:\>
```

Figure 4-5   The operation of the Directory command

Note that a directory listing doesn't include the period that separates the name portion of the file name from the extension. Instead, it lists the name portions in the first column of the listing and the extensions in the second column. So the root directory that's listed in figure 4-5 contains three files named:

AUTOEXEC.BAT
COMMAND.COM
CONFIG.SYS

To read a directory listing properly, you must mentally convert the file names in the listing to this form.

In figure 4-5, the directory listing contains five directories as indicated by <DIR> in the column that gives the file size. Although a directory name can have an extension, most don't. And because all DOS directories are the same size, there's no point in displaying their file size. Remember, though, a directory is just a special type of file that contains entries for other files.

Incidentally, the three files that are listed in figure 4-5 must always be stored in the root directory of the C drive so you shouldn't delete them. Since the COMMAND.COM file contains the DOS command processor and the internal DOS commands, it is critical to the operation of your system. Similarly, the CONFIG.SYS file contains information about your system that is required for it to function properly. And the AUTOEXEC.BAT file tells your system what commands to execute as part of its start-up procedure.

If you look at the format for the Directory command in figure 4-3, you can see two of the switches that are available for it. The independent operation of these switches is illustrated in figure 4-6, but you can use both of these switches in a single Directory command. In figure 4-6, I've highlighted the commands to distinguish them from the command output. As you can see, the /W switch causes DOS to display a directory in a wide format with only the name and extension for each file. And the /P switch causes DOS to pause when the screen is filled. Then, when you press any key on the keyboard, the directory command displays the next screen full of entries and pauses again. If you don't use this switch for a directory that fills more than one screen, the directory entries scroll by so fast you can't read them, and the scrolling continues until the last screen of entries is displayed.

If you look again at the directory displays in figure 4-6, you can see that they start with entries for a directory designated by a single period (.) and for another directory designated by two periods (..). You'll always see these entries for a directory that isn't the root directory because DOS uses them to keep track of where it is in the directory structure. The single period represents an entry for the current directory, and the double period represents an entry for the parent directory.

The *parent directory* is just the directory that's above the current directory. In figure 4-6, the parent directory is the root directory on drive C. I mention this because you'll sometimes see the dots and the term parent directory when you're using an application program.

The files listed in figure 4-6 are the files that come with DOS 3.3. Here, these files are stored in the DOS directory on the C drive. If you search the first listing, you'll find files named PRINT.COM and CHKDSK.COM. These are command files for two external commands that you'll learn about later on in this chapter.

The Change-directory command   The Change-directory command lets you change the current directory, as illustrated in figure 4-7. The first command changes the current directory from the root directory to the DOS direc-

---

The format of the Directory command

```
DIR [file-spec] [/p] [/w]
```


The /W switch displays the directory listing in a wide format

```
C:\>dir \dos /w

 Volume in drive C is DISK1-VOL1
 Directory of  C:\DOS

.                    ..               4201     CPI   5202     CPI   ANSI      SYS
APPEND   EXE   ASSIGN   COM   ATTRIB   EXE   BACKUP   COM   CHKDSK    COM
COMMAND  COM   COMP     COM   COUNTRY  SYS   DEBUG    COM   DISKCOMP  COM
DISKCOPY COM   DISPLAY  SYS   DRIVER   SYS   EDLIN    COM   EGA       CPI
EXE2BIN  EXE   FASTOPEN EXE   FC       EXE   FDISK    COM   FIND      EXE
FORMAT   COM   GRAFTABL COM   GRAPHICS COM   GWBASIC  EXE   JOIN      EXE
KEYB     COM   KEYBOARD SYS   LABEL    COM   LCD      CPI   LINK      EXE
MODE     COM   MORE     COM   NLSFUNC  EXE   PRINT    COM   PRINTER   SYS
RAMDRIVE SYS   RECOVER  COM   REPLACE  EXE   RESTORE  COM   SELECT    COM
SHARE    EXE   SORT     EXE   SUBST    EXE   SYS      COM   TREE      COM
XCOPY    EXE
        51 File(s)    5904384 bytes free
```


The /P switch pauses the directory listing after it fills the screen

```
C:\>dir \dos /p

 Volume in drive C is DISK1-VOL1
 Directory of  C:\DOS

.              <DIR>        8-01-90    4:46p
..             <DIR>        8-01-90    4:46p
4201     CPI   17089   7-24-87   12:00a
5202     CPI     459   7-24-87   12:00a
ANSI     SYS    1647   7-24-87   12:00a
APPEND   EXE    5794   7-24-87   12:00a
ASSIGN   COM    1530   7-24-87   12:00a
ATTRIB   EXE   10656   7-24-87   12:00a
BACKUP   COM   29976   7-24-87   12:00a
CHKDSK   COM    9819   7-24-87   12:00a
COMMAND  COM   25276   7-24-87   12:00a
COMP     COM    4183   7-24-87   12:00a
COUNTRY  SYS   11254   7-24-87   12:00a
DEBUG    COM   15866   7-24-87   12:00a
DISKCOMP COM    5848   7-24-87   12:00a
DISKCOPY COM    6264   7-24-87   12:00a
DISPLAY  SYS   11259   7-24-87   12:00a
DRIVER   SYS    1165   7-24-87   12:00a
EDLIN    COM    7495   7-24-87   12:00a
EGA      CPI   49065   7-24-87   12:00a
EXE2BIN  EXE    3050   7-24-87   12:00a
FASTOPEN EXE    3888   7-24-87   12:00a
FC       EXE   15974   7-24-87   12:00a
Strike a key when ready . . .
```

Figure 4-6   How the /W and /P switches of the Directory command affect the screen display

The format of the Change-directory command

```
CD [directory-spec]
```

Examples

```
C:\>cd \dos

C:\DOS>cd \

C:\>cd \dos

C:\DOS>cd \wp50

C:\WP50>cd mma

C:\WP50\MMA>cd \123\mma

C:\123\MMA>
```

Figure 4-7   Six examples of how to change directories with the Change-directory command

tory. The second one changes the current directory back to the root directory. And so on.

When you start the parameter of a Change-directory command with a backslash, DOS assumes that your specification starts with the root directory. When you start the parameter without a backslash, DOS assumes that the parameter is a subdirectory contained within the current directory, as illustrated by the fifth command in figure 4-7.

How to start an application program from the DOS command prompt

With the four commands I've just presented, you should be able to start any application program from the command prompt. You should be able to do this easily if you know what directory the program is in and what the name of the program is. You should also be able to do this if you know the name of the program but you can't remember the name of the directory that the program is in.

How to start a program when you know its directory   When you talk about a word processing or spreadsheet program, it sounds like you're talking about a single program file. However, if you use the Directory command to display the files in the directory for an application program, you'll see that a typical application program consists of many files. For instance, my directory for *WordPerfect 5.0* contains 140 files. These include three COM files, eight EXE files, and dozens of other files that contain supporting data like tables, dictionaries, and thesauruses.

To start an application program, you need to know the name of the command file (the COM or EXE file) that is designed to start the program. Often, you also need to know the name of the directory that contains the program so you can make that the current directory. Then, you use the procedure shown in figure 4-8 to change the directory and start the program. Here, the three examples start *WordPerfect, Lotus 1-2-3*, and *Q&A*.

In all three examples, the first command is a Change-directory command that sets the current directory to the one that contains the program. The second command is the name of the command file that starts the program. You can start programs in other ways, but this procedure is the only one that works on all systems for all programs.

Of course, these examples assume that all program directories are on the C drive. If they aren't, you have to use a three-step procedure for starting a program from the command prompt. First, use the Change-drive command to change the default drive to the one that contains the program directory you want. Second, use the Change-directory command to change the current directory to the program directory. Third, enter the name of the command file that starts the program.

How to start a program when you don't know its directory   If you're working on someone else's PC or you're trying to start a program that you use infrequently, you may not remember the name of the directory it's in. Usually, though, you'll be able to start the program by using the commands you've learned in this chapter. Sometimes, you'll even be able to start a program when you can't remember the name of its command file.

Example 1:	Starting *WordPerfect 5.0* from the WP50 directory with the name WP

```
C:\>cd \wp50
C:\WP50>wp
```

Example 2:	Starting *Lotus 1-2-3* from the 123 directory with the name 123

```
C:\WP50>cd \123
C:\123>123
```

Example 3:	Starting *Q&A* from the QA directory with the name QA

```
C:\123>cd \qa
C:\QA>qa
```

Figure 4-8   How to start an application program when you know its directory and name

To find the directory for a program, you can start by using the Directory command to display the root directory on the C drive. Often, this directory will contain the program directories for the system, and you'll be able to figure out which directory contains the program you're trying to start. If the root directory on the C drive doesn't contain the directory you're looking for, you can display the root directories of the other drives. One of these directories ought to contain the directory you're looking for.

Once you know the drive and path of the program directory, you can start the program in three steps or less. First, use the Change-drive command to set the default drive to the one that contains the program directory. Second, use the Change-directory command to set the current directory to the program directory. Third, enter the name of the command file that is designed to start the program.

If you don't know the name of the command file that starts the program, you can look in its program manual to get the correct name. Otherwise, you can use the Directory command to list the files in the directory. If you look for files with COM and EXE extensions, you can usually figure out which file is the one that is designed to start the program.

```
Example 1:      C:\>promp $p$g
                Bad command or file name


Example 2:      C:\>dir \mma
                Volume in drive C is DISK1_VOL1
                Directory of C:\

                File not found


Example 3:      C:\>dir /a
                Invalid switch


Example 4:      C:\>dir a:
                Not ready reading drive A
                Abort, Retry, Fail? f
                Current drive is no longer valid>c:

                C:\>
```

Figure 4-9   The most common DOS error messages as they appear on your screen

How to handle the most common DOS error messages

If you've been trying the commands on your own system as you've read this chapter, you've probably encountered one or more *DOS error messages*. Some of the ones you'll see most often are shown in figure 4-9.

As you can see in the first example, if you spell the keyword of a command wrong, DOS will tell you that you've used a "bad command or file name." However, DOS also displays this message when it can't find the command file you tried to execute. If, for example, you haven't changed the current directory to the program directory before you issue the command for starting an application program, you'll usually get this error message.

The second example shows you the message you get if DOS can't find the file you've specified within a command: "File not found." Here, DOS looks for a file named MMA in the root directory, but none exists. Sometimes, you get this message because you've entered the file name wrong. But sometimes you get this message because you didn't give a complete file specification and the file isn't in the current directory of the default drive. Then, to correct the problem, all you have to do is give a complete specification.

If you give a parameter or switch that isn't valid for a command, DOS gives you this message: "Invalid parameter" or "Invalid switch," as shown in the third example. To correct this problem, you just have to check the format for the command to find out which parameter or switch is invalid; then, you reissue the command. Often, you get this message when you accidentally use a slash (/) instead of a backslash (\ ) within a path specification.

The last message in figure 4-9 is this:

```
Not ready reading drive A
Abort, Retry, Fail?
```

You get this message when you specify diskette drive A, but that drive doesn't contain a diskette or the door for that drive isn't closed. Often, you get this message because you forgot to put the diskette in drive A before you issued a command that requires the drive. Then, to correct the problem, you put the diskette in the drive, close the door, and enter the letter *r* for Retry.

If you get that error message because you specified drive A by accident, you just enter the letter *f* for Fail. Then, DOS displays this error message as shown in figure 4-9:

```
Current drive is no longer valid>
```

This means that DOS no longer knows what its default drive should be. To correct this problem, you just enter a drive specification like C: to reset the default drive.

Although DOS has many other error messages, these are the most common ones. If DOS displays a message you're not familiar with, you can often figure out what's wrong by carefully inspecting the command you entered. Otherwise, you can look in the back of your DOS manual for a summary of all of the DOS error messages. This summary should tell you how to respond to each message.

Name	Format	Function
Clear screen	CLS	Clears the monitor screen.
Version	VER	Displays a message that tells what version of DOS is installed.
Date	DATE	Lets you inspect and change the current date.
Time	TIME	Lets you inspect and change the current time.
Path	PATH=directory-list	Tells DOS to search the directories given in the list for any subsequent commands or programs. If the directory list is omitted, this command displays the directory list from the last Path command.
Check disk	CHKDSK [drive-spec]	Displays messages about the disk drive that's specified and about the PC's internal memory.
Type	TYPE file-spec	Displays the contents of a text file.
Print	PRINT file-spec	Prints the contents of a text file.

Figure 4-10   Eight DOS commands that can help you use your system

How to use eight other DOS commands that can help you use your system

Figure 4-10 presents eight other commands that can help you use your system. Although you'll rarely need them, you should know how to use them.

The Clear-screen command   The Clear-screen command clears the screen of any messages and puts the command prompt at the top of the screen. It has no parameters or switches. You can use this command to clear the screen before you issue a command that displays information.

```
C:\>ver

MS-DOS Version 3.30
```

Figure 4-11   The operation of the Version command

```
C:\>date
Current date is Tue 12-03-1991
Enter new date (mm-dd-yy): 12-01-91

C:\>time
Current time is 20:10:57.07
Enter new time: 20.12
```

Figure 4-12   The operation of the Date and Time commands

The Version command   Figure 4-11 shows how to use the Version command. As you can see, this command displays a message that tells what version of DOS you're using. Since some application programs require specific versions of DOS, this command can tell you whether you have the right version of DOS for the program you're trying to use.

The Date and Time commands   Figure 4-12 shows you how to use the Date and Time commands. Here, I've highlighted the commands as well as the date and time entries made by the PC user. If your system displays these commands as part of your start-up procedure, you probably know how to use them already. But you should realize that you can issue them from the DOS prompt whenever you need to correct the date or time.

    If your system doesn't have a real-time clock, you should enter the correct date and time each time you start the system. Otherwise, the date and time that's stored in the directory information for a new or updated file won't be correct. Also, the date and time won't be correct when one of your application programs gets this information from the system.

The format of the Path command

```
PATH=directory-list
```

Example 1:   A Path command that displays the current directory list

```
C:\>path
PATH=C:\DOS;C:\UTIL
```

Example 2:   Three Path commands that show how to add the DOS directory to the current
                   directory list

```
C:\>path
PATH=C:\UTIL;C:\WP50

C:\>path=c:\dos;c:\util;c:\wp50

C:\>path
PATH=C:\DOS;C:\UTIL;C:\WP50
```

Figure 4-13   The operation of the Path command

On the other hand, if your system has a real-time clock, both the date and time should be kept current for you. Then, when one of your application programs gets the current date or time from the system, it should be correct. Occasionally, though, you may find you need to correct the date and time. Twice a year, for instance, you need to set the clock when the time changes to standard time and back again to daylight savings time.

As you can see in figure 4-12, the versions of DOS before 4.0 use a 24-hour clock. As a result, 8:12 p.m. must be entered into the system as 20:12. Beginning with DOS 4.0, however, this changed. Although you can still enter the time in 24-hour form when you use DOS 4.0, you can also enter 8:12 p.m. as 8:12p or 8:12pm.

The Path command   Figure 4-13 shows you how to use the Path command. This command can be used to establish a list of directories that DOS searches whenever it receives an external command. When DOS receives a command, it always starts by looking for the command in the current directory. Then, DOS continues the search by looking through the directories given by the last Path command. This list stays in effect until you issue another Path command.

If you enter a Path command at the prompt without a directory list, DOS tells you what the current path list is. This is illustrated by the first example in figure 4-13. Here, DOS displays the directory list that was established by the last Path command. This list includes two directories on the C drive: the DOS directory and the UTIL directory. On most systems, the current list will include the directory that contains the DOS files, but the directory name isn't always DOS.

If your system isn't set up so DOS knows where to find its external commands, you can issue a Path command that adds the DOS directory to the directory list. This is illustrated by the second example in figure 4-13. Here, the first Path command doesn't include a directory list so DOS displays the current list, which consists of the UTIL and WP50 directories. Then, the second Path command includes a directory list that consists of the DOS, UTIL, and WP50 directories. The third Path command in this example doesn't have a directory list so DOS displays the new directory list. This shows that the second Path command worked correctly.

When you want to add a directory to the current directory list, you should do it as shown in this second example to make sure that the list includes all of the required directories. If you establish the DOS directory with a command like this

```
path=c:\dos
```

the DOS directory will be the only one in the list. In other words, DOS doesn't add the directories given in the Path command to the current directory list. Instead, it replaces the current directory list with the list given in the Path command.

In the next chapter, you'll learn how to issue a Path command as part of your PC's start-up procedure. Once you set that up, you won't have to issue Path commands from the command prompt. As a result, you'll rarely use this command.

The Check-disk command   Figure 4-14 shows you how to use the Check-disk command that displays information about a specific disk. Here again, I've highlighted the commands to separate them from the data that's displayed by DOS. Note that the first Check-disk command doesn't have to specify a disk drive because the default drive is C. In contrast, the second command specifies drive D.

The Check-disk command is the first external command that I've presented in this chapter. As a result, DOS may not be able to find its command file when you issue the command. If it can't, DOS will display this message:

```
Bad command or file name
```

If that happens, you can use the Change-directory command to change the current directory to the one that contains the DOS files. Or you can use the Path command to add the DOS directory to the current directory list. Then, you can issue the Check-disk command again.

In the examples in figure 4-14, you can see that this command shows the total number of bytes of storage available on each disk; how that storage is used; and how much storage is available for new files. Each command shows how many bytes of storage are used for *hidden files* (files that DOS doesn't want you to access), how many for directories, and how many for user files. When you need to know whether a hard disk or diskette has enough space for a program or data file, you can use this command to find out.

This command also shows how many bytes are in *bad sectors*. These are sectors that are damaged so they can't store data reliably. Since DOS knows about these bad sectors and doesn't use them, they're nothing to worry about. In fact, most disk drives and diskettes have some bad sectors.

The last two lines of information for each drive tell how many bytes of conventional internal memory your system has and how many bytes aren't being used. In figure 4-14, these lines tell you that the PC has 655,360 bytes (about 640KB), and that 570,496 are free. If you subtract the second number from the first, you can see that 84,864 bytes of memory are used by the resident portion of DOS.

Besides getting the information shown in figure 4-14, the Check-disk command looks for various types of disk errors. If it finds any, it displays messages about these errors along with the other information. If you get one

```
The format of the Check-disk command

    CHKDSK [drive-spec]


Example 1

    C:\>chkdsk
    Volume DISK1_VOL1  created Dec 23, 1987 1:34p

     33421312 bytes total disk space
        53248 bytes in 2 hidden files
        69632 bytes in 27 directories
     31113216 bytes in 1071 user files
      2185216 bytes available on disk

       655360 bytes total memory
       570496 bytes free


Example 2

    C:\>chkdsk d:
    Volume DISK1_VOL2  created Dec 23, 1987 1:38p

     10421312 bytes total disk space
        79872 bytes in 27 directories
      9822208 bytes in 1071 user files
       135168 bytes in bad sectors
       384064 bytes available on disk

       655360 bytes total memory
       570496 bytes free

    C:\>
```

Figure 4-14   The operation of the Check-disk command

of these error messages, you often need to get technical help. But if you want to learn how to handle some of the most common error conditions on your own, you can refer to *The Only DOS Book You'll Ever Need*.

The Type and Print commands   The Type command lets you display the contents of a file; the Print command lets you print the contents of a file. However, these commands only work on *text files*. These files only contain characters that are in a standard code called ASCII. As a result, you can't use these commands to display or print the contents of the data files used by your application programs such as word processing, spreadsheet, or database files.

Figure 4-15 shows how I used these commands to display and print the contents of a DOS text file named CONFIG.SYS. Here again, I highlighted the commands to help you separate them from the DOS output. Since the commands don't specify a drive or directory for the CONFIG.SYS file, DOS looked for it in the current directory (the root directory) on the default drive (the C drive). As you can see, this file contains three lines of text.

Since the Print command is another external command, you may have to change the current directory to the one that contains the DOS files. Or you can use a Path command to add the DOS directory to the current directory list. Also, the Print command displays a message like the one in figure 4-15 that asks you to name the list device. If your system has been set up properly, all you have to do is press the Enter key when this message appears.

You can use the Type and Print commands to display or print the contents of the README files that come with software products. These are text files that usually contain corrections and changes to the manuals that come with the products. Because the files are often lengthy, it's usually better to print them than to display them. But if you want to read a file while it's displayed, you can control the scrolling of the text by using the Pause key.

How to shut down your PC

As I explained in chapter 2, you shouldn't turn your PC off when you're using an application program. If you do, you'll lose the work that is stored in internal memory. Instead, you should save your work and exit properly from the application program. Then, when DOS displays the command prompt, you can turn off your PC. It's also a good idea to remove diskettes from the diskette drives and leave their doors open before you turn your system off, but that isn't essential.

```
The formats of the Type and Print commands

    TYPE file-spec

    PRINT file-spec

The display of the Type and Print commands

    C:\>type config.sys
    BUFFERS = 20
    FILES = 20
    DEVICE = MOUSE.SYS

    C:\>print config.sys
    Name of list device [PRN] :
    Resident part of PRINT installed

        C:\CONFIG.SYS is currently being printed

    C:>

The printed output of the Print command

    BUFFERS = 20
    FILES = 20
    DEVICE = MOUSE.SYS
```

Figure 4-15   The operation of the Type and Print commands

Some perspective on DOS

The hardest part about learning to use DOS is getting started. Before you can do much of anything, you need to know how to enter a command, what the command formats are, and how to handle DOS error messages. That's why this chapter is the longest and most difficult one in this book.

Now that you've seen how twelve of the DOS commands work, you should have a better idea of why you need to learn DOS. First, if your PC doesn't have a shell utility that you use for starting your programs, you have to start your application programs from the command prompt. Second, even if your PC does have a shell utility, you need to be able to start programs from the command prompt when you add new programs to your system. Third, you can do some jobs with DOS commands that you can't do any other way. For instance, you can set the date and time of your system, you can check the available capacity of your disk drives, and you can use the Path command to tell DOS where to look for commands so DOS and your application programs work right.

Perhaps the most important reason for learning DOS, though, is that it helps you understand your system. As much as the software developers would like you to believe that you can use an application program without any knowledge of DOS, that just isn't true. If you want to have more control over your PC, you need to know more about DOS.

Terms

self test
POST routine
Power-On-Self-Test routine
booting the system
command prompt
keyword
command name
parameter
switch
resident DOS
internal command
external command
command file
parent directory
DOS error message
hidden file
bad sector
text file

Exercises

1.   Use the Prompt command as shown in figure 4-4 to change the prompt so the current directory is displayed.

2.   Use the Change-drive command to find out what drive letters are valid on your system.

3.   Use the Directory command to display the directory listing for the root directory of the C drive. If the listing for this directory is more than one screen long, use the /P switch to display the directory again. Next, use the /W switch to display the directory again. While the listing is displayed, note the names of the directories that are listed. Then, find the entries for the COMMAND.COM, CONFIG.SYS, and AUTO-EXEC.BAT files. If you can't find one for the AUTOEXEC.BAT file, you're going to want to create one after you read the next chapter.

4.   If there are no directories in the root directory of the C drive, use the Directory command to display the directories that are stored in the root directory of the D drive. While the directory is displayed, note the names of the directories that are listed.

5.   Use the Change-directory command to change from one of the directories to another. Note how the command prompt changes as the current directory changes. If your system has both C and D drives, experiment with the Change-drive and Change-directory commands so you see that each drive has its own current directory.

6.   Find out which directory contains the DOS files for your system. Normally, that directory will be on the C drive, and it will be named DOS. On some systems, however, all of the DOS files will be stored in the root directory of the C drive.

7.   Use the Change-directory command to change the directory to the one that contains the DOS files. Next, use the Directory command with the /P and /W switches to display the current directory.

8. To see how the F3 key works, press it to run your last command again. Then, while the DOS directory is being displayed, cancel the command using one of the keystroke combinations of figure 4-2.

9. Start one of your application programs from the command prompt using the procedure shown in figure 4-8. If the program directory isn't on the default drive, change to the correct drive before you start the procedure.

10. Put a diskette in the A drive. Next, use the Directory command to display its contents. Then, remove the diskette and run the last command again. When DOS displays its error message, put the diskette back in the drive and enter the letter *r* to retry the command.

11. Use the Clear-screen command to clear the monitor screen. Then, use the Version command to find out what version of DOS you're using on your PC.

12. Use the Date and Time commands to find out whether the date and time are set correctly for your system. If they aren't, correct them.

13. Use a Path command without a directory list to see whether your system has a current directory list. If it does, check to see whether the DOS directory is included in the list, but don't change the list.

14. Use the Check-disk command to find out the capacities of the disk drives on your system. Also, find out how many bytes are available for new files on each disk drive. You can do this for diskette drives as well as for the hard disk drives, but remember that the A drive on some PCs can handle both standard and high capacity diskettes. Then, the capacity depends on the diskette, not the drive.

    Remember that this command is an external command. To execute it, the DOS directory must either be in the current directory list as shown by the Path command, or the current directory must be set to the DOS directory.

15. Use the Type and Print commands to display and print the CONFIG.SYS file in the root directory of the C drive. Next, use the Type command to display the COMMAND.COM file in the root directory of the C drive. Since this isn't a text file, the command will display illegible output.

Chapter 5

How to use batch files to start your application programs more efficiently

If you start your programs from the command prompt for a while, you know that you have to enter the same commands over and over again. Usually, you have to enter at least two commands to start a program, and sometimes you have to enter three or more.

In this chapter, though, you'll learn how to start your programs from the command prompt by using *batch files*. Once you set these files up, you can execute a series of commands with a single command entry. That means you can start your programs from the command prompt with fewer keystrokes.

If someone has already set up batch files for you that start your application programs, you may never need to set up your own batch files. Nevertheless, it's worth taking the time to learn how to use batch files. Once you know how to use them, you may decide to modify some of the ones on your system so they work exactly the way you want them to work.

Similarly, if you use a shell utility to start your application programs, you may never need to use batch files. But knowing how they work can help you set up the shell so it works more efficiently. In some cases, you may decide to set up the utility so it starts one of your batch files. At the least, knowing how batch files work will help you understand how your shell works.

How a batch file works

A *batch file* is a file that contains one or more commands. The file names for all batch files have BAT as the extension so DOS can distinguish these from other types of files. Then, when you want to execute the commands in a batch file, you just enter the name of the batch file without the extension at the command prompt.

Figure 5-1 gives an example of a batch file named 123.BAT that contains six commands. To execute these commands, you just enter 123 at the command prompt. The first four commands in this batch file start *Lotus 1-2-3* from the 123 directory on the C drive. Then, when the PC user exits from *Lotus*, DOS returns to the batch file and executes the last two commands in the file. The fifth command changes the directory to the root directory; the last command clears the monitor screen. DOS then displays the command prompt and waits for your next command.

If you look closely at the commands in the batch file in figure 5-1, you can see that the fourth command is 123, the same as the name that starts the batch file. That's okay, but you have to make sure that you set your system up so this works correctly. I'll show you how to do that later on in this chapter.

How to use the Echo command in a batch file

Figure 5-2 presents the Echo command. This command is designed specifically for batch files. You can use it to specify whether or not you want batch file commands displayed as they are executed. You can also use it to display messages.

In the batch file in figure 5-1, "off" is specified so the commands in the file aren't displayed as they are executed. However, if the commands in the batch file generate any messages, they are displayed. Since "on" is the default condition, you need to use an Echo-on command only if an Echo-off command has been issued previously. Usually, it doesn't matter whether or not the commands in a batch file are displayed as they are executed, so an Echo-off command at the start of a batch file isn't necessary.

If the parameter is anything other than "on" or "off," the Echo command treats it as a message you want displayed on the monitor. The message is

A batch file named 123.BAT in the UTIL directory

```
echo off
c:
cd \123
123
cd \
cls
```

The command you enter at the command prompt to execute the six commands in the batch file named 123.BAT

```
C:\UTIL>123
```

Figure 5-1   How a batch file works

Format

```
ECHO [on] [off] [message]
```

Function

If the parameter is ON, this command tells DOS to display all batch file commands as they are executed. If the parameter is OFF, this command tells DOS not to display the batch file commands as they are executed. The OFF parameter stays in effect until the next Echo command is executed. If there's a Message parameter, the message is displayed. If no parameters are used, DOS displays a message that tells whether the Echo command is on or off.

Examples

```
echo on

echo off

echo Please record your PC time at the computer center
echo after each session.
```

Figure 5-2   The Echo command for use in batch files

displayed whether or not the current Echo status is "on" or "off." This is illustrated by the third and fourth examples in figure 5-2, and I'll show you how this works in a batch file later in this chapter.

Two ways to start an application program from a batch file

Whether you're issuing commands at the command prompt or from a batch file, there are two methods you can use to start an application program. As you will see, you can't use both methods with all programs. But you should understand both of them so you can select the one that's best for each of your programs.

Method 1: Set the default drive and current directory to the program directory before issuing the command name   In the first batch file in figure 5-3, the first two commands set the default drive and the current directory to those that contain the program. Then, the third command starts the program. This method will work no matter what version of DOS you're using or what application program you're trying to start. This, of course, is the method that I showed you in the last chapter for starting application programs from the command prompt, but it also works in a batch file.

Method 2: Enter the program's path along with the command name (DOS 3.0 or later)   If you're using a version of DOS that's 3.0 or later, you can code a program's path along with its program name. This is illustrated by the second example in figure 5-3. This command tells DOS to look on the C drive in the WP50 directory for a program named WP. Although you can start a program this way at the command prompt as well as in a batch file, this method is more useful in a batch file because it requires so many keystrokes.

If the program name and the directory name are the same, the command you enter looks a bit peculiar. If, for example, the program named WORD is stored in a directory named WORD, the command to execute the program looks like this:

```
c:\word\word
```

Set the default drive and current directory to the program directory

```
c:
cd \wp50
wp
```

Code the program's path along with the program name (DOS 3.0 or later)

```
c:\wp50\wp
```

Figure 5-3   Two ways to start an application program from a batch file

This just tells DOS to execute the command file named WORD that is stored in the WORD directory on the C drive.

Before you try to start a program this way, you should realize that it won't work with many application programs. For instance, both *Lotus 1-2-3* and *Q&A* require that the current directory be set to the program directory before the program is run. That way, the program can find the files that it requires for operation. As a result, you have to use the first method in figure 5-3 for starting programs like these.

How to use parameters with a batch file

Many DOS commands accept parameters. The Directory command, for instance, accepts parameters that specify which drive and directory you want to display. And the Type command accepts a parameter that specifies the file you want to display.

Similarly, many application programs accept one or more parameters. When you start *WordPerfect*, for example, you can use a parameter to specify the name of the file that you want the program to retrieve as in this example:

```
C:\WP50>wp \wp50\mma\c1figs
```

```
A batch file named WP.BAT that provides for one parameter

c:
cd \wp50
wp %1
cd \
cls


A command that causes the batch file to retrieve a file

C:\>wp c:\wp50\mma\c1figs
```

Figure 5-4   How to use a replaceable parameter in a batch file

Then, after DOS loads the program, *WordPerfect* retrieves the file you specified. Many application programs provide for a retrieval parameter like this,
and some programs provide for several other parameters as well.

You can also use parameters in batch files. For example, suppose you
want to create a batch file named WP.BAT that starts *WordPerfect* and provides for a filename parameter. Figure 5-4 shows how you can do this.
Notice the second line of the batch file:

```
wp %1
```

Here, the %1 is a *replaceable parameter*. When DOS executes this line of
the batch file, it replaces the %1 with the value of the first parameter you
type when you start the batch file. So if you start the batch file using the command shown in the figure, DOS substitutes \WP50\MMA\C1FIGS for %1
when it executes the second line. As a result, *WordPerfect* will load the
C1FIGS file as its initial document.

Two examples of batch files that start application programs

With this as background, you should understand the examples of batch files
in figure 5-5. They start a spreadsheet and a word processing program.

```
The 123.BAT file

    c:
    cd \123
    123
    cd \
    cls


The WP.BAT file for use with DOS 3.0 or later

    c:
    cd \wp50\mma
    \wp50\wp %1
    cd \
    cls
```

Figure 5-5   Typical batch files for starting a word processing and a spreadsheet program

A batch file for starting *Lotus 1-2-3*   The first batch file in figure 5-5 starts a spreadsheet program. Because this program requires that the current directory be set to the program directory, you use the first method in figure 5-3. This batch file doesn't provide for any replaceable parameters because *Lotus 1-2-3* won't accept a parameter that lets you specify the spreadsheet file that you want to use.

A batch file for starting *WordPerfect*   The second batch file in figure 5-5 sets the current directory to the data directory before starting the program. This saves time, because you don't have to use *WordPerfect* to change the current directory to your data directory once the program is started. Also, because this batch file provides for one replaceable parameter, you can specify the first file that you want to work on when you execute the batch file.

For example, if the first file you want to work on is named C1FIGS, you start the program by issuing this command at the prompt:

```
C:\>wp c1figs
```

Because this batch file sets the current directory to the data directory before it starts the word processing program, this command causes the word processing program to retrieve the file named C1FIGS from the MMA directory within the WP50 directory.

Unfortunately, you can't use this batch file with a version of DOS that precedes 3.0. That's because the second command specifies the path for the word processing program, and earlier versions of DOS don't let you do that.

How to set up the AUTOEXEC.BAT file so your batch files work correctly

When you start a hard disk system, DOS looks for three files in the root directory of the C drive. First, it loads the resident portion of DOS from the COMMAND.COM file. Second, it reads the CONFIG.SYS file and sets up your PC based on the specifications in this file. Third, it looks for a special batch file named AUTOEXEC.BAT. If your PC has an AUTOEXEC.BAT file, DOS executes the commands in the file. If it doesn't, DOS executes the Time and Date commands and then displays the command prompt.

Since the AUTOEXEC.BAT file is a batch file, it can contain any DOS commands. As a result, the AUTOEXEC.BAT file can have a significant effect on the way your system works. If you set this file up properly, DOS will always know where to find its external commands and where to find your batch files.

Two commands that should be in every AUTOEXEC.BAT file   In general, the AUTOEXEC.BAT file should include at least two commands. One should be a Prompt command that tells DOS to display the default drive and current directory in the command prompt. The other command should be a Path command that tells DOS what directories to search when it looks for its external commands and for batch files.

Figure 5-6 shows a simple AUTOEXEC.BAT file. The second command in this file is the form of the Prompt command that you learned about in the last chapter. This command enhances the command prompt by causing it to display the current directory along with the default drive.

The third command in this AUTOEXEC.BAT file is a Path command that establishes a list of directories that DOS searches whenever it receives a

```
echo off
prompt $p$g
path=c:\dos;c:\util
cls
```

Figure 5-6   A simple AUTOEXEC.BAT file

command. In figure 5-6, this command tells DOS to search two directories on the C drive in this order: first DOS, then UTIL.

At the least, the Path command in the AUTOEXEC.BAT file should include the DOS and batch file directories. Beyond this, you may want to include one or more of the directories that contain application programs, but that depends on the requirements of your programs. Often, you don't gain anything by putting the directory of an application program in the directory list because the current directory has to be set to the program directory anyway before you can start the program. Then, since DOS always starts its search for a command in the current directory, it never gets to the current directory list.

Since DOS doesn't use the Path command when it's looking for data files, you shouldn't include data directories in your Path command. Similarly, you shouldn't include the root directory of the C drive in your Path command unless it contains command or batch files that aren't executed automatically as part of the start-up procedure.

In general, you shouldn't include diskette drives in your Path command either. If you do, DOS will search them when it can't find a command in the directories that precede the diskette directories in the search path. Then, if you don't have a diskette in the drive that's specified, DOS will display an error message indicating that the drive isn't ready. That just slows you down.

Other commands for your AUTOEXEC.BAT file   Beyond the Path and Prompt commands, your AUTOEXEC.BAT file should contain whatever commands are appropriate for your system. If you use certain types of utility programs, for example, you should start them from this file. And some hardware components require that special commands be put in this file. If you're

---

An AUTOEXEC.BAT file that displays a message

```
echo off
prompt $p$g
path=c:\dos;c:\util
cls
echo Please record your PC time at the computer center when
echo you're done. We're trying to keep track of the usage of
echo each system this month.
echo Thanks for your cooperation.
```

An AUTOEXEC.BAT file that starts _Lotus 1-2-3_

```
echo off
prompt $p$g
path=c:\dos;c:\util
cd \123
123
```

An AUTOEXEC.BAT file that starts the DOS 5.0 shell

```
echo off
prompt $p$g
path=c:\dos;c:\util
dosshell
```

Figure 5-7   Expanded versions of AUTOEXEC.BAT files

interested, chapter 14 introduces you to some of the commands that are commonly put in this file.

To illustrate expanded versions of AUTOEXEC.BAT files, figure 5-7 presents three more. The first file ends with several Echo commands that display a message for the PC user who starts the system. The second file ends with two commands that start an application program. This is useful if you regularly use just one program. The third file ends with a Dosshell command that starts the DOS 5.0 shell. If you don't end the AUTOEXEC.BAT file with this command, DOS 5.0 starts with the command prompt just like earlier versions of DOS.

1. Keep your batch files simple.

2. Store your batch files in a utilities or batch file directory.

3. Make sure the directory that contains your batch files is in the path that's established by the AUTOEXEC.BAT file.

4. Make sure you understand how DOS searches for commands so your batch files work correctly.

Figure 5-8   Four guidelines for using batch files

How to test an AUTOEXEC.BAT file   When you finish creating or changing an AUTOEXEC.BAT file, you should test it to make sure it works right. One way to do that is to turn the PC off and turn it back on again. Then, the PC performs its self test and boots DOS. As part of the booting process, the commands in the AUTOEXEC.BAT file are executed.

A more efficient way to restart DOS is to press this key combination: Ctrl+Alt+Delete. This means to press the Delete key while holding down the Ctrl and Alt keys. This boots DOS, but doesn't force the PC to go through its self test again. This is a useful combination of keys to know since you can use it whenever you need to restart the system due to a software or hardware problem.

Four guidelines for using batch files

If you use batch files correctly, they don't take much time to set up or maintain. And they improve your efficiency. To use your batch files to best advantage, though, you should follow the guidelines in figure 5-8.

Keep your batch files simple   Besides the commands you've learned in this chapter, DOS provides many others that are specifically designed for use in batch files. These commands make it possible for you to create batch files that do elaborate functions. But even without these commands, it's tempting to try to do too much with a batch file.

So the first guideline is to keep your batch files simple. Most of the time that means your batch files should have just four or five commands, like the batch files in figure 5-5. If your batch files are more complicated than those, you're likely to find that you're spending more time using DOS and less time using your application programs to do productive work.

Store your batch files in a utilities or batch file directory   To keep your batch files under control, you should store them all in the same directory. Then, you can use one Directory command to list all of them when you need to review what you have on your system. On my system, I keep all of the batch files in a directory named UTIL that includes some utility programs. However, you can also keep your batch files in their own directory. A good name for this directory is BAT.

Make sure the directory that contains your batch files is in the path that's established by the AUTOEXEC.BAT file   To execute the commands in a batch file, DOS needs to be able to find the file. As a result, you should put the directory that contains your batch files in the list established by the Path command in the AUTOEXEC.BAT file. If, for example, your batch files are stored in the UTIL directory, the AUTOEXEC.BAT file in figure 5-6 will get your PC started right.

Make sure you understand how DOS searches for commands so your batch files work correctly   When DOS receives a command, it always starts looking for it in the current directory. If it doesn't find the command there, it searches through the directories in the current directory list, one directory at a time. In each directory, DOS looks first for a COM file, then for an EXE file, and last for a BAT file.

If you use the same name for a batch file that is used for a COM or EXE file, this search order can cause a problem as illustrated by the batch file in figure 5-9. Here, the WP.BAT file is in the UTIL directory. Then, when the WP command is entered at the command prompt, DOS starts the batch file because it finds the WP.BAT file in the UTIL directory before it finds a WP.COM or WP.EXE file in another directory. After the second command in this batch file changes the directory to WP50\MMA, the third command issues the WP command to start *WordPerfect*. That's when the problem starts.

The AUTOEXEC.BAT file

```
echo off
prompt $p$g
path=d:\dos;c:\util;c:\wp50
cls
```

The WP.BAT file in the UTIL directory

```
echo off
cd \wp50\mma
wp %1
cd \
cls
```

The command that starts the batch file

```
C:\>wp
```

Figure 5-9   A batch file that won't work correctly

If you look at the Path command in the AUTOEXEC.BAT file, you can see that the UTIL directory is before the WP50 directory in the search list. That means that DOS finds the WP.BAT file before it finds the WP.EXE file when the WP command is executed. As a result, the WP command in this batch file starts the batch file again, not *WordPerfect*. This starts a loop that will continue until you restart the system.

If you're using DOS 3.0 or later, the best way to solve this problem is to include the program's path along with its name in the batch file. For example, the third line of the WP.BAT file in figure 5-9 should be:

```
\wp50\wp %1
```

That's the way it is in the WP.BAT file in figure 5-5. Then, DOS looks for the program in the correct directory, and you get the result you want.

Another solution is to use a name for the batch file that is different from the name for the program's command file. If, for example, you name the batch file MMA.BAT, the file will work the way you want it to.

A third solution is to change the current directory to the one that contains the program instead of the one that contains the data before you issue the program command. For *WordPerfect*, though, it's more efficient to use one of the first two solutions. That way the data directory is set the way you want it as soon as you start using the program.

Four ways to create or change a batch file

By now, I hope you understand how batch files work. If so, you can decide whether or not you want to create your own batch files or change those that are already in use on your system. In particular, you should decide whether or not your AUTOEXEC.BAT file is okay. You can review this file or any other batch file by using the Type or Print command.

Remember that the AUTOEXEC.BAT file is always stored in the root directory on the C drive. If your PC doesn't have an AUTOEXEC.BAT file, you definitely should create one. And if the file doesn't contain the proper Prompt and Path commands, you should take the time to change it.

If you decide that you are going to create or change one or more batch files, please read on. Otherwise, you can skip to the end of this chapter.

Because a batch file is just a *text file*, you can use several different methods to create or change one. No matter what version of DOS you're using, you can use the Copy command to create simple text files. If you have a text editor on your PC like the one that comes with DOS 5.0, the easiest way to work with a text file is to use that editor. If you have a word processing program like *WordPerfect* that makes it easy to work with text files, you can use that for creating and changing batch files. And if none of these three methods works for you, you can use the Edlin program that comes with all versions of DOS, although this is the most difficult of the methods. These methods are now presented in the sequence I've just given, but remember that you only need to know how to use one of them.

How to use the Copy command to create or change a batch file   One of the easiest ways to create a new batch file is to use a special form of the

---

The format of the Copy-con command

```
COPY CON target-spec
```

How the command is used to create a batch file named 123.BAT in the current directory

```
C:\UTIL>copy con 123.bat
c:
cd \123
123
cd \
cls
^Z
            1 File(s) copies

C:\UTIL>
```

Figure 5-10   How to use a special form of the Copy command to create a batch file

DOS Copy command as illustrated in figure 5-10. Here, the first parameter in the Copy command is the word "con," which means that the source file will come from the keyboard, or console, of the PC. The second parameter specifies the name that you want to use for the batch file that the command will create. When you issue the Copy command using these parameters, DOS automatically moves the cursor to the next line so you're ready to type in the commands for the batch file.

After you've entered the commands that you want in the batch file, you enter an end-of-file character, which appears as ^Z. To make this entry, you hold down the Ctrl key while you press the letter z. Or you can press the F6 key. Although this entry appears as two characters on the monitor, it's read as a single character that tells DOS that the source file contains no more commands. To complete the Copy command, you press the Enter key. Then, DOS copies the commands you entered into the file you specified.

If you want to change an existing batch file, you can still use the Copy command. You just create a new file with the same name as the file you want to change. Then, when you end the command, the original file will be replaced with the file you created. Obviously, though, this isn't efficient because you have to enter a whole file even if you want to change only one character.

How to use a full-screen text editor to create or change a batch file   A full-screen *text editor* is a program that is designed for creating and changing text files. Unlike the Copy-con command, a text editor lets you change existing batch files. Also, a full-screen text editor is easier to use and more flexible than the other programs presented here. So you'll probably want to use a full-screen text editor if you have one.

Most shell utilities, like *PC Tools*, come with a text editor. And DOS 5.0 provides a full-screen text editor called *Edit*. To start the DOS 5.0 text editor, you type *edit* followed by the name of the file you want to edit as in this example:

```
C:\UTIL>edit 123.bat
```

This starts the Edit program and displays the file you specified as shown in figure 5-11.

If you're creating a new file, you just start adding commands to the file. If you're modifying an existing file, you make the necessary modifications. When you're done with the file, you save it to the hard disk.

Like a word processing program, the Edit program lets you use the arrow keys or a mouse to move the cursor to where you want it, and any text you type will be added at the cursor location. In addition, you can use the Delete or Backspace keys to delete characters. And you can use the Insert key to change from insert to type-over mode or vice versa.

You can also highlight the text you want to copy, move, or delete. To highlight text using the keyboard, you move the cursor to the beginning of the text. Then, you hold down the Shift key as you use the arrow keys to highlight the text you want to edit. To highlight text using a mouse, you move the mouse cursor to the beginning of the text. Then, you hold down the left mouse button as you move the cursor to highlight the text.

The Edit program also provides menus that make it easier to select the commands that you need to edit a file. Figure 5-12, for example, shows the commands on the Edit menu. Here, the Cut option temporarily deletes the

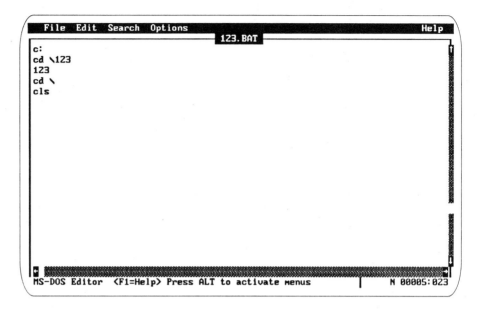

Figure 5-11   A batch file displayed by the DOS 5.0 Edit program

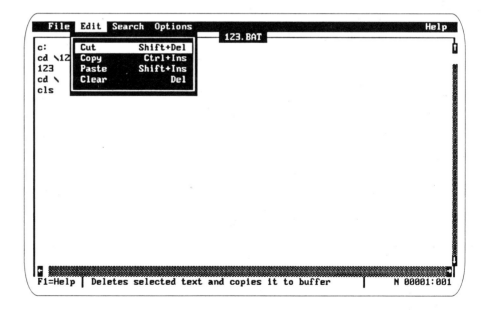

Figure 5-12   The Edit menu of the DOS 5.0 Edit program

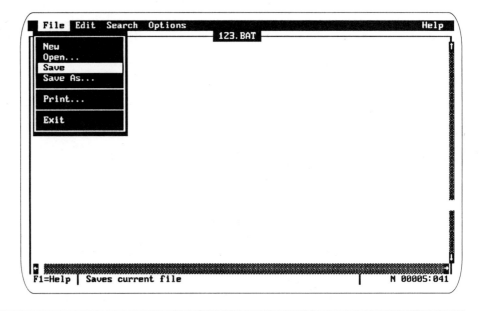

Figure 5-13   The File menu of the DOS 5.0 Edit program

highlighted text; the Copy option copies the highlighted text; the Paste option inserts text that you deleted using the Cut option; and the Clear option permanently deletes highlighted text.

To select one of the commands the Edit program provides, you can use two techniques. To select a command using the keyboard, you press the Alt key to activate the menu system and use the Left and Right arrow keys to move to the menu you want. Next, you press the Enter key and use the Down arrow key to move to the command option you want. When you press the Enter key again, the command starts.

To select a command using a mouse, you move the mouse cursor to the menu you want and press the left button once. Then, you move the mouse cursor to the command you want and press the left button again to start the command.

After you have created or edited a file, you save it using one of the commands on the File menu shown in figure 5-13. Here, the New option clears the screen so you can create a new file. The Open option loads an existing file from disk storage so you can edit it. The Save option saves the file using the current file name. The Save-as option lets you specify the file name you want to use to save the file. The Print option prints the file. And the Exit option stops the program and returns you to the command prompt.

Although this is just a brief introduction to the Edit program, that's all you need to know for editing small files. If you work with this program for a few minutes, you'll see that it's quite easy to use. So if you have DOS 5.0, you'll probably want to use this program for creating and changing your batch files.

How to use a word processing program to create or change a batch file

If you don't want to use the Copy-con command and if you don't have a text editor, you can use the text feature of your word processing program to create and change batch files. In this case, you must make sure that you retrieve an existing batch file as a text file, not as a word processing file. Also, after you create a new batch file or change an existing one, you must make sure you save the file as a text file, not as a word processing file.

When you use *WordPerfect*, for example, you use the Text-In feature to retrieve a batch file. Then, you use the regular word processing commands to change the file. When you're done, you use the Text-Out feature to save the file as a DOS text file. Not all word processing programs make it that easy to work with text files, though, so this isn't always practical with other programs.

How to use Edlin to create or change a batch file

If the other methods don't work for you, you can always use the Edlin program that comes with all versions of DOS. Edlin is a program that you can use to create or change a batch file or any other text file. But unlike a text editor, Edlin lets you edit only one line at a time. This makes Edlin awkward to use when compared to a text editor. In addition, the Edlin commands are likely to be confusing at first. So if you have another method you can use for editing batch files, you'll probably want to skip this information on Edlin.

Figure 5-14 presents some of Edlin's most useful commands. As you can see, the format of these commands use line numbers and single letters to invoke functions. This figure also shows the most useful keystrokes that you can use to edit a line or insert lines into a batch file.

Edlin commands

Command	Format	Function
`Insert`	`(line-number)I`	Inserts one or more lines before the line-number indicated.
`Edit`	`line-number`	Edits the line indicated by the line number.
`Delete`	`(line-number or numbers)D`	Deletes the line or lines indicated by the line numbers.
`List`	`L`	Lists the current version of the file.
`End`	`E`	Ends the editing session and saves the file.
`Quit`	`Q`	Quits the editing session without saving the file.

Keystrokes for the Edit command

Key	Editing function
F1	Copies one character from the old file.
F3	Copies the remaining characters in the old line.
Delete	Skips one character in the old line, thus deleting it.
Insert	Starts or stops the insertion of the characters you type in the new line.

Keystrokes for the Insert command

Keys	Editing function
Ctrl+Pause or Ctrl+C	Ends the Insert command.

Figure 5-14   A summary of the most useful commands and keystrokes for Edlin

```
C:\UTIL>edlin 123.bat
End of input file

*1              1:*c:
                2:  cd \123
                3:  123
                4:  cls
*2
                2:*cd \123
                2:*cd \lotus
*4d
*1
                1:  c:
                2:  cd \lotus
                3:  123
*4i
                4:*cd \
                5:*cls
                6:*^C
*1
                1:  c:
                2:  cd \lotus
                3:  123
                4:  cd \
                5:  cls
*e

c:\>
```

Figure 5-15   How to use Edlin to modify a batch file

In figure 5-15, you can see how Edlin is used to change a batch file. Here, all of the entries made by the PC user are shaded. And the file specification that's entered with the Edlin command indicates the file you want to edit or create. If this file doesn't exist, Edlin assumes you're creating a new file. If the file does exist, Edlin displays the following message:

End of input file

Then, on the next line, it displays an asterisk (*) that indicates it's waiting for a command.

In figure 5-15, the first command is the letter *l*. This List command tells Edlin to list the current version of the file. As you can see, the file consists of four commands.

The second command in figure 5-15 is the line number 2. Because no command code is given with the line number, this tells Edlin that you want to edit line 2. In this case, the name of the directory that contains the program files was changed from 123 to Lotus. When you edit a line, you can use the F3 key to copy the characters from the old version of the line. You can also use the Delete and Insert keys to delete or insert characters within a line.

The third command in figure 5-15 (4d) tells Edlin to delete the fourth line in the file. Then, the fourth command (l) tells Edlin to list the current version of the file. Now, the file has only three lines because one has been deleted.

The fifth command in figure 5-15 (4i) tells Edlin that lines are going to be inserted into the file before the fourth line. Since the file has only three lines, the lines are inserted after the last line in the file. Because you can insert one or more lines with this command, you need to tell Edlin when you're through. To do this, you hold down the Ctrl key and press the letter *c*. Note that this is the same keystroke combination you use to cancel a command that's being executed by DOS. When this combination is used within Edlin, it appears as ^C, and it ends the Insert command.

The sixth command in figure 5-15 is the List command again; it lists the changed version of the file. Since the file is now in the form that the user wants, the next command is the End command. The keystroke for this command is the letter *e*. This command ends Edlin and saves the edited file. As a result, the command prompt appears on the monitor. If you want to end Edlin without saving the edited file, you enter the letter *q* for the Quit command.

Although Edlin is a bit confusing when you first start to use it, you can get used to it after a short time. That's particularly true if you limit yourself to the commands and keystrokes shown in figure 5-14. Although Edlin provides several other commands and several other keystrokes and keystroke combinations, they just make Edlin that much harder to use.

When you use Edlin to edit an existing file, it automatically creates a backup file for you. If, for example, you're editing the 123.BAT file, Edlin saves the original version of the file under the name 123.BAK. Then, if the

new version of the file doesn't work right, you still have the original version
to work with. To reinstate the original as the 123.BAT file, you can use this
Copy command:

```
copy c:\123.bak c:\123.bat
```

The use of this command is explained in the next chapter.

If you're using Edlin to create a new batch file, you get this message
after you enter the command and file name at the command prompt:

```
New file
```

Then, you use the Insert command to insert the commands you want in the
batch file. After you enter the last command, you turn off the Insert
command using the Ctrl+C key combination. Next, you save the file and return to the prompt by pressing the letter *e*.

Some perspective on batch files

Once you learn how to create and maintain a batch file, you should be able to
set one up in just a few minutes. Although each batch file saves you just a
few keystrokes each time you use it, this set up time pays off because it simplifies your operational procedures. As a result, you don't have to remember
as many DOS details in order to use your application programs.

Once you've set up your batch files for starting application programs,
you can execute the batch file in several ways. If, for example, you want to
start an application program from the AUTOEXEC.BAT file, you can
include the command for the batch file that starts the application program. In
other words, a batch file can execute other batch files. You can also execute a
batch file from the DOS shell or from another shell utility. And you can execute a batch file from the command prompt.

Although this chapter shows you how to use batch files just for starting
application programs, you can also use batch files for simplifying DOS commands. In chapter 8, for example, you'll learn how to use a batch file to simplify the use of the Backup command. By using the batch file instead of
entering the command, you don't have to remember the details of using the
command.

With this in mind, you should consider using a batch file to simplify your operational procedures whenever you're bothered by the continual need to remember DOS details. Once you've got your batch files set up, you'll spend more time using your application programs and less time using DOS.

Terms

batch file
replaceable parameter
text file
text editor

Exercises

1. Start one of your application programs from the command prompt by using the second method in figure 5-3. But remember, if the program requires that the current directory be set to the program's directory, this method won't work properly.

2. Use Directory commands to find which directories (if any) contain batch files. To display only batch files, you can use the *.BAT wildcard specification in each Directory command.

3. Enter a Path command without any parameters at the command prompt to see whether a directory list has been established by the AUTO-EXEC.BAT file. If so, check to see whether the directories that contain batch files are included in the directory list.

4. Create a batch file for starting one of your application programs. If the program provides for a parameter, set up the batch file so it provides for the parameter. Store the batch file in a directory that's appropriate for batch files. To test your batch file, enter its name at the command prompt. If its directory isn't listed in the current path, you must change the current directory to the one that contains the batch file before you enter the name of the batch file.

5. Use a Directory command to see whether the root directory of the C drive contains an AUTOEXEC.BAT file. If it does, use the Print command to print the file. Then, check to see whether this file contains an appropriate Prompt and Path command as prescribed in this chapter.

6. If the AUTOEXEC.BAT file doesn't include an appropriate Prompt and Path command, modify the file so it does. But if you don't understand what some of the commands in the existing file do, don't delete or modify them because they may have an important effect on your system. To test your AUTOEXEC.BAT file, press the Ctrl+Alt+Delete key combination to restart the PC. Then, use the system for a while to make sure the AUTOEXEC.BAT file has worked correctly.

Section 3

The least you need to know about DOS to manage your files

No matter what application programs you use, you need to know how to manage the directories and files on your hard disk. You also need to know how to work with diskettes. And you need to know how to back up the files on your hard disk to diskettes. So those are the skills you'll learn in this section.

If you use a shell program on your PC for managing directories and files, you should still read the chapters in this section for four reasons. First, you can do some of these jobs more easily by using DOS commands than you can by using a shell. Second, if you're using a shell program like the DOS 5.0 shell, you'll learn the parameters and switches that you need when you use the shell to perform functions like formatting diskettes and backing up the hard disk. Third, you'll learn file management guidelines that you should follow whether or not you use a shell. Last, you'll be able to use your shell program more effectively if you understand how the shell functions are done by DOS commands. After all, a shell program merely converts the functions you request into DOS commands so you don't have to be concerned about the details of the commands.

Chapter 6

How to manage the directories and files on a hard disk

When you use a hard disk, its directories and files can quickly get out of control. If you use three or four different application programs for a year or two, it's not unusual to have more than one thousand files spread over a couple dozen directories. By that time, you're likely to have dozens of files that you no longer need and at least a few files that you need but can't find. That's why it's important that you learn how to do an effective job of managing your directories and files.

In this chapter, you'll learn how to use five DOS commands to manage your directories and three commands to manage your files. Next, you'll learn how to use the two DOS wildcards within the commands for managing files. Then, you'll learn how to use the directory commands and file commands together for some common maintenance tasks. Last, you'll learn 12 guidelines that will help you manage your directories and files more effectively.

If you have a shell program on your PC that makes it easy to manage directories and files, you should use it for most of those tasks. But you should also know how to manage directories and files from the command prompt for at least two reasons. First, you can perform some file management jobs more efficiently from the command prompt. Second, you'll be able to use your shell program more effectively if you understand how the shell functions are done with DOS commands. All a shell program does is convert the functions that you request into DOS commands so you don't have to be concerned about the details of the commands.

Five commands for working with directories

Figure 6-1 summarizes five commands you can use for working with directories. In chapter 4, you learned how to use the first two, so you shouldn't have any trouble learning to use the others.

The Directory command   As you already know, this command displays a directory. But if you use DOS 5.0, you can use another switch with the Directory command: the /S switch. When you use this switch, DOS not only displays the contents of the directory you specified, but it also displays the contents of any subdirectories that are subordinate to the directory you specified.

This switch is useful when you can remember the name of the file, but you can't remember the name of the subdirectory that contains the file. In figure 6-2, for example, I used the /S switch to find out the path for the file named PROFORMA.WK1. As you can see, the complete path for this file is:

```
123\MMA\PROFORMA.WK1
```

Finding a file this way is a simple task that you can do more efficiently from the command prompt than you can from a shell program.

The Change-directory command   As you already know, you use this command to change the current directory. But there's another form of this command that is often useful:

```
cd ..
```

The two dots in the directory specification represent the parent directory. The parent directory is always the directory in the path that immediately precedes the current directory. So with this specification, you can change the current directory to the parent directory.

Name	Format	Function
Directory	DIR [file-spec] [/p] [/w] [/s]	Displays a directory listing for the specified files. The /P switch causes a pause when a screen is full; the /W switch causes a wide display format; the /S switch provided by DOS 5.0 displays subordinate directories and their files.
Change directory	CD [directory-spec]	Changes the current directory. If the parameter is omitted, this command displays the path of the current directory.
Make directory	MD directory-spec	Makes a new directory.
Remove directory	RD directory-spec	Removes a directory. However, a directory must be empty before it can be removed. As a result, you can't remove a directory when it's the current directory.
Tree	TREE [drive-spec] [/f]	Displays the directory structure for a drive. The /F switch also causes a display of the files within each directory.

Figure 6-1   Five commands for working with directories

The Make-directory command   You use the Make-directory command to make a new directory. As you can see in figure 6-1, you enter a directory specification in this command to indicate the directory you want to create. This specification gives the name of the new directory, and it also locates the new directory within the directory structure of the drive. You'll learn how to use this command for directory maintenance tasks later in this chapter.

When you name a directory, you use the same naming rules that you use for files. Thus, a directory name can be up to eight characters long with an extension of up to three characters. In practice, though, it makes sense to create short, meaningful directory names with no extensions.

```
C:\>dir proforma.wk1 /s

 Volume in drive C is DOS-C
 Volume Serial Number is 159A-7E41

Directory of C:\123\MMA

PROFORMA WK1       16709 06-12-89    4:36p
        1 file(s)        16709 bytes

Total files listed:
        1 file(s)        16709 bytes
                       1757184 bytes free

C:\>
```

Figure 6-2   The use of the /S switch in the DOS 5.0 Directory command

The Remove-directory command   You use this command to remove a directory. However, you can't remove a directory if it contains any subdirectories or files. And you can't remove a directory if it's the current directory. You'll learn how to use this command for directory maintenance tasks later in this chapter.

The Tree command   If you have more than a few directories, it's hard to visualize the directory structure. The Tree command is designed to help you review that structure. It displays the directories on a disk drive. If you use the /F switch, it also displays the files in each directory.

To illustrate, figure 6-3 shows the output that's displayed by the Tree command for versions of DOS before 4.0. As you can see, this command displays a list of the directories and the subdirectories that they contain. Unfortunately, it's difficult to work with this information in this form so this command isn't used much.

In contrast, figure 6-4 shows how the output of the Tree command is displayed for DOS 4.0 and 5.0. With these versions, this command displays a graphic tree that gives you a quick view of the directory structure. In general,

```
C:\>tree

DIRECTORY PATH LISTING

Path: \DOS

Sub directories:   None


Path: \UTIL

Sub directories:   None


Path: \WP50

Sub directories:   MMA
                   PROJ1


Path:  \123

Sub directories:   MMA
                   DOUG


Path:  \QA

Sub directories:   MMA
```

Figure 6-3   The output displayed by the Tree command in DOS versions before 4.0

the more directories you have on your drives, the more valuable the graphic tree structure becomes and the less valuable the tree listing becomes.

Three commands for working with files

Figure 6-5 summarizes three commands you can use for working with files. Once you master the Copy command, you shouldn't have any trouble learning how to use the Delete and Rename commands.

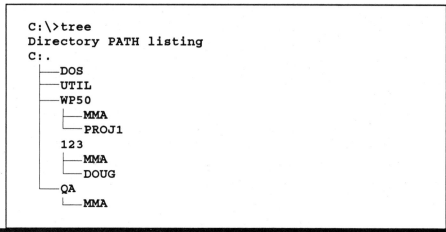

Figure 6-4   The output displayed by the Tree command for DOS 4.0 and 5.0

Later in this chapter, I'll show you how you can use these commands to operate on more than one file at a time. For example, I'll show you how to copy, delete, and rename several files at once. But for now, just concentrate on learning how to use these commands on single files.

The Copy command   You use the Copy command to copy files. You can use this command to copy files within a single directory, from one directory to another, from the hard disk to a diskette, or from a diskette to a hard disk. As a result, you're likely to use the Copy command frequently.

If you look at the format of the Copy command shown in figure 6-5, you can see that it has two parameters. The first parameter is the file specification for the *source file*; the file that's going to be copied. The second parameter is the file specification for the *target file*; the file that's going to be created by the Copy command.

Figure 6-6 shows five examples of Copy commands along with explanations of what happens when they are executed. In all of these examples, the command prompt tells you what the default drive and current directory are. If you specify the drive, directory, and file name for both the source and target files, it doesn't matter what the default drive and the current directory are. But if you omit the drive specification for a file, the default drive is assumed. And if you omit the directory specification, the current directory is assumed.

Name	Format	Function
Copy	`COPY source-spec [target-spec]`	Copies the file identified by the source specification to the path and file name given by the target specification. If the target specification is omitted, this command copies the source file to the current directory on the current drive using the source file name for the target files too.
Delete	`DEL file-spec [/p]`	Deletes the file identified by the file specification. The /P switch provided by DOS 4.0 and later versions of DOS asks you for confirmation before the file is deleted.
Rename	`REN source-spec target-spec`	Renames the file identified by the source specification with the name given in the target specification.

Figure 6-5   Three commands for working with files

If you omit the file name for the target file, DOS uses the file name of the source file for the target file. Since that's frequently what you want, you'll often omit the target file name, whether or not you give a drive and directory specification. For instance, example 2 gives a drive and directory specification but no file name, and example 4 gives a drive specification but no file name.

When you use the Copy command, you must realize that it will replace an existing file if the file specification for the target file is the same as one for an existing file. Worse, DOS will replace the existing file without warning you that it's going to be replaced. If, for example, you copy a file named C1.DOC to a diskette that already has a file named C1.DOC on it, DOS will replace the existing file with the new file. Although that might be what you want, you must use the Copy command with care so you don't replace files accidentally.

The format of the Copy command

```
COPY source-spec [target-spec]
```

Example 1:   Copies the file named ADMGOALS.TXT in the current directory to a new file named
ADMGOALS.BAK in the same directory

```
C:\WP50\MMA>copy admgoals.txt admgoals.bak
```

Example 2:   Copies the file named ADMGOALS.TXT in the current directory to a file with the
same name in the WP50\MMA91 directory on the D drive

```
C:\WP50\MMA>copy admgoals.txt d:\wp50\mma91
```

Example 3:   Copies the file named ADMGOALS.TXT in the WP50\MMA directory on the C drive
to a new file with the same name in the current directory on the default drive

```
D:\DATA\MMA91>copy c:\wp50\mma\admgoals.txt
```

Example 4:   Copies the file named ADMGOALS.TXT in the current directory to a file with the
same name on a diskette in the A drive

```
C:\WP50\MMA>copy admgoals.txt a:
```

Example 5:   An invalid command that tries to copy a file within the current directory but doesn't
give a name for the new file

```
C:\WP50\MMA>copy admgoals.txt
```

Figure 6-6   The Copy command

The Delete command   You use the Delete command to remove a file
from a directory. In this command, the file specification identifies the file
that you want to delete. When you use the Delete command without the /P
switch, you must be careful because it deletes the file you've specified

---

The format of the Delete command

```
DEL file-spec [/p]
```

Example 1:   Deletes the file named ADMGOALS.TXT from the current directory

```
C:\WP50\MMA>del admgoals.txt
```

Example 2:   Deletes the file named ADMGOALS.WK1 from the WK1 directory on the D drive

```
C:\WP50\MMA>del d:\wk1\admgoals.wk1
```

Example 3:   Asks you for confirmation before deleting the file named ADMGOALS.WK1 from the
WK1 directory on the D drive

```
C:\WP50\MMA>del d:\wk1\admgoals.wk1 /p

D:\WK1\ADMGOALS.WK1,   Delete (Y/N)?
```

Figure 6-7   The Delete command

without giving you any warning or a chance to cancel the command before
the damage is done.

Figure 6-7 shows three examples of the Delete command. In example 1,
the command deletes a file named ADMGOALS.TXT from the current directory. In example 2, the command gives a complete file specification to delete
a file named ADMGOALS.WK1 from the WK1 directory on the D drive. In
example 3, the /P switch causes DOS to ask you for confirmation before it
deletes the file.

The Rename command   You use the Rename command to change the
name of a file. In this command, the source specification identifies the file
you want to rename, and the target specification gives the name you want to
use for the renamed file. Note, however, that you can't specify a drive and
directory in the target specification because this command can only rename a
file; it can't move the file to another directory.

The format of the Rename command

```
REN source-spec target-spec
```

Example 1: Renames REVSUM.TXT in the current directory to REVSUM91.TXT

```
C:\WP50\MMA>ren revsum.txt revsum91.txt
```

Example 2: Renames REVSUM.WK1 in the WK1 directory on the D drive to REVSUM91.WK1

```
C:\WP50\MMA>ren d:\wk1\revsum.wk1 revsum91.wk1
```

Example 3: An invalid command that tries to rename a file in the current directory with a target file specification that's in another drive and directory

```
C:\WP50\MMA>ren revsum91.txt d:\wk1\revsum91.txt
```

Figure 6-8 The Rename command

Figure 6-8 shows three examples of Rename commands. In example 1, the command renames a file named REVSUM.TXT in the current directory to REVSUM91.TXT. In example 2, the command renames a file named REVSUM.WK1 in the WK1 directory on the D drive to REVSUM91.WK1. In example 3, the command is invalid because its target specification includes drive and directory information.

How to use wildcards within a DOS command

DOS provides two *wildcards* that you can use within the file specifications of DOS commands. These wildcards are summarized in figure 6-9. When you use wildcards within a command, a single DOS command can operate on more than one file.

The * *wildcard* (asterisk wildcard) represents one or more characters of any kind, and it is the wildcard that you'll use the most. Sometimes, this wild-

Wildcard	Meaning
*	One or more characters of any kind
?	One character of any kind

Examples	Meaning
.	All files (any name, any extension)
*.com	All files with COM as the extension
*.	All files that don't have an extension
c1.*	All files named C1 no matter what the extension is
c*.*	All files with names that start with C
c?.*	All one or two character file names that start with C
c?.com	All one or two character file names that start with C and have an extension of COM
c???????.	All file names that start with C and that don't have an extension (same as c*.)
????.exe	All one, two, three, or four character file names that have an extension of EXE

Figure 6-9   The * and ? wildcards

card is called the *star wildcard*, and a specification like *.* is referred to as "star-dot-star." This wildcard makes it easy for a single command to operate on all of the files within a directory or all the files in a directory that have a specific extension.

The *? wildcard* (question mark wildcard) represents one character of any kind. Although you may never need it, it can be useful once in a while. It's used to select files that have any character in each ? wildcard position. For instance, a specification like this

```
C?FIGS
```

includes files with names C1FIGS, C2FIGS, and C9FIGS, but it excludes files with names like C19FIGS and C20FIGS.

Perhaps the best way to get comfortable with the use of the wildcards is to practice using them in Directory commands, as illustrated in figure 6-10. Here, the first command displays only the files with COM as the extension. The second command displays the files that have an extension of COM and that start with the letter C. The third command displays the files that have no extension and that start with the letter C. The fourth command uses ? wildcards to display file names of four characters or less that start with the letter C and that have COM as the extension. The fifth command uses ? wildcards to display file names of three characters or less no matter what the extensions are.

Once you're sure that you know how wildcards work, you can use them in Copy and Rename commands as illustrated in figure 6-11. Here, the examples only show the use of * wildcards, but you can use ? wildcards whenever they are appropriate.

If you have any doubt about the way wildcards are going to work in Delete commands, I recommend that you use a two-step procedure like the one in figure 6-12. In step 1, you use the Directory command with the file specification for the files you want to delete. Then, if the correct files are displayed, use exactly the same file specification in a Delete command, as shown in step 2.

If you have DOS 4.0 or later, you can use the /P switch to avoid deleting the wrong files. When you use this switch, the Delete command ask you for confirmation before it deletes a file. If you respond with *Y* when DOS asks you if you want to delete a file, the file is deleted. If you respond with *N*, the command proceeds to the next file specified by the command or ends the command if no other files are specified.

Typical command sequences for managing directories and files

Although DOS provides commands for making a new directory and removing an existing directory, it doesn't provide commands for renaming a directory, and it doesn't provide commands for moving a directory and its files

```
C:\DOS>dir *.com /w

 Volume in drive C is DISK1_VOL1
 Directory of  C:\DOS

ASSIGN   COM     BACKUP   COM     CHKDSK   COM     COMMAND  COM     COMP     COM
DEBUG    COM     DISKCOMP COM     DISKCOPY COM     EDLIN    COM     FDISK    COM
FORMAT   COM     GRAFTABL COM     GRAPHICS COM     KEYB     COM     LABEL    COM
MODE     COM     MORE     COM     PRINT    COM     RECOVER  COM     RESTORE  COM
SELECT   COM     SYS      COM     TREE     COM
        23 File(s)    5611520 bytes free


C:\DOS>dir c*.com

 Volume in drive C is DISK1_VOL1
 Directory of  C:\DOS

CHKDSK   COM      9819    7-24-87   12:00a
COMMAND  COM     25276    7-24-87   12:00a
COMP     COM      4183    7-24-87   12:00a
        3 File(s)    5611520 bytes free


C:\DOS>dir c*.

 Volume in drive C is DISK1_VOL1
 Directory of  C:\DOS

File not found


C:\DOS>dir c???.com

 Volume in drive C is DISK1_VOL1
 Directory of  C:\DOS

COMP     COM      4183    7-24-87   12:00a
        1 File(s)    5611520 bytes free

C:\DOS>dir ???

 Volume in drive C is DISK1_VOL1
 Directory of  C:\DOS

.    <DIR>                 8-01-90    4:46p
..   <DIR>                 8-01-90    4:46p
EGA      CPI     49065    7-24-87   12:00a
FC       EXE     15974    7-24-87   12:00a
LCD      CPI     10752    7-24-87   12:00a
SYS      COM      4725    7-24-87   12:00a
        6 File(s)    5611520 bytes free

C:\DOS>
```

Figure 6-10   The use of wildcards in Directory commands

Example 1:   A Copy command that copies all of the files in the WP50\MMA directory on the
C drive to a diskette in the A drive.

```
C:\>copy \wp50\mma\*.* a:
```

Example 2:   A Copy command that copies all of the files with an extension of WK1 in the
current directory to a diskette in the A drive.

```
C:\DATA\123>copy *.wk1 a:
```

Example 3:   A Copy command that copies all of the files on the diskette in the A drive to the
current directory.

```
C:\DATA\123>copy a:*.*
```

Example 4:   A Rename command that renames all files named PRSUM in the current directory,
no matter what the extensions are, to PRSUM91.

```
C:WP50\MMA>ren prsum.* prsum91.*
```

Example 5:   A Rename command that changes the extensions of all files in the current
directory with the extension of WK1 to the extension of BAK.

```
C:\123\MMA>ren *.wk1 *.bak
```

Figure 6-11   The use of wildcards in Copy and Rename commands

from one point in the directory structure to another. To do these tasks, you
have to use a combination of DOS commands.

When you use a shell program for managing directories and files, you
can do most directory functions more easily from the shell than you can from
the command prompt. For instance, the DOS 5.0 shell provides specific functions for creating, renaming, and deleting directories. As a result, you don't
have to know how to do these functions from the command prompt. However, the DOS 5.0 shell doesn't provide a function for moving a directory and
its files from one point in the directory structure to another. To do that, you
must use the series of DOS commands that I'll describe in a moment. You

Step 1:   Use the Directory command with the wildcard specification that you intend to use in the
Delete command.

```
C:\>dir d:\wp50\mma\*.bak
```

Step 2:   If the files that are displayed are the ones that you want to delete, use the Delete command
with exactly the same wildcard specification that you used in step 1.

```
C:\>del d:\wp50\mma\*.bak
```

Figure 6-12   How to use wildcards in Delete commands

can start these commands from the command prompt or from the shell, but
you must understand what has to be done before you can do it.

How to make a new directory   Figure 6-13 shows you two ways to use
the Make-directory command when you want to make a new directory. In
example 1, the Change-directory command changes the current directory to
the one that the new directory should be subordinate to. Then, the Make-
directory command specifies only the new directory name as a parameter. In
example 2, the Make-directory command gives a complete path for the new
directory as a parameter.

How to remove a directory   Figure 6-14 shows you one way to remove a
directory from a drive. In step 1, you change the current directory to the one
that you want to remove. In step 2, you delete all the files in the directory
because a directory has to be empty before you can remove it. When you use
wildcard specifications to delete all of the files in a directory, DOS displays
this message

```
Are you sure (Y/N)?
```

to give you a chance to change your mind. If you are sure, you respond with
a *Y*. In step 3, you use the Change-directory command to change the current
directory to the root directory because you can't use the Remove-directory

---

Example 1

```
C:\>cd \123

C:\123>md becky
```

Example 2

```
C:\>md \123\becky
```

Figure 6-13   Two ways to make a new directory named 123\BECKY

Step 1:   Change the current directory to the one that you want to remove.

```
C:\>cd \qa\nancy
```

Step 2:   Delete all the files in the directory.

```
C:\QA\NANCY>del *.*
Are you sure (Y/N)?y
```

Step 3:   Change the current directory to the root directory.

```
C:\QA\NANCY>cd \
```

Step 4:   Remove the empty directory.

```
C:\>rd \qa\nancy

C:\>
```

Figure 6-14   How to remove a directory named WP50\NANCY

command to remove the current directory. And in step 4, you use the Remove-directory command to remove the empty directory.

If you like, you can simplify this procedure by specifying the directory path in the Delete command. Then, you can delete the files and remove the directory with just two commands:

```
C:\>del \QA\NANCY\*.*
Are you sure (Y/N)?y

C:\>rd \QA\NANCY
```

How to rename a directory   Because there's no single DOS command for renaming a directory, you have to use the combination of commands shown in figure 6-15. In step 1, you use the Make-directory command to make a new directory with the name that you want to rename the existing directory with. In step 2, you copy all of the files in the existing directory to the new directory. In step 3, you delete all the files in the existing directory. In step 4, you remove the existing directory from the disk. The result is a renamed directory.

Unfortunately, in order to use this technique, you must have enough space on your hard disk to hold two copies of the files in the directory. If you don't have enough free disk space, you have to delete some files to free up some disk space before you begin. In addition, the process is more complicated if the directory you want to remove has subdirectories. In that case, you must copy each of those subdirectories as well.

How to move a directory   There's no single DOS command for moving a directory from one point in a directory structure to another. Also, as I mentioned earlier, the DOS 5.0 shell doesn't provide for this function. As a result, you have to use the combination of commands shown in figure 6-16 to move a directory. As you can see, moving a directory requires basically the same steps as renaming a directory, so I won't go through the commands again. Here again, the process is more complicated if the directory you want to move has subdirectories.

Step 1:   Make a new directory that has the name you want to rename the old directory with.

```
C:\>md \123\mma91
```

Step 2:   Copy the files from the old directory to the new directory.

```
C:\>copy \123\mma\*.* \123\mma91
BALSHEET.WK1
PROFORMA.WK1
SALARIES.WK1
MKTGEXP.WK1
ADMEXP.WK1
         5 File(s) copied
```

Step 3:   Delete the files in the old directory.

```
C:\>del \123\mma\*.*
Are you sure (Y/N)?y
```

Step 4:   Remove the old directory.

```
C:\>rd \123\mma

C:\>
```

Figure 6-15   How to rename a directory from 123\MMA to 123\MMA91

Twelve guidelines for managing your directories and files

Now that you've learned the commands for managing your directories and files, here are 12 guidelines that will help you do a better job of managing them. You need to know these guidelines whether you use a shell or DOS commands to manage your directories and files. Because these guidelines are all quite straightforward, I'll go through them quickly. They are summarized in figure 6-17.

Keep the number of files in each root directory to a minimum   If you do this, it's easier to manage the directories and files on your system. In

Step 1:   Make a new directory in the location that you want to move the old directory to.

```
C:\>md \mma
```

Step 2:   Change the current directory to the new directory.

```
C:\>cd \mma
```

Step 3:   Copy the files from the old directory to the new directory.

```
C:\MMA>copy \123\mma\*.*
BALSHEET.WK1
PROFORMA.WK1
SALARIES.WK1
MKTGEXP.WK1
ADMEXP.WK1
          5 File(s) copied
```

Step 4:   Delete the files in the old directory.

```
C:\MMA>del \123\mma\*.*
Are you sure (Y/N)?y
```

Step 5:   Remove the old directory.

```
C:\>rd \123\mma
```

Figure 6-16   How to move a directory

general, each root directory should contain only entries for subordinate directories. In addition, the root directory of the C drive must contain the
COMMAND.COM, CONFIG.SYS, and AUTOEXEC.BAT files.

You can't always keep other files out of the root directories, though,
because some application programs and utility programs put files of their
own in the root directory of the default drive. For example, *PC Tools* rou-
tinely puts files in my root directories. Nevertheless, you shouldn't put any

1. Keep the number of files in each root directory to a minimum.

2. Don't use more than two directory levels below the root directory.

3. Use simple directory names.

4. Store DOS files in a DOS directory.

5. Store utility programs in a utility directory.

6. Store all batch files in one directory.

7. Store application programs in their own directories.

8. Store data files in logically organized data directories.

9. Keep your data directories small.

10. Don't keep files you don't need.

11. Use consistent file names.

12. Include the file name in the heading of each document that's prepared from a file.

Figure 6-17   Twelve guidelines for managing directories and files

more files in your root directories than are required. Instead, you should store your files in directories that help you keep them organized.

Don't use more than two directory levels below the root directory

Sometimes, it's tempting to use more than two levels of directories below the root directory. For instance, you start by adding a directory (WP) for your word processing program that's subordinate to the root directory. Next, you add a data directory (WP\PROJECTA) for the files you'll create as part of an extensive writing project. Then, because several of you are working on the project, you are tempted to add more directories that are subordinate to the PROJECTA subdirectory. That way, there's a directory for each person's work: WP\PROJECTA\DOUG, WP\PROJECTA\PAT, and so on.

As tempting as this may be from an organizational point of view, you should resist doing this because it leads to paths that are too long for efficiency. After you enter the complete path specifications a few times, you'll be convinced of that. Also, you can get the same effect without going to a third structural level. Just make the directories for each person as well as the PROJECTA directory subordinate to the word processing directory. Or make the PROJECTA directory subordinate to the root directory instead of the word processing directory. Either way, by limiting yourself to two directory levels below the root directory, you'll simplify your directory and file management.

Use simple directory names   You'll type directory and subdirectory names often as you use your PC, so keep them short and simple like the ones illustrated in this book. Don't use special characters in your directory names because they're more difficult to type than letters and numbers, and don't use extensions in your directory names either. For program directories, try to use the name suggested by the program's installation instructions. For data directories, try to use a short but meaningful name.

Store DOS files in a DOS directory   Many users keep all of their DOS files in the root directory of the C drive. But rather than clutter up the root directory, I suggest that you store the DOS files (except for COMMAND.COM, CONFIG.SYS, and AUTOEXEC.BAT) in a directory named DOS. Then, add the DOS directory to the Path command in your AUTOEXEC.BAT file.

If your DOS files are already stored in the root directory, you can move them to a DOS directory. But you may have to work around other files that are in the root directory. As a result, you'll need to perform six steps to move your DOS files to a DOS directory. First, create a DOS directory that's subordinate to the root directory. Second, copy all of the files from the root directory to the DOS directory. Third, delete all of the files in the root directory. Fourth, copy the COMMAND.COM, CONFIG.SYS, and AUTOEXEC.BAT files and any files that aren't DOS files from the DOS directory to the root directory. Fifth, delete the COMMAND.COM, CONFIG.SYS, and AUTO-EXEC.BAT files and any files that aren't a part of DOS from the DOS directory. Sixth, add the DOS directory to the search list in the Path command in the AUTOEXEC.BAT file.

Store utility programs in a utility directory   If you own any utility programs, I suggest you store them in a directory named UTIL. Then, add the UTIL directory to the Path command in your AUTOEXEC.BAT file. If you purchase a large utility that comes with many files, you can create a separate directory for that program.

Store all batch files in one directory   I mentioned this in chapter 5, but it's worth repeating. To control the batch files on your system, you should store them in one directory. This can be the UTIL directory, or you can create a separate directory for them named BAT. If you create a separate directory, it should be added to the search list in the Path command in your AUTOEXEC.BAT file.

Store application programs in their own directories   Because most application programs require dozens of files, you should store each program in its own directory and make that directory subordinate to the root directory. If you look back to the tree in figure 6-4, you can see three directories for application programs: WP50 for *WordPerfect*; 123 for *Lotus 1-2-3*; and QA for *Q&A*.

Store data files in logically organized data directories   Although some programs require it, you shouldn't store data files in program directories if you can avoid it. Otherwise, your program directories will quickly become unmanageable. Instead, you should store your data files in logically organized data directories.

Figure 6-18 illustrates five ways to organize data directories. In the first structure, word processing documents are stored in a directory called DOC, and spreadsheets are stored in a directory called WK1 (the normal extension for *Lotus 1-2-3* spreadsheets). This one-level structure is sensible if you don't have too much software or data on your system.

In the second structure in figure 6-18, the two data directories (DOC and WK1) are subordinate to a directory named DATA. And all of the program

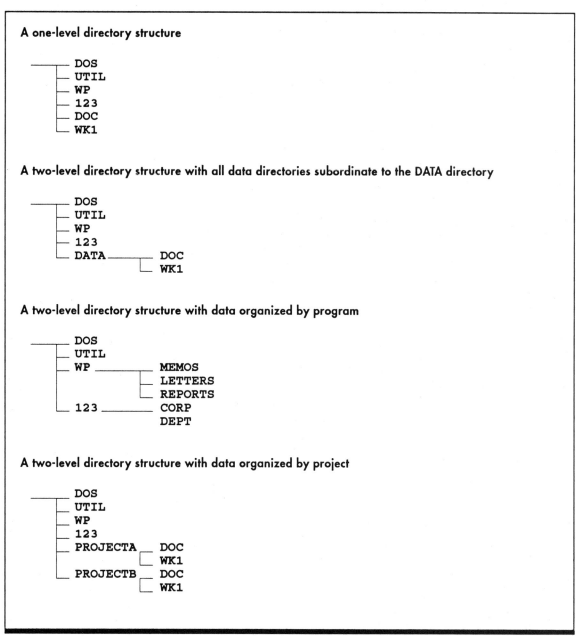

Figure 6-18   Five ways to organize data directories (part 1 of 2)

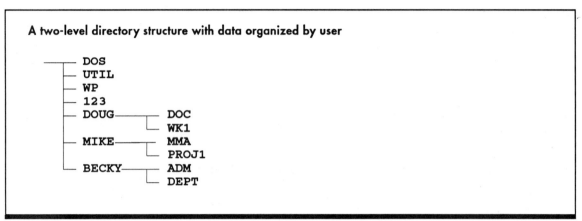

A two-level directory structure with data organized by user

```
─────┬──── DOS
     ├──── UTIL
     ├──── WP
     ├──── 123
     ├──── DOUG────────┬──── DOC
     │                 └──── WK1
     ├──── MIKE────────┬──── MMA
     │                 └──── PROJ1
     └──── BECKY───────┬──── ADM
                       └──── DEPT
```

Figure 6-18   Five ways to organize data directories (part 2 of 2)

directories are subordinate to the root directory. As chapter 8 explains, this two-level structure can simplify your backup procedures.

The third structure in figure 6-18 is a two-level structure that's organized by application program. Here, the data directories are subordinate to the program directories. As a result, you know that the MEMOS, LETTERS, and REPORTS directories contain word processing documents. And you know that the CORP and DEPT directories contain spreadsheets.

The fourth structure in figure 6-18 is a two-level structure that's organized by project. Here, the DOC directories contain word processing documents related to each of the two projects, and the WK1 directories contain spreadsheets related to the projects.

The last structure in figure 6-18 is a two-level structure that's organized by PC user. This is sensible when several people use the same PC. Then, the users decide how they want to organize their subdirectories.

The point I'm trying to make is that there should be some logic to the structure of your directories. If there is, it will be easier for you to manage your files. You'll also be able to find whatever files you're looking for.

Keep your data directories small   At some point, a data directory holds so many files that it becomes unmanageable. Then, it's time to delete files you no longer need. It may also be time to regroup the files into two or more subdirectories based on some logical structure. If you keep your data directories small, you'll be able to manage your files more effectively.

Don't keep files you don't need   This guideline is pretty obvious, and it's closely related to the previous one. However, I've included it as a separate guideline because most PC users don't follow it. Since they've usually got millions of bytes of free space on their disk drives, they just don't worry about a few unnecessary files. But the few files add up, and eventually the clutter makes it more difficult to manage the directories and files.

For instance, many PC users keep a copy of each letter they write on their systems. But they rarely refer to any of them. Similarly, they keep several versions of reports and proposals on their systems, but they only use the final versions. If you're guilty of either of these practices, delete the files you never use and you'll simplify file management.

To complicate matters, some programs automatically create files that you don't need. For instance, many programs create backup files for each file that you work on so you won't lose your work in case of a power failure. Normally, these files have a distinctive extension such as BAK or BK. Also, some programs create temporary files while you're using them. If you end the program normally, these files are deleted. But if you don't, these files with extensions like TMP, $$$, or 001 stay on your system. Occasionally, then, you should take a few minutes to delete the backup and temporary files that have accumulated. You can delete them by using a wildcard with an appropriate extension as in this command:

```
C:\WORD>del *.tmp
```

Use consistent file names   A good file name is one that is descriptive enough to tell you what's in the file, and distinct enough to distinguish it from other files with similar names. Unfortunately, you can't always create good file names with a limit of eight characters for the name and three for the extension. That's why it's so important that you organize your data files in logical directories and that you keep those directories small.

Within each data directory, you should try to create file names that are consistent. In a word processing directory, for example, you may want to use the extension RPT for reports, LTR for letters, and MEM for memos. If the program doesn't let you use your own extensions, you can start the file names with three-character identifiers. Similarly, you may want to start spreadsheet names with PF for proforma analyses, SLS for sales summaries, and FIN for financial summaries. Although this consistency may not help you find the exact file you're looking for, it will at least help you narrow down the possibilities.

Include the file name in the heading of each document that's prepared from a file   Because you can't always create distinctive file names, you should include the file name in the heading of any document or spreadsheet that's printed from a file. In figure 6-19, for example, you can see a word processing document with ADMGOALS in the heading. Then, if you want to modify this document, you look for a file with that name in the directory that's logically related to it. Usually, you don't need to include the path along with a file name in the heading, but if there's any chance for confusion, include the path too.

How a shell program can help you manage directories and files

If you follow the 12 guidelines I've just presented, you can do an effective job of managing your directories and files whether or not you use a shell program. If you're not using a shell program, though, you should probably consider getting one.

To start, you can learn how to use the DOS 5.0 shell for managing directories and files in chapter 11 of this book. If you like that shell, you can upgrade from your current version of DOS to DOS 5.0. Otherwise, you can install a commercial shell program on your system without changing your current version of DOS.

From a practical point of view, it's usually best to use some combination of DOS commands and shell functions to manage your directories and files. If you want to carefully select files for deletion by reviewing their names and creation dates, a shell is usually more efficient. But if you want to copy or delete entire directories or portions of directories that can be selected by wildcards, the DOS commands are usually more efficient.

```
January 1, 1991            ADMGOALS                    Page 1
Administrative goals for 1991


Customer service    Although our customer service is already
excellent, our goal is to continue to improve it.  For instance, I
would like us to ship all orders within one day from the time we
receive them.

Productivity standards   In 1990, salaries and wages for the
administrative group went up 38.3 percent, but sales only
increased 13 percent.  To some extent, that means that our people
weren't as productive in 1990 as they were in 1989.  That's why
our goal for 1991 is to not only provide the best (and most
personal) customer service in the industry, but also to do it with
maximum efficiency and productivity.

Training  In 1991, I'd like to continue to emphasize training.
Our goal should be to train all the people in the department so
that next year at this time they're more valuable to us...and to
themselves.  That means on-the-job training for everyone and in-
class training for some.
```

Figure 6-19   A word processing document with the file name in the heading

Terms

source file
target file
wildcard
* wildcard
star wildcard
? wildcard

Exercises

1. Use the Directory command to experiment with the * and ? wildcards until you understand how they work.

2. Copy all the files that start with A, C, or D from your DOS directory to an empty diskette in drive A. That will require three Copy commands with wildcards. Next, change the default drive to drive A. Then, use the Directory command to get a directory listing of the files in the current directory of the default drive.

3. Use the Make-directory command to create a COM directory on the diskette in the A drive. Next, copy all the files in the root directory of the C drive with an extension of COM to the COM directory on the diskette. Then, use Directory commands to list the files in the root directory and the COM directory to make sure your commands worked correctly.

4. Use a single Rename command to rename all the files in the COM directory on the diskette in the A drive so the extensions are CBK. Then, use a Directory command to list the files in the COM directory to make sure the Rename command worked correctly.

5. Change the name of the COM directory to CBK.

6. Remove the CBK directory from the diskette in the A drive.

7. Use the Directory command to get directory listings of the root directories on the drives of your hard disk. Do these directories contain acceptable minimums of files? Are the DOS files in the root directory of the C drive? Are any other programs in the root directory of the C drive? What directory and file reorganization do these listings suggest?

8. Run the Tree command for the C drive of your system to see what output you get. If you have other drives on your hard disk, run the Tree command for those drives too. How are the program directories on your system organized? How are the data directories organized? What directory and file reorganization is suggested by the current directory structure?

Chapter 7

How to work with diskettes

When a PC has a hard disk, you won't have much need for diskettes. Most of the time, you'll retrieve the files you need from the hard disk, and you'll save the files you create on the hard disk.

Nevertheless, one diskette drive is an essential component of a hard disk system because the hard disk isn't removable. As a result, software for a hard disk system is usually delivered on diskettes. You often use diskettes when you want to transfer data from one PC to another. And the most common way to back up a hard disk is to transfer its data to diskettes.

In this chapter, you'll learn how to work with diskettes. First, I'll review the diskette characteristics I presented in the first chapter. Then, I'll present two DOS commands you can use when you work with diskettes. Last, I'll present three specific skills that are related to diskette use.

When you finish this chapter, you will know how to use diskettes for transferring data from one system to another. You will also know how to work with diskettes when you use them for backing up data as presented in the next chapter. You need to have these skills whether or not you use a shell program on your PC.

A review of diskette characteristics

In chapter 1, I described the two types of diskettes that are in widespread use today: the 5-1/4 inch diskette and the 3-1/2 inch diskette. Now, I'll review some of the characteristics of these diskettes. These characteristics are summarized in figure 7-1.

Size	Capacity	Common labelling notation	Tracks	Sectors
5-1/4"	360KB	5-1/4" Double-Sided Double-Density 5-1/4" DSDD	40	9
5-1/4"	1.2MB	5-1/4" Double-Sided High-Density 5-1/4" DSHD	80	15
3-1/2"	720KB	3-1/2" Double-Sided Double-Density 3-1/2" 2DD 3-1/2" 1.0M formatted capacity	80	9
3-1/2"	1.44MB	3-1/2" Double-Sided High-Density 3-1/2" 2HD 3-1/2" 2.0M formatted capacity	80	18

Figure 7-1   A summary of diskette characteristics

5-1/4 inch diskettes   These diskettes are most commonly used with PCs, XTs, and ATs. The standard capacity is 360KB; the high capacity is 1.2MB. Although a high-capacity diskette drive can read and write both types of diskettes, a standard-capacity drive can only read and write 360KB diskettes.

Although these diskettes are tough, they're not indestructible. In fact, reading and writing errors often occur when you use this type of diskette. So to get the best results from them, you should handle them with care. That means you shouldn't write on them with a pencil or a ballpoint pen; you shouldn't touch the surface that's exposed through the diskette opening; you shouldn't get them close to anything magnetic (including paper clips that have been in a magnetic paper clip holder); and you shouldn't leave them anywhere that will expose them to extremes of heat or cold. You should also keep them in their protective sleeves when they're not in use.

3-1/2 inch diskettes   Although these diskettes were popularized by laptop computers and the PS/2s, you can now get a 3-1/2 inch drive for other types of PCs. The standard capacity is 720KB; the high capacity is 1.44MB. Here again, a high-capacity diskette drive can read and write both types of diskettes, but a standard-capacity drive can only read and write 720KB diskettes.

These diskettes are more reliable than the 5-1/4 inch diskettes, so reading and writing errors rarely occur when you use them. Also, these diskettes don't require as much care. With sensible handling, you shouldn't have any problems with them.

Two commands for working with diskettes

Figure 7-2 summarizes the two commands you need for formatting and copying entire diskettes. Otherwise, you use the same file-handling commands for diskettes that you use for hard disks including the Copy, Delete, and Rename commands. You can also use the directory commands on a diskette, although the root directory is usually the only directory you need on a diskette.

The Format command   Before you can use a diskette, it has to be formatted. Today, you can buy diskettes that are already formatted, but otherwise you have to use the Format command to format them.

The Format command prepares the surface of the diskette so it can record information. It does this by defining the tracks on a diskette. The Format command also sets up the root directory for the diskette, and it checks the reliability of the diskette.

When you format a diskette that already has data on it, all of its data is destroyed. Similarly, if you unintentionally format your hard disk, all of its data is destroyed. To avoid this disaster, you should make sure that the drive specification in this command is always drive A or drive B. If you specify drive C, DOS will give you a warning message. But if you ignore it, the disaster is in progress.

The first example of a Format command in figure 7-3 shows you how to enter the command when you want to format the diskette with the default format of the drive. As you can see, no switches are required so the only parameter is the drive specification. Then, if the drive is standard capacity, the Format command formats the diskette in standard capacity. If the drive is

---

The format of the Format command

```
FORMAT drive-spec [switches]
```

Function

This command formats a diskette for use by DOS. To format a diskette in the default format of the diskette drive, you don't need any switches. Otherwise, you must use one or more of the switches as illustrated in figure 7-3.

Switch meanings

/4	Formats a 360KB diskette in a 1.2MB drive
/n:sectors **/t:tracks**	DOS 3.2 and 3.3 switches used to format a standard capacity diskette using a high-capacity drive
/f:capacity	DOS 4.0 and 5.0 replacement for the /N and /T switches
/q	DOS 5.0 switch for reformatting a diskette quickly
/s	Formats a system diskette that's used to boot DOS

The format of the Diskcopy command

```
DISKCOPY source-drive target-drive
```

Function

This command copies an entire diskette including any directories and all of its files. It works most efficiently if you copy the diskette in one drive to a diskette in another drive. But you can also use this command when your PC has only one diskette drive.

Figure 7-2 Two commands for working with diskettes

How to format a diskette in the default format of the drive

```
C:\>format a:
```

How to format a 360KB diskette in a 1.2MB drive

```
C:\>format a: /4
```

How to format a 720KB diskette in a 1.44MB drive (DOS 3.2 and 3.3)

```
C:\>format a: /n:9 /t:80
```

How to format a 720KB diskette in a 1.44MB drive (DOS 4.0 and 5.0)

```
C:\>format a: /f:720
```

How to format a diskette quickly (DOS 5.0)

```
C:\>format a: /q
```

How to format a system diskette

```
C:\>format a: /s
```

Figure 7-3   How to use the Format command

high capacity, the command formats the diskette in that capacity. This is the way you'll enter the command most of the time.

The next three examples in figure 7-3 show you how to enter this command when you want to use a high-capacity drive to format a standard-capacity diskette. Here, the switches tell DOS what the formatting requirements are. In the third example, you can see that the switches specify the number of tracks and sectors for a 720KB diskette. In the fourth example, the /F switch that's allowed by DOS 4.0 and 5.0 simplifies the third example. If you frequently use commands in any one of these forms, you may want to set up batch files for them so you don't have to remember how to enter the switches.

The fifth example in figure 7-3 shows how you can use the /Q switch that DOS 5.0 provides to reformat a diskette quickly. When you use this switch, DOS doesn't format every track on the diskette. Instead, DOS just erases the directory and file entries on the diskette. This reduces the time required to reformat a previously formatted diskette. If you try to use the /Q switch to format an unformatted diskette, it won't work because this switch only works on previously formatted diskettes.

The last example in figure 7-3 shows you how to use the /S switch. When you use this switch with the Format command, it copies three DOS files from the hard disk to the diskette after it finishes formatting the diskette. One of the files is the COMMAND.COM file. The other two files are hidden files so they won't show up in a directory listing. When you use the /S switch, the default drive has to be the C drive, so DOS can find the three files it needs. After you format a diskette in this way, you can use it to boot DOS from the A drive. I'll explain more about this in a moment when I tell you about preparing a system diskette.

Figure 7-4 shows the Format command in operation. When you issue the command, DOS prompts you to insert the diskette to be formatted into the disk drive. After you insert the diskette and close the drive door, you press any key to start the formatting. As DOS formats the disk, it displays its progress. If you're using DOS 3.3 or earlier, it displays the track and side that's currently being formatted. If you're using DOS 4.0 or 5.0, it displays the percent of the disk that has been formatted.

When DOS has completed the formatting operation, it displays the storage information shown in figure 7-4. This display shows the total number of bytes on the diskette, the number of bytes in bad sectors, and the number of bytes of available disk storage. In this figure, for example, you can see that there are more than 60,000 bytes of bad sectors on the diskette. You don't have to worry about these bad sectors, though, because DOS locks them out and doesn't use them to store data.

After DOS has formatted one diskette, it asks if you want to format another. If you respond with a Y for Yes, DOS repeats the process I just

```
C:\>format a:
Insert new diskette for drive A:
and strike ENTER when ready

    1213952 bytes total disk space
      61280 bytes in bad sectors
    1152672 bytes available on disk

Format another (Y/N)?n

C:\>
```

Figure 7-4   The operation of the Format command

described. If you have just opened a box of diskettes, it's often worth taking the time to format all of them.

With some versions of DOS, the Format command displays a message that asks you to supply a *volume label* for the diskette that's going to be formatted. Because you don't need to assign a volume label to a diskette, you can just press the Enter key to ignore the message.

The Diskcopy command   Occasionally, you will want to make a copy of an entire diskette. Then, you can use the Diskcopy command. Because this command copies the entire source diskette, whether it's filled with data or not, all data on the target diskette is destroyed. So choose your target diskette carefully. You should also know that you can't use this command to copy a diskette of one capacity onto a diskette of another capacity.

If you have two drives on your system, you enter this command as shown in the first example in figure 7-5. Then, DOS tells you to put the diskette you want to copy (the source diskette) in the A drive and the diskette you want to create (the target diskette) in the B drive. This is illustrated in the first part of figure 7-6. When the copy operation is finished, DOS asks if you want to copy another diskette.

If you have only one drive on your system, you enter the command as shown in the second example in figure 7-5. The operation of this command is illustrated in the second part of figure 7-6. After DOS tells you to put the source diskette in drive A, this command reads as much data as it can from

```
How to copy a diskette from one drive to another

    C:\DOS>diskcopy a: b:

How to copy a diskette on a PC with one diskette drive

    C:\DOS>diskcopy a: a:
```

Figure 7-5   How to use the Diskcopy command

the source diskette into internal memory. If, for example, your PC has 640KB of memory and you're copying a 360KB diskette, this command reads the entire diskette into internal memory. Next, the command asks you to remove the source diskette from the drive and insert the target diskette. When you do that, the data in memory is copied onto the target diskette. If the entire diskette can't be read into internal memory all at once, the command repeats this procedure until all the data has been copied to the target diskette.

With some versions of DOS, you can use an unformatted diskette for the target diskette of a Diskcopy command. For instance, all versions of PC-DOS will automatically format the target diskette if it's not already formatted. However, the versions of MS-DOS before 4.0 require that you format the target diskette before you use this command.

Three related skills

Now that you know how to use the Format and Diskcopy commands, you shouldn't have any trouble working with diskettes. Along with knowing those commands, you should also know how to do the specific skills that follow.

How to use diskettes to transfer data from one PC to another   Figure 7-7 shows you how to copy data from a hard disk to a diskette. The first example shows you how to copy just one file; the second example shows you how to use wildcards to copy all the files in a directory; and the third

The format of the Diskcopy command

```
DISKCOPY source-drive target-drive
```

Copying a diskette from drive A to drive B

```
C:\>diskcopy a: b:

Insert SOURCE diskette in drive A:

Insert TARGET diskette in drive B:

Press any key when ready . . .

Copying 40 tracks
9 Sectors/Track, 2 Side(s)


Copy another diskette (Y/N)?n

C:\>
```

Copying a diskette from drive A to drive A

```
C:\>diskcopy a: a:

Insert SOURCE diskette in drive A:

Press any key when ready . . .

Copying 40 tracks
9 Sectors/Track, 2 Side(s)

Insert TARGET diskette in drive A:

Press any key when ready . . .


Copy another diskette (Y/N)?n

C:\>
```

Figure 7-6   The operation of the Diskcopy command

Example 1:	A command that copies a file named PROJSUM.WK1 from the PROJECTB directory of the C drive to the diskette in the A drive.

```
C:\>copy \projectb\projsum.wk1 a:
```

Example 2:	A command that copies all the files in the BECKY directory on the C drive to the diskette in the A drive.

```
C:\>copy \becky\*.* a:
```

Example 3:	A command that copies all the files with the DOC extension from the current directory on the hard disk to the diskette in the A drive.

```
C:\DATA\MMA>copy *.doc a:
```

Figure 7-7   How to use the Copy command for copying selected files to a diskette

example shows you how to copy just the files in a directory that have a specific extension. Once you have the data copied to a diskette, you can use the Copy command to copy the data to the hard disk of another PC.

You should realize, though, that you can't use the Copy command to copy a file that is larger than the capacity of a single diskette. Similarly, you can't use this command to copy all the files in a directory if the files require more bytes than are available on a single diskette. In either case, the Copy command is cancelled when it tries to copy a file that requires more bytes than are in the remaining capacity of the diskette. To get around this limitation, you can use the Backup command that is presented in chapter 8.

You should also be aware of the compatibility problems you can encounter when you transfer files from one PC to another. The most obvious problem is trying to use a standard-capacity drive to read a high-capacity diskette. Although that won't work, you should remember that a high-capacity drive is able to read a standard-capacity diskette. As a result, you shouldn't have any trouble transferring data from a PC with a standard-capacity drive to a PC with a high-capacity drive.

When you want to transfer data from a high-capacity drive to a standard-capacity drive, you should use the standard-capacity drive to do the formatting whenever possible. If the diskettes are formatted by the high-capacity drive, they may be incompatible with the standard-capacity drive due to some technical differences in how the two types of drives do the formatting.

One other compatibility problem occurs when you try to format a standard-capacity diskette in the high-capacity format. Although the format command may appear to work when you do this, DOS won't be able to write data on the diskette reliably or read data from it.

How to write-protect a diskette   Occasionally, you may want to protect the files on a diskette so no one can delete them or destroy them by reformatting the diskette. You can provide this protection by *write-protecting* the diskette. Then, DOS can read data from the diskette, but it can't change the data on the diskette in any way.

Figure 7-8 shows how to write protect a diskette. For a 5-1/4 inch diskette, you cover the notch on the diskette with one of the write-protect tabs that comes with a box of diskettes. For a 3-1/2 inch diskette, you slide the plastic tab on the diskette up to open the write-protect window.

When you use a program or command that tries to write on a write-protected diskette, DOS displays a message like this:

```
Write protect error writing drive A
Abort, Retry, Fail?
```

If that happens, you can remove the write-protect tab, put the diskette back in the drive, and reply with an *R* for retry. Or, you can reply with an *A* for abort. But you should never replace the write-protected diskette with another diskette and reply with an *R* for retry. If you do, the data won't be written in the right location on the replacement diskette. Although DOS won't alert you to the problem, it won't be able to retrieve the file correctly later on.

How to prepare a system diskette   Normally, when you start your PC, it boots the DOS files it needs from the hard disk. Sometimes, though, you will want to boot your PC from a diskette. If, for example, something goes wrong with the hard disk, you may have to boot from a diskette to get your PC started again. For this purpose, you need a special type of diskette called a

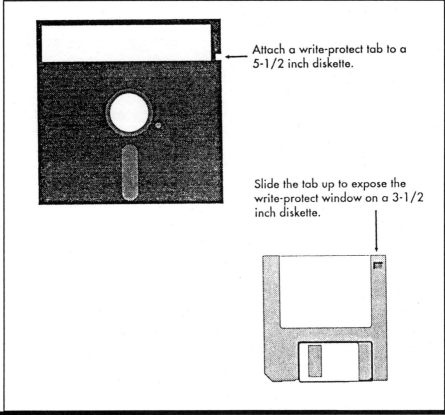

Attach a write-protect tab to a 5-1/2 inch diskette.

Slide the tab up to expose the write-protect window on a 3-1/2 inch diskette.

Figure 7-8   How to write-protect a diskette

system disk, or *system diskette.* This diskette contains the files that DOS needs for getting itself started.

If you have DOS 3.3 or an earlier version, the easiest way to prepare a system diskette is to use the Diskcopy command to make a copy of the system diskette that DOS came with. For most versions of DOS, you'll use the diskette labelled "DOS diskette" or "DOS Operating Diskette."

If you have a later version of DOS, you can't use the Diskcopy command to copy the system diskette that comes with DOS. Instead, you must use the installation program to create a system diskette.

Sometimes, you will want to customize your system diskette instead of making an exact duplicate of the DOS system diskette. For example, you may want to put just a few of the DOS commands on the diskette. Then, you'll have room on the diskette for a utility or a small application program.

To customize a system diskette, you use the Format command with the /S switch as in the last example in figure 7-3. Then, DOS copies three files onto the diskette: the COMMAND.COM file and two hidden files. After that, you can copy whatever DOS command files you want to use from the hard disk. You can also copy the program files for the utility or application programs that you want to put on the diskette. This procedure works with all versions of DOS.

Some perspective on diskettes for hard disk users

As I said at the start of this chapter, you shouldn't have much need for diskettes if you have a hard disk system. However, they're still the best medium for transferring data from one PC to another. And, as you'll learn in chapter 8, they're still the least expensive medium for backing up the data on a hard disk.

Terms

volume label
write-protection
system disk
system diskette

Exercises

1. Use the Directory command to display the directory of a diskette in the A drive. Next, if the diskette is unformatted or if you don't need any of the files on the diskette, use the Format command to format the diskette in the default format of your A drive. Then, use the Directory command to display the directory of the newly formatted diskette.

2. Use the Copy command to copy all of the files in a directory on the hard disk to a diskette in the A or B drive. If possible, choose a directory that

exceeds the capacity of a single diskette. When the command is finished, use the Directory command to display the directory of the diskette.

3. Use the Diskcopy command to copy the files on the diskette you've just created to another diskette.

4. Use the Format command to create a system disk from your hard disk. Then, restart the PC with the system disk in the A drive to make sure that it works.

Chapter 8

How to back up the data on a hard disk

Eventually, the hard disk on your PC will fail, and all of the data on it will be lost. This could happen the first month you have the disk drive, or it could happen after five years of heavy use. But even before it fails, you can lose all the data on the disk by an operational error like someone accidentally reformatting drive C. You can also lose all the data due to theft, fire, or vandalism.

Sooner or later, you'll also lose one or more of the files on your hard disk due to a programming or an operating error. If, for example, you're working on two proposals at the same time and you replace the first one on the disk with the second one, the first one is lost. Or, if while using the Delete command, you accidentally delete all the files in the current directory when you meant to delete all of the files on the diskette in the A drive, dozens of files may be lost. Mistakes like that happen to even the most proficient PC users.

So think about it right now. Can you afford to lose all of the data on your hard disk? Can you afford to lose one of your largest and most important files? If you can't, you should protect yourself by *backing up* your hard disk to diskettes. Then, if a disaster happens, you can recover from it by *restoring* the diskette files to the hard disk.

In this chapter, you'll learn how to back up and restore the files on your hard disk. Since many PC users don't back up their disks regularly because backup takes too long, the emphasis will be on efficient backup procedures. After you learn how to use the DOS Backup and Restore commands, you'll learn three ways to design your backups and five guidelines that will help do your backups as quickly and as effectively as possible. You need to have these skills whether or not you use a shell program on your PC. Then, you'll learn about two hardware improvements and one software improvement that can make your backups even more efficient.

Two types of backup

The key to efficient backups is realizing that there are two kinds of backups. These are illustrated in figure 8-1. Here, the system is backed up on Monday using a *full backup*. On the other days of the week, the system is backed up using an *incremental backup*.

Full backup   A full backup is a backup of every file on one of the drives of your hard disk. That includes program and command files as well as data files. A full backup is illustrated in figure 8-1 by the procedure for Monday. When a hard disk fails, the full backup is the starting point for recovery.

Unfortunately, full backups are time consuming. If, for example, you have 20MB of files on a hard disk and you're using 1.2MB or 1.44MB diskettes, a full backup can take 30 minutes. And it will take even longer if you're using 360KB or 720KB diskettes.

Incremental backup   An incremental backup is a backup of just the files that have been created or changed since the last backup. This is illustrated in figure 8-1 by the procedures for Tuesday through Friday. Even if you have hundreds of files on your system, you probably use only a few files each day. As a result, incremental backups are much faster than full backups. On my PC, for example, I do an incremental backup each day before I leave the office, and that procedure takes less than 30 seconds.

Incremental backups are possible because the directory entry for each file on a DOS system has an *archive bit*. This bit indicates whether or not the file needs to be backed up. Whenever you create or change a file, this bit is set so the Backup command knows that the file should be backed up during an incremental backup. Then, when the Backup command is executed, all of the archive bits are reset so they won't be backed up the next time. Usually,

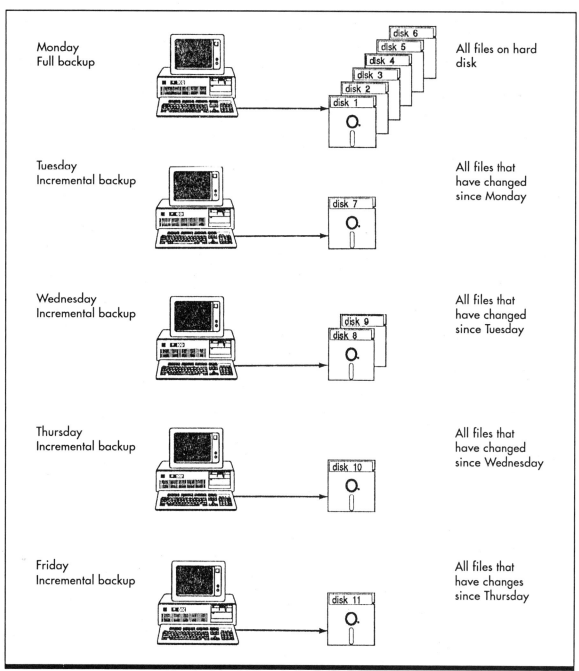

Figure 8-1   A weekly schedule of full and incremental backup

---

The format of the Backup command

```
BACKUP source-spec target-spec [switches]
```

Switch meanings

/s   Includes files that are in the subdirectories of the specified directory.

/m   Backs up only those files that have been modified since the last backup.

/a   Adds the new files to the files that are already on the backup diskette (DOS 3.3 or later).

The format of the Restore command

```
RESTORE source-spec target-spec [switch]
```

Switch meaning

/s   Restores all files in all subdirectories

Figure 8-2   The Backup and Restore commands

when you use an application program, only the data files that you work on are changed, so your program files aren't included in an incremental backup.

Two commands for backing up data and restoring it

Figure 8-2 summarizes the two DOS commands for backing up and restoring a hard disk. Although you should use the Backup command frequently, you only use the Restore command when you need to restore data to your hard disk.

The Backup command   If you study the Backup command in figure 8-2, you can see that this command backs up the files in the source specification to the target specification. When you use this command, the source specification is for a directory on the hard disk, while the target specification is a diskette drive. When the command is run, the files in the source directory are backed up to the diskette drive.

If you use the /S switch with the Backup command, the files in the source directory are backed up, and all the files in directories that are subordinate to the source directory are also backed up. If, for example, the source directory is the root directory of a drive, all the files on that drive are backed up because all the directories are subordinate to the root directory.

Whether or not the /S switch is on, the /M switch provides for an incremental backup. If the /M switch isn't specified, the Backup command does a full backup.

Figure 8-3 shows how to use the Backup command. Here, the first command does a full backup of the C drive. In this case, the /S switch is required because it tells DOS to include the files in all the subdirectories of the source specification. If the /S switch wasn't included, only the root directory would be backed up.

When a backup is in progress, DOS displays messages that tell you which diskette to insert into the drive next. For instance, a message like this is displayed when the command needs diskette number 3:

```
Insert backup target diskette 3 in drive A:
Strike any key when ready
```

As you can see, you need to keep your backup diskettes organized, so you should label and number them.

The second command in figure 8-3 shows how to use the Backup command for an incremental backup. Here, the /S switch tells the command to include subdirectories, and the /M switch tells it to do an incremental backup. If you don't include the /A switch for an incremental backup, the backed up files will be directed to a new diskette. In figure 8-1, for example, you can see that each incremental backup starts with a new diskette number.

The third command in figure 8-3 shows the use of the /A switch. When it is used, the backed up files are added to the last backup diskette. Since this saves diskettes, you usually want to use this switch for incremental backups. Then, you can refer to the backup as an *appended incremental backup* because the new files are appended to the last diskette in the set. Note,

---

The format of the Backup command

```
BACKUP source-spec target-spec [/s] [/m] [/a]
```

How to back up all the files on a drive (a full backup)

```
C:\>backup c:\*.* a: /s
```

How to back up only those files that have been changed since the last backup
(an incremental backup)

```
C:\>backup c:\*.* a: /s/m
```

How to do an appended incremental backup (DOS 3.3 or later)

```
C:\>backup c:\*.* a: /s/m/a
```

How to back up all the files in one data directory

```
C:\>backup c:\123\mma\*.* a:
```

Figure 8-3   How to use the Backup command

however, that you can only do an appended backup with a version of DOS that's 3.3 or later.

The last command in figure 8-3 shows you how to back up just one directory on a hard disk. This is useful when you work on the files in only one directory. And it's usually better than the DOS Copy command because the Backup command will use as many diskettes as are needed for the backup operation. It will also back up a single file that is so large it can't be stored on a single diskette. In contrast, the Copy command stops as soon as the first diskette is full.

If you use the Directory command to display the root directory of a backup diskette, you'll realize that the Backup command doesn't work at all like a Copy command. Instead of one entry for each file that has been backed

The format of the Restore command

```
RESTORE source-spec target-spec [/s]
```

How to restore all of the files from a full backup

```
C:\>restore a: c:\*.* /s
```

How to restore a single file from a full backup

```
C:\>restore a: c:\account\dist5.dbf
```

How to restore all of the files from a backup of the QA\DATA directory on the C drive

```
C:\>restore a: c:\qa\data\*.*
```

Figure 8-4   How to use the Restore command

up, you'll find just two directory entries for an entire backup diskette. One entry is for a file named BACKUP; the other is for a file named CONTROL. The first file contains all the files that have been backed up to the diskette; the second one contains control information that is required for the proper operation of the Backup and Restore commands.

The Restore command   Because of the special format used by the Backup command, you must use the Restore command to restore files that have been backed up. You can't use the Copy command.

The first example in figure 8-4 shows you how to use the Restore command if you want to restore all of the files from a full backup. Because the /S switch is used, this command will restore the files in all of the subdirectories. If you insert all of the backup diskettes in the sequence they were created, this command restores all the files from a full backup as well as all the files from the incremental backups that were done after the full backup.

The second example in figure 8-4 shows you how to use this command if you want to restore just one file from a full backup. Because this command is entered in an unusual way, you should take a moment to study it. As you can see, the A drive is given as the source drive, just as you would expect. However, the path and name of the file that you want restored from the A drive are given in the target specification. When the Restore command is executed, the restored file is always stored in the directory that it was backed up from.

Whether you restore one file or many, the Restore command has you insert each diskette from your set of backup diskettes. As a result, if you're restoring only one file, you may spend several minutes inserting diskettes before you get to the one that has the file you want restored. Then, if you've done incremental backups, you must continue through your set of backup diskettes to make sure that you restore the most recent version of the file. However, if you want to restore an earlier version, you can stop when you've restored that version.

The third example in figure 8-4 shows you how to use this command if you want to restore the files from just one directory of a backup. You use a command like this to restore the files from a full backup. But you must also use a command like this if the backup diskettes contain only the files from one directory. In other words, if the backed up files came from a directory, you must give that directory name in the target specification. And the restored files are always stored in the directory that they were backed up from.

Even if it takes several minutes to restore a file, you'll be delighted to discover that the file has been restored and you haven't lost all the hard work that went into it. If you ever have to restore hundreds of files, you'll be thankful indeed that you took the time to do an effective job of backing up your hard disk.

Three ways to back up your hard disk

To make your backups as tolerable as possible, you should design them so they're as efficient and easy as possible. That almost certainly means you should use incremental backups in combination with full backups. But that can also mean you should do two different types of backups: one for program files and one for data files.

Here, then, are three practical ways to run your backups. If you're like most PC users, one of these methods will be appropriate for your system. If you don't use your system often enough to justify daily backups, you can use the same methods on a less frequent backup schedule.

Daily backup of all files   If you want to keep your backups as simple as possible, don't distinguish between program and data files. Then, you can back up your hard disk by doing a full backup on the first day of each month or each week and an incremental backup on the other days of the month or week. That way, all the files on your hard disk are backed up daily.

However, because program files usually don't change, you spend more time doing backups than you need to when you use this method. If, for example, your hard disk has 6MB of files on it but only 2MB of data files, you're backing up 4MB of files unnecessarily. To improve the efficiency of your backups, you can use one of the two methods that follow.

Daily backup of data drive and periodic backup of program drive
On my PC, all the program files are stored on drive C, and all the data files are stored on drive D. Then, I do a full backup of drive C once a month, and I don't do daily incremental backups for this drive. In contrast, I do a full backup for drive D on every Monday, and I do daily incremental backups for this drive the rest of the week. By using separate backup procedures for the program drive and the data drive, my total backup time for the month is less than 30 minutes.

If you buy a new PC or a hard disk, you can easily set up the drives so you can use this method of backup. But it's time consuming to set up the drives in this way after you've used a PC for a while. Often, it takes several hours to back up the hard disk, repartition it into two or more drives, and restore the old files to the new drives. As a result, you may be better off using a different backup method.

Daily backup of data directories and periodic backup of program directories   If you commonly work within several data directories, you can sometimes simplify your backup procedures by reorganizing your directories. If, for example, all of your data directories are subordinate to one data directory as shown in figure 8-5, you can back them up using one command for a full backup and another one for an incremental backup. By combining a backup procedure for the entire hard disk with a backup procedure for the

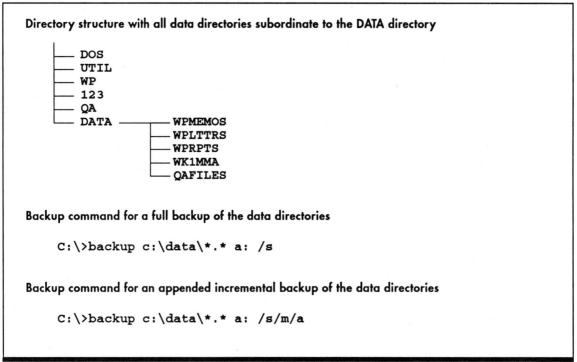

Directory structure with all data directories subordinate to the DATA directory

```
├── DOS
├── UTIL
├── WP
├── 123
├── QA
└── DATA ──────┬── WPMEMOS
               ├── WPLTTRS
               ├── WPRPTS
               ├── WK1MMA
               └── QAFILES
```

Backup command for a full backup of the data directories

```
C:\>backup c:\data\*.* a: /s
```

Backup command for an appended incremental backup of the data directories

```
C:\>backup c:\data\*.* a: /s/m/a
```

Figure 8-5   A directory structure that can simplify backups

DATA directory and its subordinates, you can reduce the time you spend doing your daily backups.

Five guidelines for simple and effective backups

Now that you know how to back up your hard disk, here are five guidelines for simple and effective backups. They are summarized in figure 8-6.

Set a schedule for your backups   Because backing up a hard disk takes time away from your other activities, it's always tempting to skip your backup procedure for a day, a week, or a month. Even if you're doing incremental backups that take less than a minute each, it's tempting to skip them. Before long, you won't even remember the last time you did a backup.

1. Set a schedule for your backups.

2. Use batch files to automate your backups.

3. Delete unnecessary files before you do a full backup.

4. Keep your diskettes organized.

5. Keep a log of your backups.

Figure 8-6   Five guidelines for simple and effective backups

That's why it's important to set a schedule for your backups. How often should you do them? That depends on how much you use your system. If, for example, you use your system more than four hours a day, you should probably do daily backups. If you use your system just an hour or two a day, you can perhaps get by with weekly backups, but you're going to be better off with daily backups. As a rule of thumb, you should schedule your backups so you'll never lose more work than you can afford to lose when a disk failure occurs. Then, you should stick to your schedule.

If you do one backup for program files and one for data files, you should set a separate schedule for each type of backup. For instance, you can schedule program backups once a month and data backups daily.

If you want to schedule both full and incremental backups, you can set full backups for a day like the first day of each month, the first day of each week, the last day of each month, or the last day of each week. Just schedule your full backups on days that usually provide the free time you need for this task. Then, schedule incremental backups on the other days. But if you don't want to schedule days for full backups, you can just do them whenever the number of diskettes you've used for incremental backups gets unwieldy.

Use batch files to automate your backups   Once you've designed and scheduled your backups, you should put the commands in batch files to make them easier to use. In figure 8-7, for example, you can see one batch file for a full backup of the C drive, and one for an incremental backup. Once you create these files, you don't have to remember the details for entering the

```
BACKFULL.BAT

    backup c:\*.* a: /s


BACKINC.BAT

    backup c:\*.* a: /s/m/a
```

Figure 8-7   Two batch files for backups

Backup command each time that you do a backup. Instead, you can execute
these batch files from the command prompt or from a shell program.

Delete unnecessary files before you do a full backup   Often, it's
quicker and easier to delete unnecessary files than it is to back them up. So
before you start a full backup, it's worth taking a few minutes to see if your
hard disk has any directories or files that you no longer need. If you find
some and delete them, your backups will run more quickly, and your directories and files will be more manageable.

Keep your diskettes organized   This is obvious, but I think it's worth
mentioning. By all means keep your diskettes organized by labelling and
numbering your backup diskettes and your diskette boxes. That way, you'll
be able to run your backups as efficiently as possible. Also, if you ever have
to use the Restore command, you'll be able to present the diskettes in the
proper sequence so that the command will work the way you want it to.

In general, the label for a backup diskette should indicate the drive or
directory that the backup is for. It should also give the sequence number of
the diskette within the backup procedure. However, a diskette label shouldn't
indicate whether it is for a full or incremental backup. If, for example, the
full backup ended with diskette 6 and the first incremental backup started
with diskette 7, you shouldn't indicate this on the diskette labels. And you
shouldn't write the date of the backup on the labels. Instead, you should keep
this information in a backup log.

Keep a log of your backups   When you use more than one type of
backup, you can easily lose track of what type of backup you should be
doing and which diskette you should start with. That's why you should keep
a log of the backups you run. You don't need anything elaborate for this, so a
simple form like the one in figure 8-8 will do.

In this log, you can see that the PC user does a full backup of the C drive
on the last day of the month. That backup includes both program and data
directories so it protects against a complete failure of the hard disk. For the
rest of the month, the user does a full backup of just the data directories on
each Monday and incremental backups of just the data directories on the
other days of the week. By using a separate procedure for backing up data
files, the user can keep backup time to a minimum and never be in danger of
losing more than a day's work. But without a backup log, a system like this
can get out of control.

Two hardware improvements that can simplify backup

If your backups take so long that you often skip them, you should do whatever you can to make them quicker and easier. One way to make an improvement in your backup procedures is to add a new hardware component to your
system. Two components that can help are a high-capacity diskette drive and
a backup tape drive.

A high-capacity diskette drive   If you don't already have a high-capacity
diskette drive on your system, buying one can quickly improve backups.
Since the 1.2MB diskettes have about four times the capacity of the 360KB
diskettes, you only have to use one-fourth as many diskettes. Similarly, you
only have to use one-half as many diskettes if you add a 1.44MB diskette
drive to a PC with only a 720KB drive. At a price of about $100 for a new
drive, this purchase can simplify your backup procedures so you're more
likely to do them as scheduled.

A backup tape drive   Backup tape drives record data on a special high-
capacity tape that's enclosed in a removable cartridge that's similar to an
audio tape cassette. Most of these tape drives fit in the space allocated for a
diskette drive in the systems unit of a PC. Depending on how much you want

Backup Log			
Date	Drive/Path	Backup Type	Last disk
3/30	C:	Full	12
4/2	C:\data	Full	2
⟨	⟨	Incremental	3
			3
			3
			4
4/9	C:\data	Full	2
⟨	⟨	Incremental	3
		⟨	3
			4
			4
4/16	C:\data	Full	2
⟨	⟨	Incremental	3
		⟨	3
			3
			3
4/23	C:\data	Full	2
⟨	⟨	Incremental	3
		⟨	3
			3
			3
4/30	C:	Full	12
5/1	C:\data	Full	2
⟨	⟨	Incremental	3
		⟨	4
			4

Figure 8-8   A simple backup log

to spend, you can get drives that handle tape capacities of from 20MB to 2,000MB. If you get a tape drive with a large enough capacity, you can run a full backup unattended because you don't have to insert diskettes as the backup program runs. You can also set up the backup program so it runs automatically after you've gone home.

The only drawback to a backup tape drive is cost; prices range from $400 to $2,000. However, if you work on many large files and those files are essential to the operation of a department or company, a tape drive can easily justify its cost. For instance, the desktop publishing system that we use to produce books has a tape drive for backup. At any given time, this system has the critical versions of many different chapters and marketing pieces, and we just can't afford to lose the hard disk data. Because the tape backup program is set up to run automatically every night at 6:00 P.M., we know that the backups are done daily.

How a commercial backup utility can improve backup

If your backup requirements are simple, the DOS Backup and Restore commands may be all that you need. For most PC users, though, a commercial backup utility will pay for itself in less than a year. In general, backup utility programs are much faster than the DOS commands, and they're also easier to use.

Figure 8-9 gives you some idea of what you can expect from a typical backup utility. This chart just summarizes the data from an informal test on my own system, but the message is clear. If a full backup takes you 15 minutes when you use the Backup command, you can probably save 10 minutes or more each time you run one. You can also save time on each incremental backup. And the more data you have on your hard disk, the more valuable a backup utility is.

At a cost of around $100 for a product like *PC Tools Deluxe*, you can figure out how soon the program will pay for itself. But the most important benefit of a backup utility is not the time you save by using one. It's the fact that you're far more likely to do scheduled backups because they take less time.

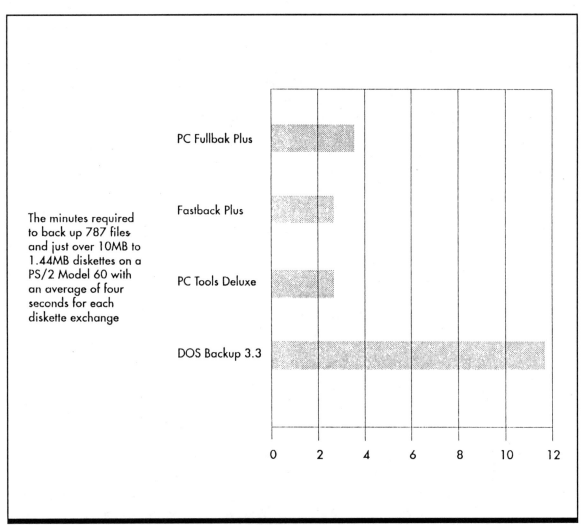

The minutes required to back up 787 files and just over 10MB to 1.44MB diskettes on a PS/2 Model 60 with an average of four seconds for each diskette exchange

Figure 8-9   Relative backup times for the Backup command and three backup utilities

Terms

backing up a hard disk   archive bit
restoring a hard disk   appended incremental backup
full backup
incremental backup

Exercises

1. Use the Backup command to do a full backup of all the files in one of the data directories of your hard disk to diskettes in the A drive. Next, use the Directory command to display the directory of one of the backup diskettes.

2. Modify one of the files that you backed up in exercise 1, but not a file that you can't afford to lose. Then, do an incremental backup of all the files in the data directory that you used for exercise 1.

3. Delete the file that you modified in exercise 2. Then, use the Restore command to restore the modified version of it.

4. Run a full backup of all the drives on your hard disk and record the time that it takes. Then, establish backup procedures for your system. Next, create the batch files for the Backup commands required by your procedures.

Section 4

How to use the DOS 5.0 shell

If you already have DOS 5.0, the four chapters in this section will show you how to use the DOS 5.0 shell. In chapter 9, you'll be introduced to the basic functions of the shell. In chapter 10, you'll learn how to use the shell to create and use menus to start your application programs. In chapter 11, you'll learn how to use the shell to manage the directories and files on your hard disk. And in chapter 12, you'll learn how to use the task switching capabilities of the shell to quickly switch between application programs. When you finish this section, you'll be able to use the DOS 5.0 shell for most DOS functions.

If you don't have DOS 5.0 on your PC, you can read this section to see what the shell can do and how it works. Then, you can decide for yourself whether upgrading to DOS 5.0 is worth the effort. If you like the idea of using a shell, but you don't want to upgrade to DOS 5.0, you can consider the purchase of a commercial shell program.

Chapter 9

An introduction to the DOS 5.0 shell

Since the introduction of the IBM PC and DOS in 1981, users have complained that DOS is hard to use. To a large extent, that's why *shell programs* have become popular. These programs let you perform many of the functions provided by DOS commands without forcing you to know the details of the commands themselves.

Beginning with DOS 4.0, Microsoft included a shell program with DOS called the *DOS shell*. With DOS 5.0, Microsoft significantly improved the shell program. Although some commercial shell programs still provide advanced features that aren't found in the DOS 5.0 shell, the 5.0 shell provides most of the shell features that you are likely to want. It also includes a few features that aren't found in any commercial shell programs. And it's easy to use. So if you have DOS 5.0 on your PC and you aren't already using another shell, I definitely recommend that you use the 5.0 shell.

In this chapter, I'll introduce you to the shell by presenting a brief overview of the shell's menu and file management functions. Then, in chapters 10 and 11, I'll show you how to use these shell functions in detail. In chapter 12, I'll present the task-switching functions that the DOS 5.0 shell provides.

If you don't have DOS 5.0 on your PC, these chapters will show you how the shell works. They will also show you the features that the shell offers. Then, you can decide for yourself whether upgrading to DOS 5.0 is worth the effort. If you like the idea of using a shell, but you don't want to upgrade to 5.0, you can consider the purchase of a commercial shell program.

As you will soon see, the quickest way to learn how to use a shell is to experiment with it. That's why the chapters in this section don't present detailed instructions for using the shell. Instead, they present general operational procedures for using the shell, and they introduce you to the capabilities of the shell. Once you have this background, you shouldn't have much trouble using the shell because most of its operations are self-explanatory.

If your PC has a mouse, you'll want to use it with the DOS shell because it simplifies some of the operations. However, you can also use the shell with the keyboard. Throughout this section of the book, I'll show you how to perform a function using both a mouse and the keyboard.

An overview of the DOS shell

Before you learn how to use the DOS 5.0 shell program, you should know that it provides functions that you can use for three distinct purposes. First, it provides a program-list function that lets you start your application programs by selecting choices from a menu rather than by typing commands. Second, it provides file-management functions that let you manage your directories and files without remembering the details of DOS command formats. Third, it provides task-switching functions that let you load several programs into memory at once and switch from one to another with just a few keystrokes.

How to start the DOS shell   When you install DOS 5.0 on your system, the installation program asks you if you would like the DOS shell program to be started automatically. If you answer "yes," the installation program puts this command in your AUTOEXEC.BAT file: DOSSHELL. This is the name of the program file that starts the shell. If your shell isn't started by the AUTOEXEC.BAT file, you can start it any time by entering the Dosshell command at the prompt.

The DOS shell display   When you start the shell, it displays the screen shown in figure 9-1. This is the standard display, but you should know that the DOS shell provides other display options you can select. If you or someone else has used the shell previously and selected another display option,

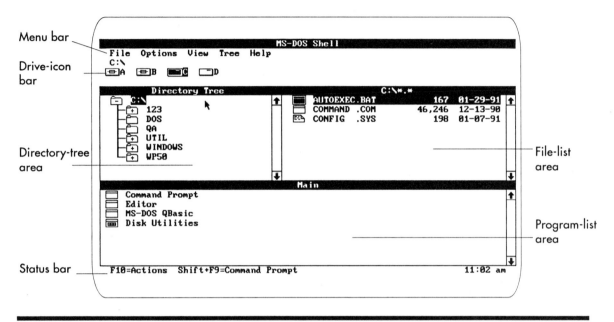

Menu bar

Drive-icon bar

Directory-tree area

File-list area

Program-list area

Status bar

Figure 9-1   The first screen of the DOS 5.0 shell

your screen won't look like this one. In just a moment, I'll show you how to reset your display to the one shown here.

In figure 9-1, you can see that the DOS shell displays a *menu bar* at the top of the screen. You use this menu bar to select DOS shell functions. Below the menu bar are the *drive icons* in the *drive-icon bar*. These icons represent each disk drive on your system, and you use them to select the drive you want to use. Below the drive icons, the display is divided into two areas: the *directory-tree area* and the *file-list area*. You use these two areas to manage your files and directories. The next area is the *program-list area*. You use it to start DOS utilities and application programs. At the bottom of the screen, the *status bar* displays the current time and indicates any function keys or keystroke combinations you can use to perform functions.

If the DOS shell display on your PC uses the same basic layout, but it looks slightly different from the one in figure 9-1, you're probably using a different monitor than the one I used for the figures. Also, I used the shell in graphics mode because the shell uses some graphics symbols. So if you're running the shell in text mode, your screen won't look exactly like the one in figure 9-1.

When you use the DOS shell, only one of the areas on the display is active at a time. If you're using a color monitor, the DOS shell identifies the active area by using a different color in the area's title bar. If you're using a monochrome monitor, the DOS shell identifies the active area by placing a small arrow next to the current item within the area.

To use one of the areas of the DOS shell, you must first make that area active. If you have a mouse, you just move the mouse cursor to the area you want to activate and press the left mouse button. If you don't have a mouse, you use the Tab key to move from one area to the next. Each time you press the Tab key, the next screen area is activated. As a result, you sometimes have to press the Tab key several times to activate the area you want.

How to use the pull-down menus   The menu bar in figure 9-1 contains five menu items: File, Options, View, Tree, and Help. To select one of these menu items, you move the mouse cursor to the item and press the left mouse button. This is referred to as *clicking the mouse*. When you do that, a *pull-down menu* is displayed. For example, figure 9-2 shows the pull-down menu that's displayed when you click on the File menu item when the program-list area is activated. As you can see, this menu has eight functions: New, Open, Copy, Delete, Properties, Reorder, Run, and Exit. To select one of these functions, you just point to it with the mouse cursor and click again.

If you don't have a mouse, you can use three techniques to use the pull down menus. One, you can activate the menu bar by pressing the F10 key. Then, you can pull down a menu by pressing the underlined letter of the menu you want (*F* for File, *O* for Options, and so on). Two, you can press the F10 key to activate the menu bar and then use the cursor keys to move the highlight to the menu you want and press the Enter key. Three, you can hold down the Alt key while pressing the underlined letter of the menu you want.

Once you've pulled a menu down, you can use the keyboard to select a function by pressing the underlined letter of the function you want (for example, *O* for Open). Or you can use the cursor keys to move the highlight to the function and then press the Enter key.

If you're running the DOS shell on your PC as you read this chapter and if the DOS shell display is different than the one in figure 9-1, take a moment

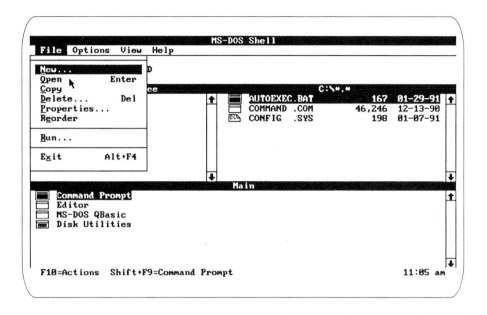

Figure 9-2   The File menu when the program-list area is active

now to change the display. First, select the View function from the menu bar. Then, select the Program/File-list view from the menu. Now, your display should match the figures in this chapter.

When you use the DOS shell, you'll probably notice that the items in the menu bar change as you move from one area to another. When the program-list area is active, for example, the Tree menu is removed from the menu bar. In addition, the functions that appear in the pull-down menus vary depending on which area of the shell is active. In some cases, menu functions are displayed in grey to show that they're unavailable because they don't apply to the area that's active. (On a monochrome monitor, these functions aren't displayed at all.) When you're using the directory-tree area, for example, the Copy function of the File menu isn't available because you can't copy a directory.

How to get Help information from the DOS shell   Whenever you're using the DOS shell, you can get information from the Help facility by pressing the F1 key. This information is displayed in a *window* as shown in figure

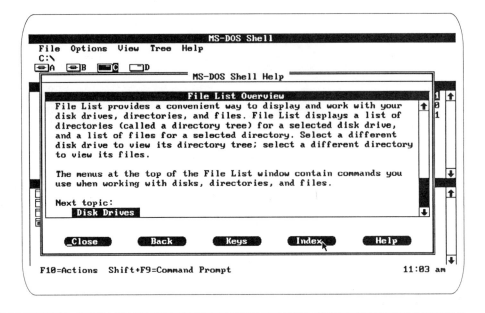

Figure 9-3   One of the Help-facility windows that's displayed when you press the F1 key

9-3, and it always relates to whatever you're trying to do at the time. If, for example, you press the F1 key while you're using the file-list area, you get the information shown in this figure. As you can see, the Help information explains what the file list does.

The five ovals at the bottom of the Help window are called *buttons*. To use any one of the button functions, you click on it with the mouse. You can also start one of these functions by using the cursor control keys to move the cursor to the desired button and then pressing the Enter key. For instance, you can cancel the Help function by clicking the mouse on the Close button, or you can move the cursor to it and then press the Enter key.

The Help button in figure 9-3 provides information about how to use the Help facility. The Index button displays an index of topics within the Help facility. By using it, you can skip directly to any Help subject that's available. The Keys button displays a list of all the functions that can be performed by keyboard and function keys when you're using the DOS shell. And the Back button moves you to the previous help screen.

How to exit from the DOS shell   You can exit from the DOS shell in two different ways. To exit from the shell completely and return to the DOS prompt, you select the Exit option from the File menu. If you want to start the DOS shell again after you use this command, you must enter DOSSHELL at the command prompt.

If you just want to exit from the shell temporarily, you can press the Shift-F9 key combination as indicated by the status bar, or you can select the Command-prompt option from the main program list. Either way, the DOS command prompt is displayed. To return to the DOS shell, you just type the word "exit" at the prompt and press the Enter key.

An introduction to the program-list functions of the shell

A *program list* is a menu that you can use for starting your application programs or DOS utilities. When you first install the DOS shell, the program-list area contains a program-list with just a few options that let you execute some of the more useful DOS commands. In this chapter, I'll show you how to use the default program list provided with the DOS shell. In the next chapter, you'll learn how to customize that program list by adding options to it that start your application programs.

The components of the DOS shell that provide the program-list functions
Figure 9-4 identifies these components. The *menu bar* displays the menu choices that are available when you're working with the program list: File, Options, View, and Help. The *program-list title bar* shows the name of the program list that's currently displayed. Here, the *main program list* is active and it has four options displayed in the program-list area: Command Prompt, Editor, MS-DOS QBasic, and Disk Utilities.

In figure 9-4, you can see that the first three options of the main program list have plain boxes to the left of them. That means these options start programs or functions. The last option, however, has a box with a pattern of smaller boxes in it. That means it leads to another program list. You can think of the main program list and its subordinate program lists as a two-level menu system. And you can think of the options in these program lists as menu choices. You'll understand how these two types of program lists work before you complete this chapter.

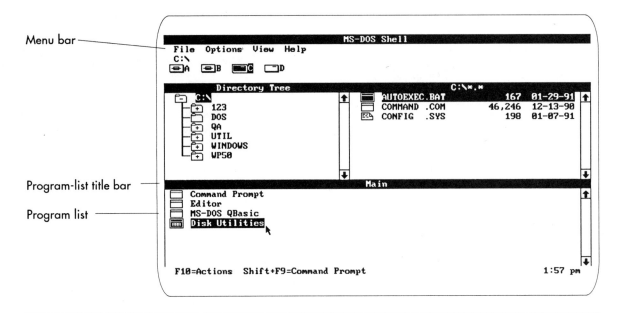

Menu bar

Program-list title bar

Program list

Figure 9-4   The components of the shell that provide the program-list functions

How to select an option from the main program list   To select one of the options on the main program list, you move the mouse cursor to it and press the left mouse button twice in rapid succession. This is referred to as *double clicking the mouse*. If you don't have a mouse, you must first press the Tab key one or more times to activate this area of the shell, then you use the cursor control keys to highlight your selection.

How to start the Edit program   The Editor option starts the Edit program that I showed you how to use in chapter 5. This full-screen text editor makes it easy to edit batch files. When you select the Editor, the DOS shell starts by displaying the *dialog box* shown in figure 9-5. After you type in the file specification and press the Enter key, DOS starts the Edit program and loads the file you specified.

How to use the Disk-utilities program list   When you select the Disk-utilities option from the main program list, the program list in figure 9-6 is

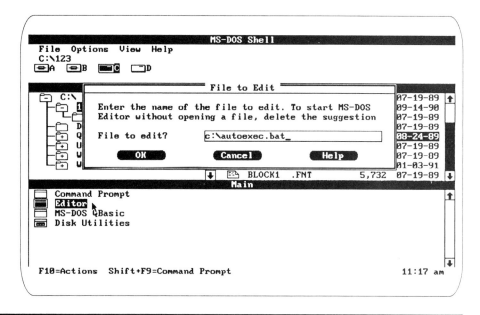

Figure 9-5   The dialog box for the Editor option of the main program list

displayed. Here, the Disk-copy option runs the DOS Diskcopy command, the Backup-fixed-disk option runs the DOS Backup command, and so on.

When you select one of these options, a dialog box asks for parameters. To illustrate, figure 9-7 shows the dialog box you get when you select the Format option. Here, the default drive is drive A. So if you want to format a 720KB diskette in drive B, which is a 1.44MB drive, you have to type in the following information:

```
b: /f:720
```

These are the parameters that I presented in chapter 7 when I showed you how to format a diskette using the Format command at the DOS prompt. So even though you're using the DOS shell, you have to know the details of the command.

Similarly, the Backup-fixed-disk option displays a dialog box like the one in figure 9-8. Here, the default parameters produce a complete backup

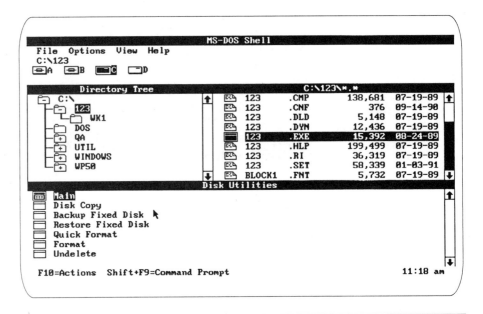

Figure 9-6   The Disk-utilities program list

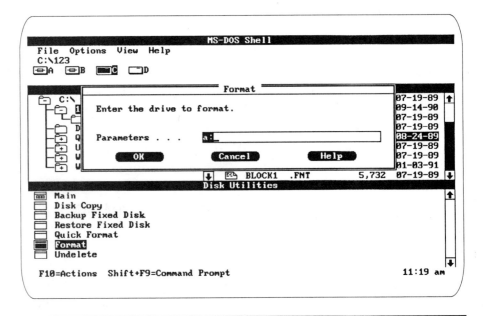

Figure 9-7   The dialog box for the Format option in the Disk-utilities program list

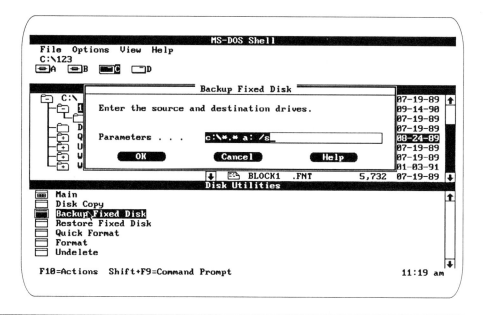

Figure 9-8   The default parameters of the dialog box for the Backup-fixed-disk option in the Disk-utilities program list

of drive C. If you want to do an incremental backup, you must replace the default parameters with the ones I showed you in chapter 8:

```
c:\*.* a: /s/m/a
```

These are the parameters you use to do an incremental backup using the Backup command at the DOS prompt.

An introduction to the file-management functions of the shell

When you use the DOS 5.0 shell to manage files, you use the directory-tree and file-list areas of the screen. After I introduce you to these and other components, I'll show you how to change the default drive, change the current directory, scroll through a file list, scroll through a directory tree, select files, and pull down the menus.

The components of the DOS shell that provide file-management functions
Figure 9-9 identifies the components you use to manage files. The menu bar
displays five choices for pull-down menus: File, Options, View, Tree, and
Help.

The drive-icon bar displays the drives and highlights the default drive. If
your monitor is in graphics mode, the shell uses a symbol to indicate whether
a drive is a diskette drive or a hard drive. In addition, the *path bar* displays
the default drive and path. In figure 9-9, this bar specifies the root directory
on the C drive.

The directory-tree area presents a *directory tree*, which is a graphic repre-
sentation of the default drive's directory structure. If your monitor is in graphics mode, folders represent directories, and plus signs on those folders identify directories that have subdirectories that aren't displayed. One directory is
highlighted to identify it as the current directory.

The file-list area displays a *file list*, which is a list of the files of the current directory in a format that is similar to one displayed by the Directory
command. In graphics mode, a symbol next to each file indicates whether the
file is a program file or a data file. The *selection cursor* is a bar in this area
that's used to select files by highlighting them.

How to change the default drive   To change the default drive, you can
use the mouse to click on the drive you want in the drive-icon bar. If you
don't have a mouse, you can hold down the Ctrl key while you press the letter of the drive you want. Or you can press the Tab key until the drive-icon
bar becomes active. Then, you can use the cursor control keys to highlight
the drive that you want and press the Enter key.

How to change the current directory   To change the current directory,
you can use the mouse in the directory-tree area to click on the directory you
want. If you don't have a mouse, you must first use the Tab key to activate
the directory-tree area. Then, you use the cursor control keys to highlight the
directory you want and press the Enter key.

How to scroll through a file list   If a directory has more files than can be
displayed in the file-list area at one time, you can scroll through the list to
view all of the files. The easiest way to do that is by using the cursor control

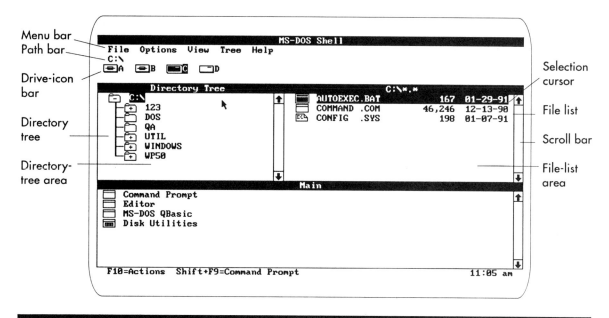

Figure 9-9   The components of the shell that provide the file-management functions

keys to move through the list one line at a time, or by using the Page-up and Page-down keys to move the list one screen at a time.

You can also scroll through the list with a mouse by using the *scroll bar* to the right of the file list. You can scroll down one line at a time by clicking on the arrow at the bottom of the scroll bar. Similarly, you can scroll up one line at a time by clicking on the arrow at the top of the scroll bar.

To scroll through varying numbers of lines with the mouse, you move the mouse cursor to the white portion of the scroll bar called the *scroll box*. Then, you hold down the left mouse button while you move the scroll box to the new position. As you move the mouse, the file list scrolls to its new position. This process is illustrated in figure 9-10. Notice that the file named APPEND.EXE, which was at the bottom of the file list in part 1, has been scrolled off of the list in part 2.

To help you gauge your position when you use the scroll bar, the height of the scroll box indicates the relative size of the file list. For instance, the scroll bar in figure 9-9 is all white, which means that all of the files in the directory are displayed. In contrast, the scroll box in the figure 9-10 indicates

Part 1:

Put the mouse cursor
on the scroll box.

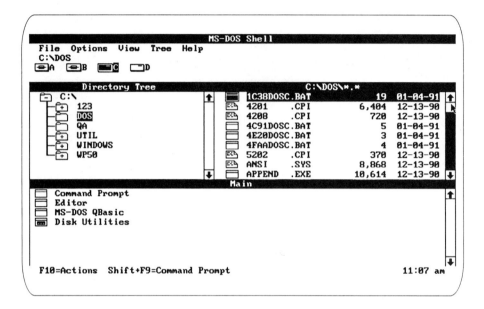

Part 2:

While holding down
the left mouse button,
drag the scroll box to
the new file position.

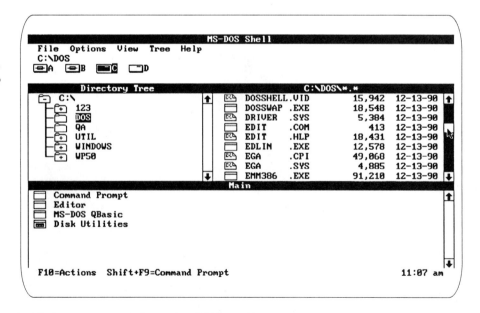

Figure 9-10   How to use the scroll bar to scroll through the file list

that about one-fifth of the files in the directory are displayed. In part 1, the scroll box indicates that the files in the first part of the directory are displayed. In part 2, the box indicates that the files in the middle part of the directory are displayed.

How to scroll through a directory tree   If a drive has more directories than can be displayed in the directory-tree area at one time, you can scroll through the directory tree just as you can the file list. Again, the easiest way to do that is by using the cursor control keys to move the tree display one line at a time or by using the Page-up and Page-down keys to move the tree one screen at a time.

You can also scroll through the directory tree with a mouse by using the scroll bar to the right of the directory tree. You can scroll up or down one line at a time by clicking on one of the arrows at the top or bottom of the scroll bar. And you can scroll varying amounts by moving the scroll box.

Figure 9-11 shows how the shell displays a typical directory structure. Here, plus signs (+) on folders indicate that these directories have at least one subdirectory. To expand a directory so you can see these subdirectories, you move the mouse to the directory folder as shown in part 1. When you click the mouse, the directory is *expanded* to display any subdirectories as shown in part 2. To use the keyboard to expand a directory, you press the Tab key to activate the directory-tree area. Then, you use the cursor control keys to move to the desired directory. When you press the Plus sign key, the DOS shell expands the directory.

When a directory has been expanded, a minus sign (-) is displayed in the directory folder to indicate that you can *collapse* the directory. To collapse a directory using a mouse, you just click on the folder with the minus sign. To collapse a directory using the keyboard, you move the highlight to the folder with the minus sign and press the Minus sign key.

The DOS shell also provides commands that you can use to expand and collapse directories. You access these commands from the Tree menu. With them, you can expand one directory or all of the directories on the tree, and you can collapse a directory.

How to select files   When you use DOS commands, you enter the names of the files you want to process as parameters. In contrast, when you use the

Part 1:

Move the mouse cursor to the folder of the directory you want to expand and click the mouse.

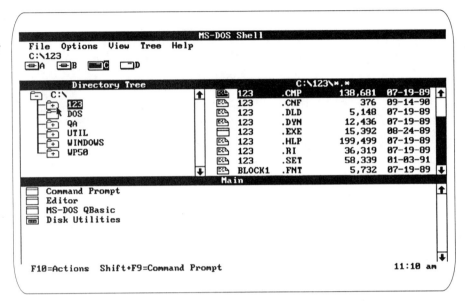

Part 2:

The expanded directory is then displayed.

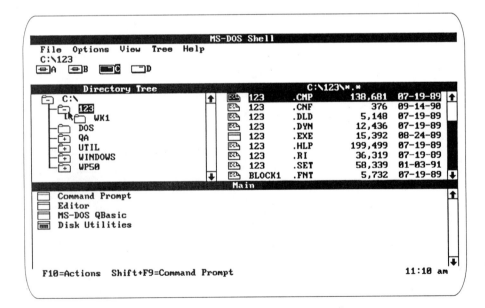

Figure 9-11   How to expand a directory

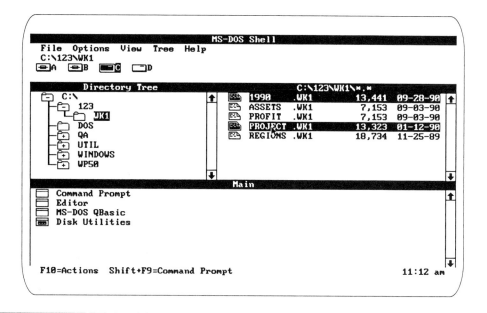

Figure 9-12   Two files selected by holding down the Ctrl key as you click the mouse on each file

DOS shell, you don't enter file names. Instead, you select the files you want to process before you start a command. Then, when you select the command that you want from a menu, all the files you selected are processed. To delete files, for example, you first select all the files you want to delete. Next, you select the Delete command from the File menu. All the selected files are then deleted.

You can use three techniques to select files using a mouse. First, you can select a single file by moving the mouse cursor to the file in the file list and clicking on it. After you select a file, it's highlighted.

Second, you can select several files by holding down the Ctrl key as you click on each file. With this technique, you can select any number of files from anywhere in the file display as shown in figure 9-12.

Third, you can select a group of files that are listed together one under the other. First, you move the mouse cursor to the first file in the group and click on it, as shown in part 1 of figure 9-13. Next, you move the mouse cursor to the last file in the group you want to select. Then, you hold down the

Part 1:

Select the first file in the group, then move the mouse cursor to the last file in the group.

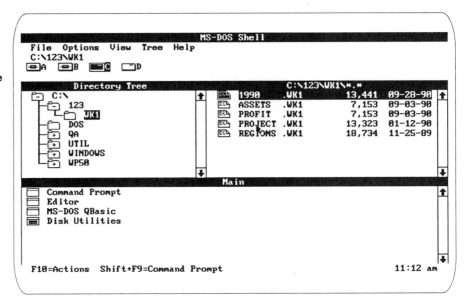

Part 2:

Select the group by holding down the Shift key while you click the mouse on the last file.

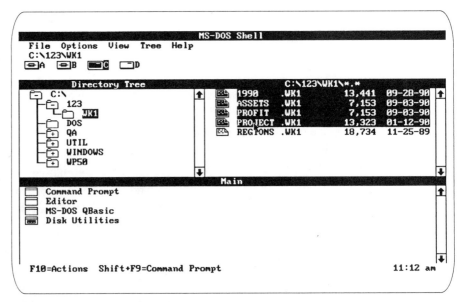

Figure 9-13 How to select a group of files

Shift key as you click on the file. All the files in the group are then selected, as shown in part 2 of figure 9-13.

To select a single file with the keyboard, you use the cursor control keys to move the selection cursor to the file. To select several files, you press the Shift-F8 key combination to turn on the Add mode. Then, you use the cursor control keys and the space bar key to select each file. To turn the Add mode feature off, you press the Shift-F8 keys again. To select a group of files, you hold down the Shift key and use the cursor control keys to select the group.

If you want to cancel a selection, all you have to do is move either the mouse cursor or the selection cursor to another area before you execute the function from one of the pull-down menus.

How to use the pull-down menus   If you look again at figure 9-9, you can see that when the file-list area is active, the menu bar contains these five selections: File, Options, View, Tree, and Help. The pull-down menu you'll use the most as you work with files and directories is the File menu, shown in figure 9-14. As you can see, it provides several groups of functions. Many of these functions correspond to familiar DOS commands, such as Copy, Delete, and Rename. Other functions, such as Associate and Move, provide functions unique to the shell. You'll learn how to use all of these functions in chapter 11.

How to start a command or program from the file-list area

When you use the DOS shell, you can start any command or program from the file-list area. To do this with a mouse, you double-click on the command or program file in the file list. To do this with the keyboard, you use the cursor control keys to highlight the command or program file and then press the Enter key.

Since you can use this method to start any file with a COM or EXE extension, you can start any of the external DOS commands in this way. You can also start batch files this way. If, for example, you have already stored one batch file for each of your application programs in the UTIL directory, you just change the current directory to UTIL, select the batch file you want to execute, and start the batch file using one of the techniques I just mentioned.

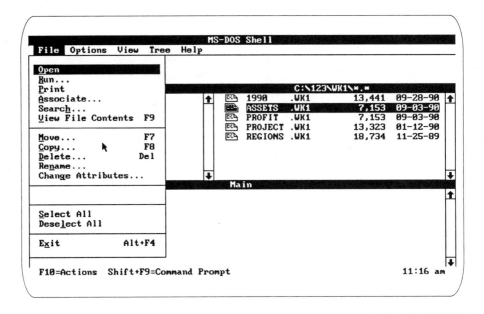

Figure 9-14 The File menu when the file-list area is active

Some perspective on the DOS 5.0 shell

If you only use the DOS shell for starting commands and programs, you won't get much benefit from it. In fact, if you already use batch files to start your application programs, you can probably start them faster from the command prompt than you can from the shell. Similarly, if you already know how to use the DOS commands, you can probably run them faster from the command prompt than you can from the Disk-utilities program list in the shell.

In the next chapter, though, you'll learn how to use the DOS shell to create and use menus to start your application programs. Then, in chapter 11, you'll learn how to use the shell to manage directories and files. After you finish these chapters, you'll have a better idea of how the DOS 5.0 shell can help you work more efficiently.

Terms

shell program
DOS shell
menu bar
drive icon
drive-icon bar
directory-tree area
file-list area
program-list area
status bar
clicking the mouse
pull-down menu
window
button
program list
menu bar
program-list title bar
main program list
double clicking the mouse
dialog box
path bar
directory tree
file list
selection cursor
scroll bar
scroll box
expand a directory
collapse a directory

Chapter 10

How to use the DOS 5.0 shell to create and use menus

The program-list functions of the DOS shell make it easy for you to create menus for starting your application programs. Once you create the menus, you can start your application programs more easily from a program list than you can from the file list. All you have to do to start a program is to double click the mouse on the selection you want. Or if you don't have a mouse, you just highlight the selection you want and press the Enter key.

In this chapter, you'll learn how to use the program-list functions to create your own menus. Then, you'll learn how to start your application programs from these menus. If you've read the last chapter, you already know the general techniques for using the DOS shell, so this chapter should be easy to follow. When you finish this chapter, you should be able to set up menus for your own programs in just a few minutes.

The menu structure of the program-list area

The program-list area in figure 10-1 shows the main program list. When you install DOS 5.0, this screen automatically has the four options shown here: Command Prompt, Editor, MS-DOS QBasic, and Disk Utilities. As you can see, the first three options have plain boxes to the left of them to indicate that they start programs. The last option, however, has a box with a pattern of

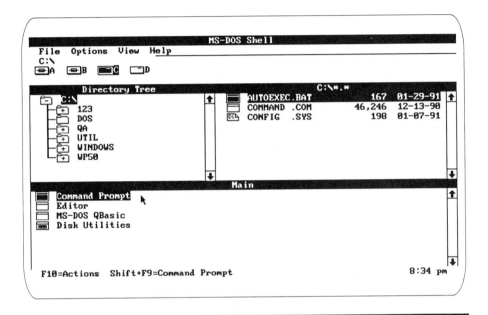

Figure 10-1   The main program list

smaller boxes in it. This symbol indicates that this option leads to another program list.

When you use the DOS 5.0 shell, you can create a multi-level menu system. The main program list can lead to other program lists, and those program lists can lead to still others. For most users, though, a two-level menu structure is adequate so the menu structure consists of just the main program list and the program lists that it leads to.

If you use just two or three application programs, it's probably best to add them to the main program list shown in figure 10-1. If, on the other hand, you use several programs, it's probably best to create a program list for them that's subordinate to the main program list. You can call this something like "Applications."

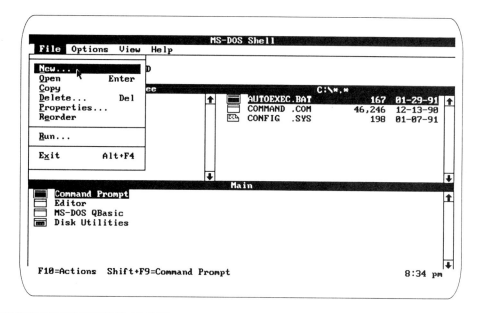

Figure 10-2   The File menu when the program-list area is active

How to add a program list to the main program list

To do this, you activate the program-list area and pull down the File menu as shown in figure 10-2. As you can see, it provides eight functions: New, Open, Copy, Delete, Properties, Reorder, Run, and Exit. In this chapter, I'll only show you how to use the New and Properties functions because all the others are easy to use once you know how to use these two.

Figure 10-3 shows the dialog boxes that appear when you select the New function from the File menu. The dialog box in part 1 lets you specify whether you want to add a new *Program Group* or a new *Program Item* to the current list. In this case, I've selected the Program-group option to add a subordinate program list to the main program list. Here, *program group* is just another name for a program list.

The dialog box in part 2 lets you enter information to identify the new program list. The Title entry is the name of the list that will be added to the main program list. This entry can be up to 23 characters long, and it's the only required entry for this dialog box.

Part 1:

First, you select the New option from the File menu. Then, you choose the Program-group option in the first dialog box.

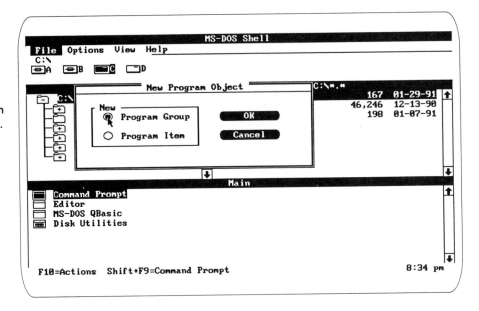

Part 2:

Next, you fill in the entries in the second dialog box that create and identify the new program list.

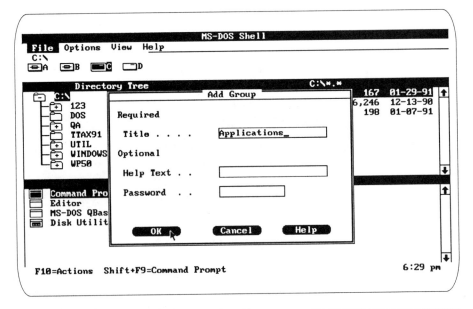

Figure 10-3 How to add a program list to the main program list

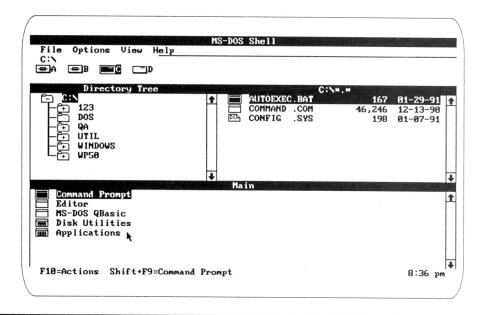

Figure 10-4   The main program list with the Applications option created by the dialog boxes in figure 10-3

The Help-text entry can be used if you want Help information to be available for the program group. If you make an entry, the text is displayed when the PC user presses the F1 key while the group is highlighted. Usually, though, the purpose of a program group is obvious so there's no reason to include a Help-text entry.

The Password entry can be used if you want to restrict access to the new program list. Then, only a PC user who knows the password can use the programs in the program list. Since passwords have a limited use, though, you usually leave this entry blank.

After you've completed the entries in this dialog box, use the OK button to add the program list to the main program list. In figure 10-4, you can see how the Title entry in figure 10-3 is displayed after this list has been added to the main program list.

As you can see in figure 10-4, the Applications option has a box with a grid of smaller boxes in it to indicate that it leads to another program list.

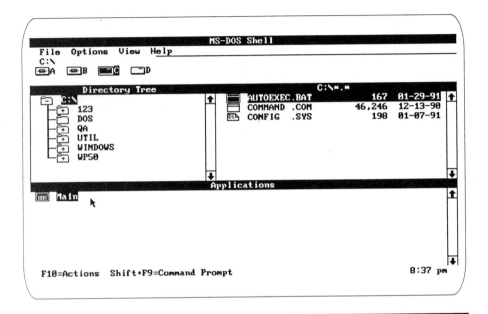

Figure 10-5   The empty program list of the Applications option

When you select the Applications option before you add any programs to the new list, you get the screen in figure 10-5. Notice the change in the program-list title bar; it now tells you that you're in the Applications program list.

How to add a program to a program list

To do this, you select the program list in the main program list that you want to add a program to. If, for example, you want to add a program to the Applications program list, you first select the Applications list from the main program list. Then, the shell displays the screen shown in figure 10-5. Here, the Applications program list is empty except for the option that takes you back to the main program list.

Next, you pull down the File menu as shown in figure 10-6. Because the Applications program list is empty, only four options are available on the menu. Now, you select the New option. Figure 10-7 shows the dialog boxes that appear.

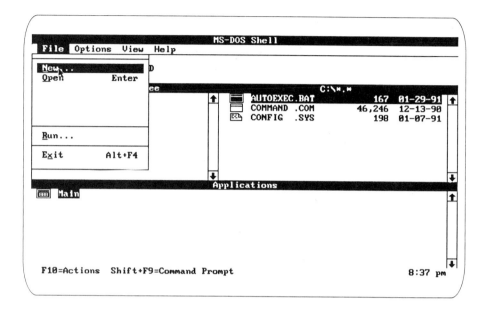

```
                              MS-DOS Shell
    File  Options  View  Help
  ┌─New...──────────┐ D
  │ Open      Enter │
  ┌────────────────────┐ ee                           C:\*.*
  │                    │      ↑  ┌─┐ AUTOEXEC.BAT         167  01-29-91 ↑
  │                    │         ├─┤ COMMAND .COM      46,246  12-13-90
  │ Run...             │         ┌─┐ CONFIG  .SYS         198  01-07-91
  │                    │
  │ Exit      Alt+F4   │
  │                    │      ↓                                         ↓
  └────────────────────┘         Applications
  ┌─┐ Main                                                             ↑



    F10=Actions  Shift+F9=Command Prompt                      8:37 pm  ↓
```

Figure 10-6   The File menu that's displayed for an empty program list

The dialog box in part 1 of figure 10-7 lets you specify whether you want to add a new Program Group or Program Item to the current list. In this case, I've selected Program Item to add a program to a program list. Here, the term *program item* just refers to the menu item that will start the program that's being added to the program list.

The dialog box in part 2 lets you enter information that's needed to start the program. The first required entry is the Title entry. This establishes the title that will be used in the subordinate program list. In this example, the title that will appear on the program list is *WordPerfect*.

The second required entry is the Commands entry. For this entry, you can enter one or more commands, provided you don't exceed 256 characters. When you enter more than one command, you separate each command with a space, a semicolon (;), and another space. In part 2 of figure 10-7, you can see that the Command entry contains these three DOS commands:

```
c: ; cd \wp50 ; wp
```

Part 1:

After you select the program list that you want to add a program to, you select the New option from the File menu. Then, you choose the Program-item option in the first dialog box.

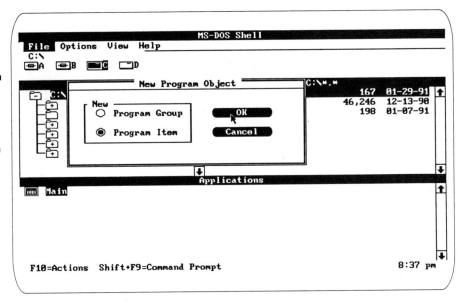

Part 2:

Next, you fill in the entries in the second dialog box that will identify and start the application program.

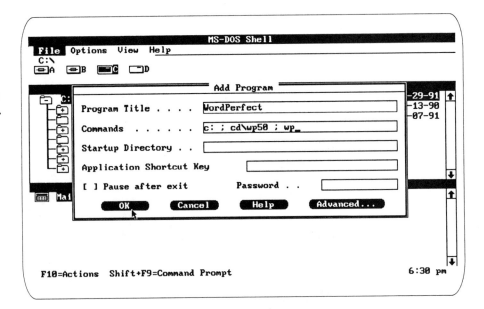

Figure 10-7   How to add a program to a program list

The first command changes the default drive to the C drive; the second command changes the current directory to the WP50 directory; and the third command starts *WordPerfect*. If you already have a batch file set up for starting *WordPerfect* that contains these three commands, you can simplify your Commands entry by entering only the command for the batch file.

As you can see, the last three entries are optional. The Startup-directory entry lets you specify the data directory that you want to use with the program. However, this doesn't work with many programs. The Applications-shortcut-key entry lets you assign a special keystroke combination to an application program. I'll show you how to use this entry in chapter 12 when I explain the task switching capabilities of DOS 5.0. The Pause-after-exit entry lets you return to the shell immediately after you exit an application program, or it lets you pause and press a key before you return to the shell. And the Password entry lets you assign a password that restricts access to the program. Most of the time, you'll leave these entries blank as shown.

After you've added one application program to a program list, you'll see how easy it is. Then, you can add the other application programs you use to the list. If you want to reorder the program items in a list, you put the highlight on the program item you want to move, and you execute the Reorder function from the File menu. When I finished adding programs to my Applications group, it looked like the one in figure 10-8.

How to set up a customized dialog box for a program item

If the command that starts an application program accepts parameters, you can set up a customized dialog box so you can enter the parameter when you start the program. For instance, you can set up a dialog box for *WordPerfect* that accepts the file name for the first document to be processed by the program.

Figure 10-9 shows you how to create a customized dialog box. First, you highlight the application program in the program list. Then, you select the Properties function of the File menu to get the dialog box shown in part 1 of figure 10-9. Next, you enter a replaceable parameter in the command that starts the program. Here, the replaceable parameter (%1) after the WP command lets you enter a file name when you start *WordPerfect*. In this example,

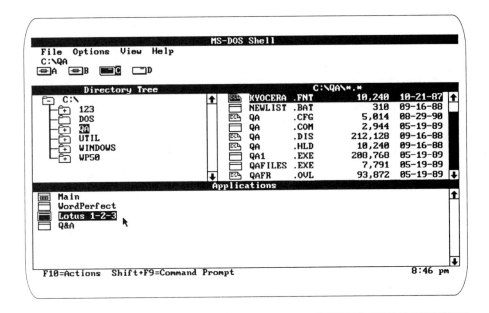

Figure 10-8   The options of the Applications program list

example, I've used the Startup-directory entry to specify a starting data directory because this works with *WordPerfect*.

Part 2 of figure 10-9 shows the dialog box that the DOS shell displays
next. You use the Window-title entry to identify the customized dialog box;
the Program-information entry to explain how you use the box; the Prompt-
message entry to prompt for the parameter; and the Default-parameters entry
to specify a default parameter (if you want one).

After you set up a dialog box like this one, the DOS shell displays it
every time you use the program list to start the program. Figure 10-10, for
example, shows the dialog box that's displayed as a result of the entries in
figure 10-9. Here, the box prompts you for the file you want to use with
WordPerfect and offers the file, letter, as a default. At this box, you can
either accept the default file specification or type in the one for the file you
want to use. After you use the OK button, the DOS shell starts *WordPerfect*
and loads the file you specified.

Part 1:

After you select the program from the program list, pull down the File menu and choose the Properties option so you can type a replaceable parameter in the command line of the dialog box.

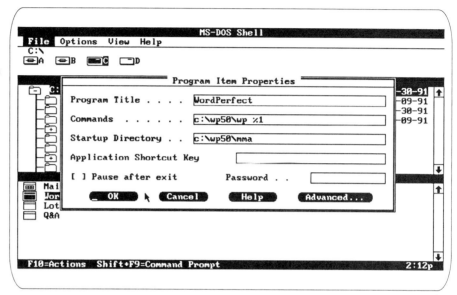

Part 2:

In the second dialog box, you create the text of the customized box and the default value for the replaceable parameter.

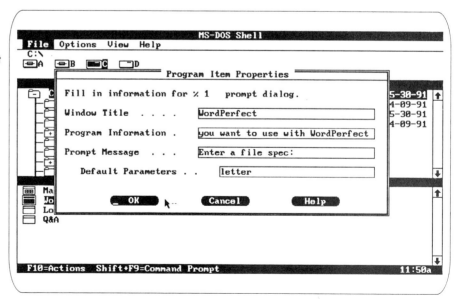

Figure 10-9   How to create a customized dialog box for a program item

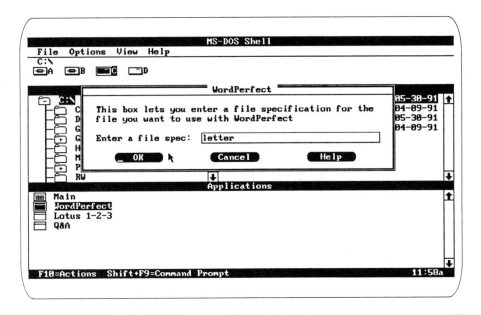

Figure 10-10 The customized dialog box created by the entries in figure 10-9

How to modify a program item in a program list

The DOS shell makes it easy for you to modify program items after you've created them. First, you highlight the item you want to change. Then, you select the Properties function from the File menu. The same dialog boxes you used to create the item are then displayed so you can change any of the entries you want. The new settings are put into effect as soon as you complete the process.

Some perspective on the DOS 5.0 shell

Without much trouble, you should now be able to set up the menus you need for starting all of your application programs. This can simplify the operation of your PC. And it can be particularly valuable if your PC is used by several people who have trouble starting programs from the DOS prompt.

If you compare the use of the program lists of the DOS shell to the use of batch files, you'll realize that you can start programs just as fast from batch files at the command prompt as you can from the shell. However, you can usually add a program to a program list faster than you can create a batch file for starting a program. Also, program lists make the PC easier to use because you don't have to remember the names of batch files. As a result, the menu capability of the DOS shell is clearly an improvement upon the capabilities of earlier versions of DOS.

Terms

program group
program item

Chapter 11

How to use the DOS 5.0 shell to manage directories and files

In this chapter, you'll learn how to use the DOS shell to manage directories and files. First, I'll review how you use the directory-tree and the file-list areas to select files for a function. Then, I'll show you how to use the most useful functions of the pull-down menus for these areas. Because you learned the basic techniques for using the DOS shell in chapter 9, you should be able to move quickly through this chapter.

How to use the directory-tree and file-list areas to select files

When you use DOS commands at the command prompt, you enter the names of the files you want to process as parameters. In contrast, when you use the DOS shell, you don't enter file names. Instead, you first select the directory and files you want to process. Then, you select the function that you want from a menu. Next, you execute the function, and all the files you selected are processed. To delete files, for example, you first select all of the files that you want to delete. Then, you select the Delete function from the File menu. When that function is executed, all of the selected files are deleted.

As a review, figure 11-1 shows the DOS shell screen. To select a file using a mouse, you first click on the directory that contains the file or files

Menu bar

Drive-icon bar

Directory-tree area

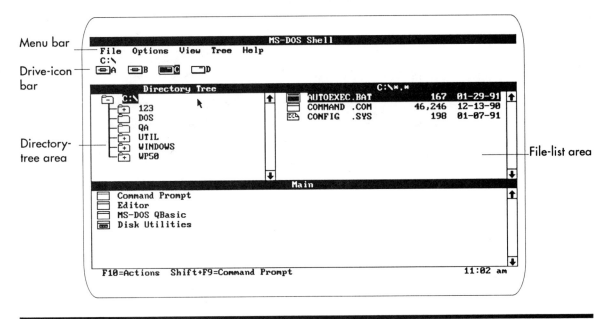

File-list area

Figure 11-1 The four components of the DOS shell you use to manage directories and files

you want to select. If required, you click on the appropriate directory folder to expand the directory listing. Then, to select a single file, you just click on that file in the file list. To select several files, you hold down the Ctrl key as you click the mouse. And to select a group of files, you select the first file of the group. Then, you move the cursor to the last file in the group and hold down the Shift key as you click the mouse. To cancel your selection, just click the mouse on another file and start the selection process again.

To select a file using the keyboard, you use the cursor control keys to highlight the file. To select several files, you press the Shift-F8 key combination to turn on the Add mode. Then, you move to each file you want to select and press the space bar. And to select a group of files, you hold down the Shift key as you press the space bar. If you change your mind after you have selected files, you can cancel the selection by pressing the space bar again after the file is highlighted. After you select a file, it's highlighted in the file list as shown in figure 11-2. Here, two files have been selected.

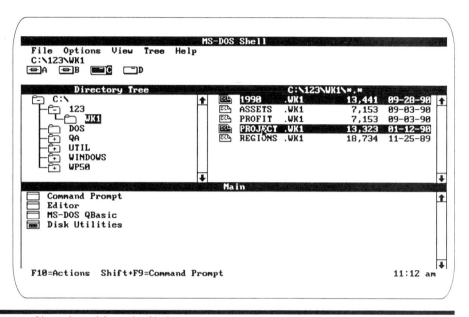

Figure 11-2   Two files selected from the file list

How to use the most useful functions of the File menu for the file-list area

Figure 11-3 shows the File menu for the file-list area. When you pull this menu down while the file-list area is active, the menu offers the 14 functions shown. Now, I'll present the eight functions you use to manage files, and I'll present the functions you use most frequently first.

The Move function   This function copies files, and then it deletes the originals. To use the Move function, you first select the files you want to move. Then, when you select this function from the File menu, a dialog box like the one in figure 11-4 is displayed. The From field lists the file or files you've selected, and the To field lets you specify the path for the new location. Here, I've entered C:\123\WK1\ as the destination for the file.

You can also use another technique for moving files. Figure 11-5 illustrates how you can use the mouse to perform this function. First, you select the files you want to move. Then, you put the cursor on the symbol next to the file, press the left mouse button, and hold it down. This symbol is called a

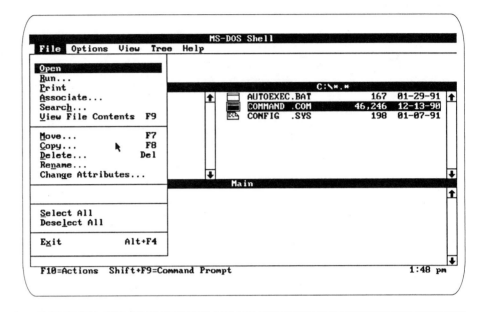

Figure 11-3 The File menu for the file-list area

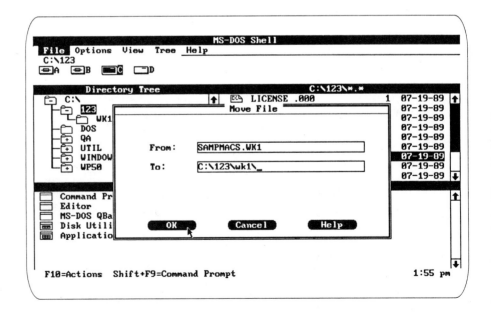

Figure 11-4 The dialog box for the Move function for moving files

Part 1:

Select the file, then click the mouse cursor on the file icon and hold down the left mouse button.

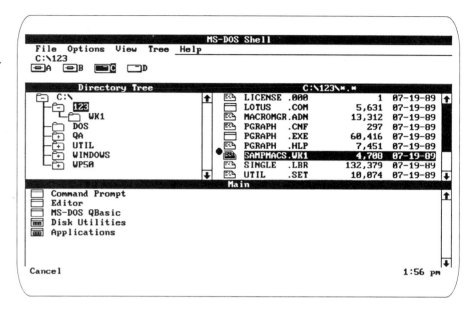

Part 2:

Drag the file icon to the directory you want to move the file to and release the mouse button.

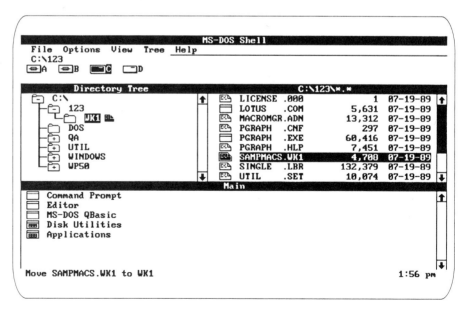

Figure 11-5   How to use the mouse to move a file (parts 1 and 2 of 3)

Part 3:

Use the dialog box to confirm the move or cancel the function

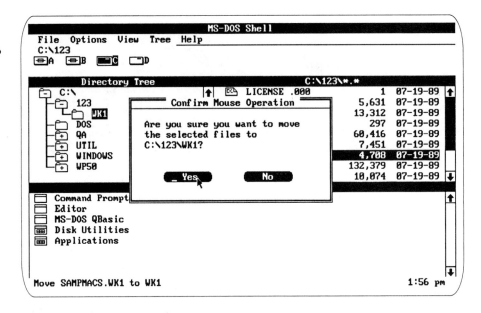

Figure 11-5   How to use the mouse to move a file (part 3 of 3)

file icon. While you hold down the button, you *drag* a copy of the icon to the directory you want to move the file to, as shown in part 2. When you release the mouse button, the DOS shell displays the dialog box shown in part 3. At this box, you can confirm or cancel the move.

The Copy function   This function works much like the Move function. First, it displays a dialog box so you can specify the location you want to use for the files. Then, it makes copies of the files in the new location.

You can also use a mouse technique to copy files. First, you select the files you want to copy. Then, after you click the mouse on the file icon, you hold down the Ctrl key and drag the icon to the drive or directory you want to use. When you release the mouse button, the DOS shell displays a dialog box like the one it uses for the Move function so you can either confirm the function or cancel it.

The Delete function   To use this function, you first select the files you want to delete. Then, after you select the Delete function from the File menu, dialog boxes like the ones in figure 11-6 are displayed. The box shown in part 1 lists the files you selected. Here, you can confirm that you want to delete these files, or you can cancel the Delete function.

If you OK the first dialog box, a dialog box like the one in part 2 is displayed for each file. Then, you can delete each file, or you can skip the file. You can also cancel the Delete function for the remaining files. In a moment, you'll learn how to use the Confirmation function of the Options menu to activate or deactivate this second dialog box.

The Rename function   To rename one or more files within a directory, you first select the files you want to rename. Then, after you select the Rename function from the File menu, a dialog box like the one in figure 11-7 is displayed for each file you've selected. Here, you just type in the new name for the file and press the Enter key. Or you can press the Esc key to cancel the function.

The Search function   The Search function makes it easy to find and compare files because it lists all the files on a disk drive that match the file name you specify, and it shows the directory for each file. This command also accepts wildcards.

Figure 11-8 shows the Search function in use. Part 1 shows the dialog box that the DOS shell displays when you select the Search function. At this box, you type in the name of file you want to find. Here, for example, I entered a file specification to find all the spreadsheet files on the disk. The screen in part 2 shows the list of files that match the file specification in part 1.

The View-file-contents function   This function displays the contents of a selected file. You can use it to help you verify that a file in the list is in fact the one you want. If the file is a text file, this function displays its contents as shown in figure 11-9. Here, the contents of the CONFIG.SYS file are displayed. Since batch files are text files, you can use this function to display their contents.

If a file isn't a text file or the DOS shell doesn't recognize it as such, this function displays the file contents in *hex code*. Even if you're familiar with

Part 1:

After you select the
files, you can confirm
or cancel the Delete
function.

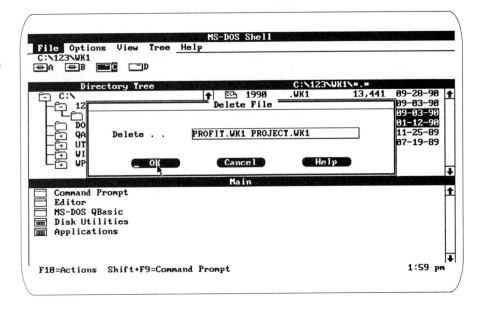

Part 2:

Confirm or cancel the
Delete function for
each selected file.

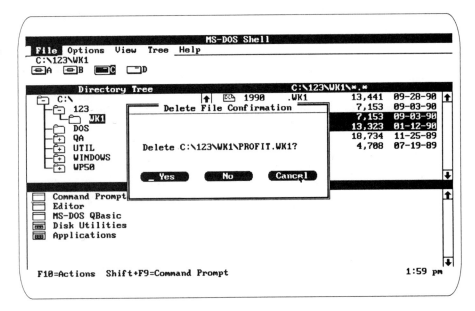

Figure 11-6 How to use the Delete function to delete files

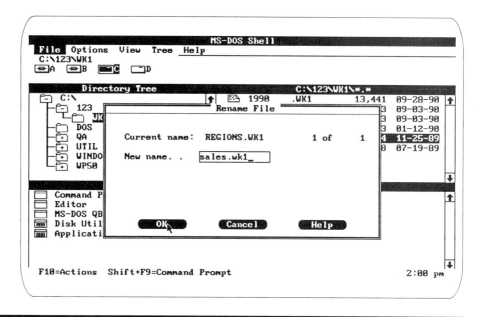

Figure 11-7   The dialog box for the Rename function for renaming files

this code, this display format usually doesn't help you identify a file. As a result, this function is only useful for text files.

The Select-all and Deselect-all functions   When you use the Select-all function, all of the files in the file list are selected. That way, you don't have to select the files one at a time. This saves you time when the file list is long and fills several screens. You can use this function when you want to move, copy, or delete all of the files in a directory.

When you use the Deselect-all function, all the selected files are deselected. This function is useful because the selected files are often moved off the screen as you scroll through the file display. Then, if you decide to perform a different function from the one you started selecting files for, you can use the Deselect-all function to make sure you've cancelled all the selections. That way, you'll avoid including files in the new operation that you didn't realize were selected.

Part 1:

Type in the file specification for the search.

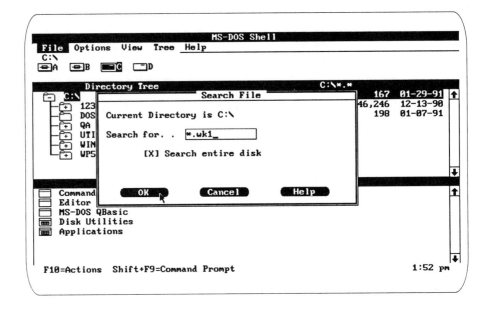

Part 2:

The list of files that matched the search specification is displayed.

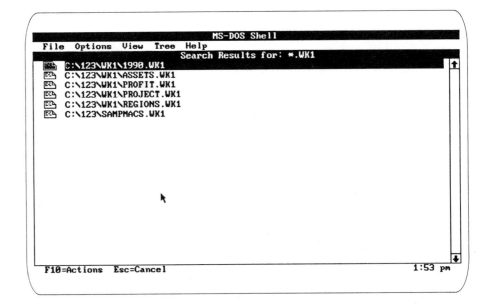

Figure 11-8   How to use the Search function

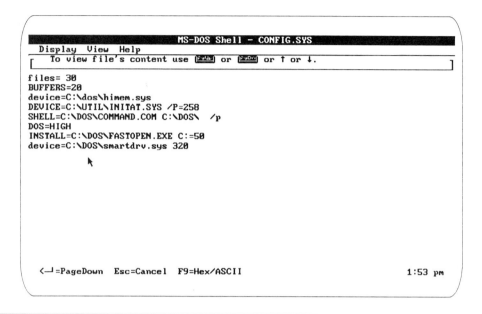

```
                        MS-DOS Shell - CONFIG.SYS
     Display  View  Help
        To view file's content use [PgUp] or [PgDn] or ↑ or ↓.

  files= 30
  BUFFERS=20
  device=C:\dos\himem.sys
  DEVICE=C:\UTIL\INITAT.SYS /P=258
  SHELL=C:\DOS\COMMAND.COM C:\DOS\  /p
  DOS=HIGH
  INSTALL=C:\DOS\FASTOPEN.EXE C:=50
  device=C:\DOS\smartdrv.sys 320

                        ▶



     <─┘=PageDown  Esc=Cancel  F9=Hex/ASCII                    1:53 pm
```

Figure 11-9   How the View-file-contents function displays a text file

How to use the most useful functions of the File menu for the directory-tree area

Figure 11-10 shows the File menu for the directory-tree area. When you pull this menu down with the directory-tree area active, it offers the seven functions shown. Now, I'll show you how to use the three functions you use to manage your directories: the Delete, Rename, and Create-directory functions. Even though the Delete and Rename functions are the same names assigned to functions on the File menu of the file-list area, they perform different functions when the directory-tree area is active.

The Delete function   To delete a directory, you first select the directory you want to delete. Next, you select the Delete function from the File menu. The DOS shell then displays the dialog box shown in figure 11-11. At this box, you can confirm the function or cancel it.

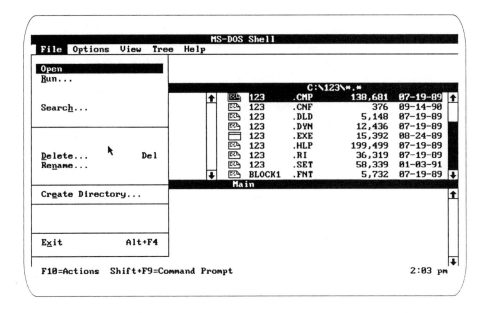

Figure 11-10   The File menu for the directory-tree area

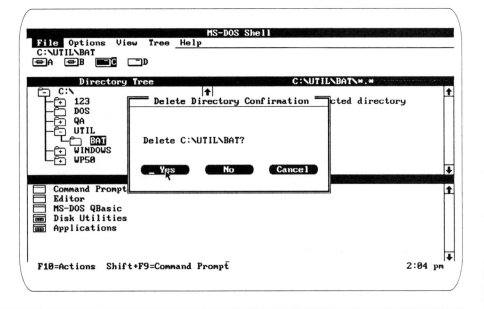

Figure 11-11   The dialog box for the Delete function for deleting directories

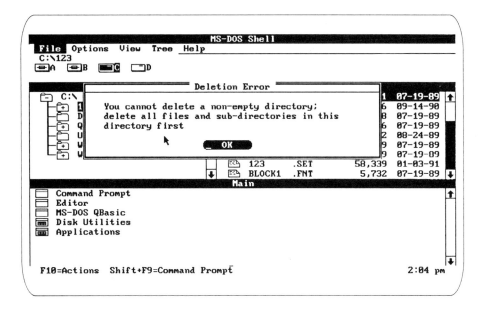

Figure 11-12 The dialog box that's displayed when you try to delete a directory that isn't empty

If the directory you're trying to delete isn't empty, the DOS shell displays the dialog box shown in figure 11-12. That's because you can't delete a directory that contains files or subdirectories.

The Rename function   To rename a directory, you first select the directory you want to rename. Next, you select the Rename function from the File menu. The DOS shell then displays the dialog box shown in figure 11-13. At this box, you can type in a new name for the directory. Since there isn't a DOS command that lets you rename a directory, this is a valuable function provided by the DOS shell.

The Create-directory function   To create a directory, first you select the appropriate drive. Then, you select the directory that you want the new directory to be subordinate to. If you're creating a top-level directory, you'll select the root directory. Next, you select the Create-directory function from the File menu. The DOS shell then displays the dialog box shown in figure 11-14. At this box, you enter the name of the new directory and press the

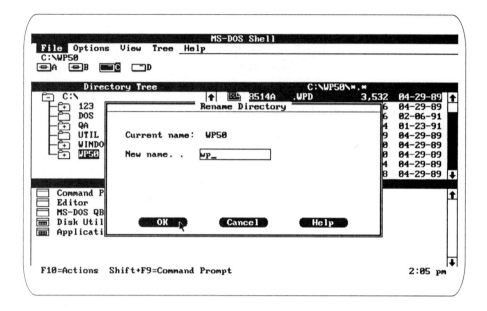

Figure 11-13   The dialog box for the Rename function for renaming directories

Enter key. After the function in figure 11-14 is executed, a directory named HG will be created in the root directory.

How to use the most useful functions of the Options menu

Figure 11-15 shows the Options menu. When you pull down this menu, it offers the seven functions shown here. Generally, you use these functions to set up the DOS shell program so it works the way you want it to. Although you probably won't need to do that often, you occasionally may want to change one of these options. That's why I'll explain when and how to use the most useful functions. Then, in the next chapter I'll show you how to use the Enable-task-swapper function.

The Confirmation function   Figure 11-16 shows the dialog box that's displayed when you select this function from the Options menu. Here, an *X* next to the option indicates it's on. To turn an option on or off, you click on it with a mouse. With a keyboard, you use the cursor control keys to move the

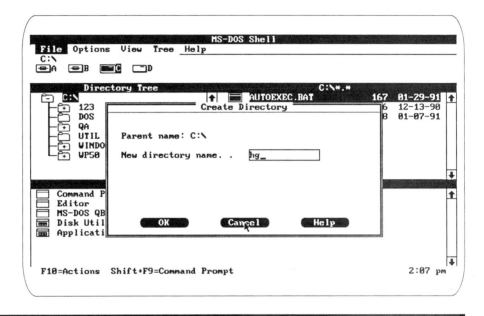

Figure 11-14 The dialog box for the Create-directory function

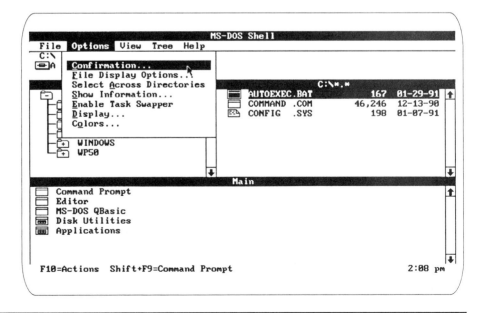

Figure 11-15 The Options menu

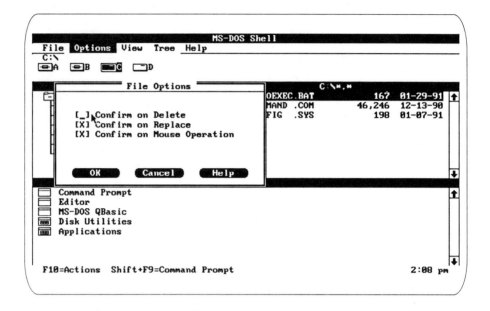

Figure 11-16 The dialog box for the Confirmation function

highlight from one option to the next, and you use the space bar to turn an option on or off.

The Confirm-on-delete option specifies whether the DOS shell should ask for confirmation before it deletes a file. If this option is on, a dialog box like the one in part 2 of figure 11-6 is displayed each time a file is about to be deleted by the Delete function. As a general rule, you should leave this option on so you won't accidentally delete any files. However, as you become more familiar with the DOS shell, you may want to turn this option off.

The Confirm-on-replace option helps protect files from being accidentally replaced when you use the Copy and Move functions. When this option is on, a Copy or Move function asks for confirmation before replacing an existing file with a new file. In contrast, the DOS Copy command replaces existing files without asking for confirmation. Although this option should be on most of the time, you may want to turn it off when you are deliberately replacing existing files with new ones of the same name.

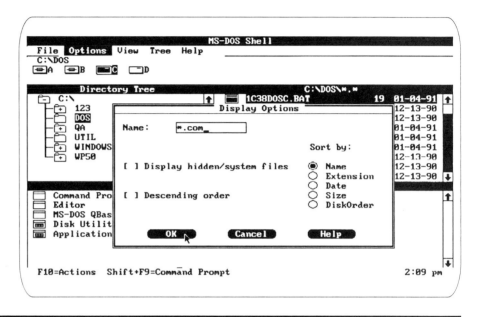

Figure 11-17   The dialog box for the File-display-options function

The Confirm-on-mouse-operation option specifies whether the DOS shell should ask for confirmation before it executes a move or copy operation that you perform using the mouse techniques I showed you earlier. If this option is on, a dialog box is displayed before the function is executed. This box tells you whether you're copying or moving a file, and it gives you a chance to cancel the function. So I recommend that you keep this option on.

The File-display-options function   Figure 11-17 shows the dialog box that is displayed when you select this function. The default setting for the Name field is *.*. That means all of the files in the current directory are displayed in the file-list area. However, you can change this default setting by entering a file name using wildcards. Here, for example, I entered *.COM to display only the files with an extension of COM. Figure 11-18 shows how the file list looks with this setting in effect.

If you want the files of a directory to be displayed in sequence by name, extension, date, size, or location in the directory, you can use the Sort-by fields in the dialog box. To select one of these fields with a mouse, you just

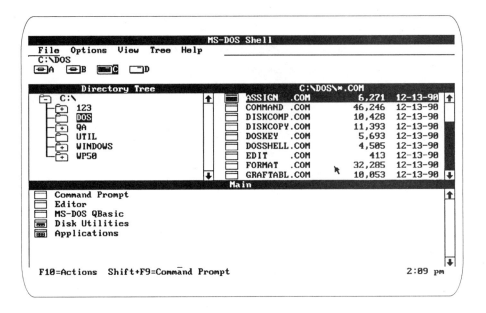

Figure 11-18   The file-list display that results from the selections in figure 11-17

click on the appropriate button. To select a field with the keyboard, you use the Tab key to activate the Sort-by portion of the dialog box. Then, you use the cursor control keys to select the field you want.

If you want to copy, move, rename, or delete files based on a wildcard specification, you can use this function to enter the wildcard specification. Then, you can use the Select-all function of the File menu to select all of the files that match the wildcard.

The Select-across-directories function   This function controls what happens to selected files when you change directories. If this function is off, all selected files are deselected when you change from one directory to another. That way, only files from one directory at a time can be selected. If this function is on, files are not deselected when you change directories. As a result, you can select files from more than one directory on your hard disk.

To turn on the Select-across-directories function, you execute it from the Option menu using either the mouse or the keyboard. When you do, a small

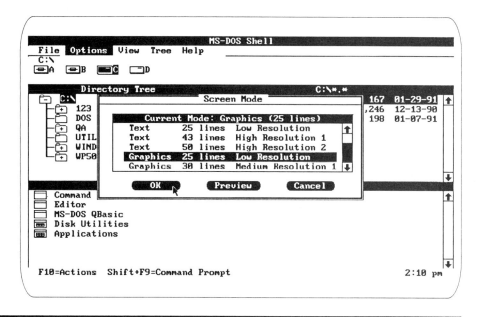

Figure 11-19   The dialog box for the Display function

dot appears next to the Select-across-directories function to show that it is on. To turn this function off, you execute it again.

Although the Select-across-directories function should be off most of the time, you may want to use it occasionally for simplifying file maintenance. When this option is on, for example, you can copy or move files from several directories in three steps: (1) select the files you want to copy; (2) select the file maintenance function (like Move or Copy); and (3) specify the directory you want to use for the files.

The Display function   Figure 11-19 shows the dialog box that's displayed when you select the Display function. This box lets you specify whether you want to use *text* or *graphics mode* for the DOS shell screen. If your monitor can display graphics, you'll generally want to select this option because it makes the DOS shell a bit easier to use. As you can see, you can also specify the number of lines you want to display on your screen.

The options that are available in figure 11-19 depend on the type of monitor you have. The options shown here, for instance, are the ones available

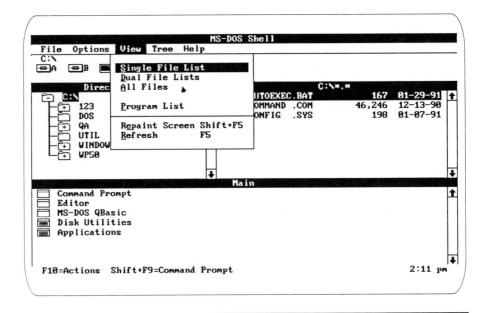

Figure 11-20   The View menu

with a VGA monitor. So if you have a different type of monitor, the DOS shell will offer you some different options.

How to use the most useful functions of the View menu

Figure 11-20 shows the View menu. When you pull this menu down, it offers the six functions shown here. These functions change the format of the DOS shell screen. Here, I'll refer to these different screen formatting functions as *views*. And I won't present the All-files view because it's too hard to use.

So far, you've learned how to use the DOS shell using only one view. If you change to one of the other views listed in figure 11-20, that view remains in effect until you select another view. Even when you exit from the DOS shell and start it again, it won't return to the default view that you've used up to this point. Instead, it will use the view that was active when you last exited from the DOS shell.

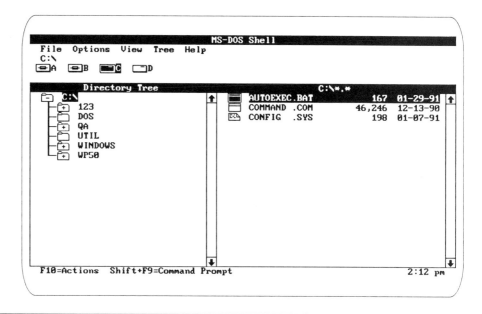

Figure 11-21   How the screen looks in Single-file-list view

The Single-file-list view   Figure 11-21 shows the Single-file-list view.
This view displays the directory-tree and file-list areas, but not the program-
list area. As a result, you can see more files and directories on the screen than
you can by using the default view. Sometimes, this is helpful when you perform maintenance tasks that involve many files or directories.

The Dual-file-lists view   Figure 11-22 shows the Dual-file-lists view. This
view lets you display the files from two directories at the same time. As a
result, the Dual-file-list view makes it easier for you to compare the files in
two directories and to copy or move files from one directory or drive to
another.

The Program/File-lists view   Figure 11-23 shows the Program/File-lists
view. You should already recognize this view because it's the one that I've
used throughout this section. It's also the default view that's active when you
start the DOS shell the first time. This choice isn't displayed on the menu in
figure 11-20 because it was active when I pulled down the menu. To change

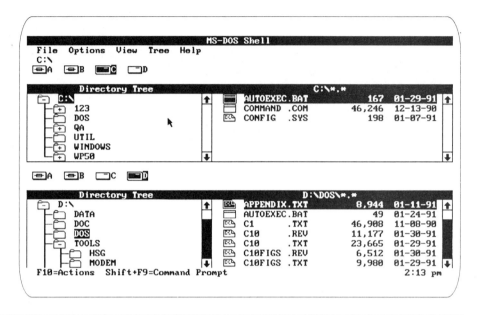

Figure 11-22 How the screen looks in Dual-file-list view

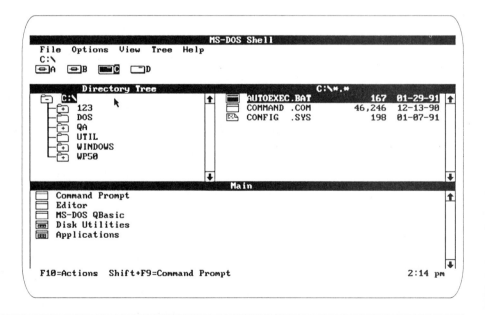

Figure 11-23 How the screen looks in Program/File-list view

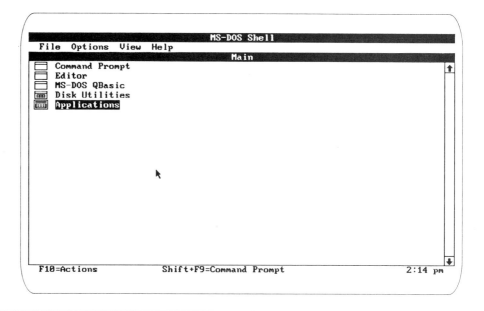

Figure 11-24   How the screen looks in Program-list view

back to this view, you simply select the Program/File-lists function from the View menu.

The Program-list view   Figure 11-24 shows the Program-list view. As you can see, it displays only the program-list area. As a result, this view is most useful if you want to set up a PC for other people to use and you don't want them to manage the files and directories on the hard disk.

The Refresh and Repaint functions   The Refresh and Repaint functions on the View menu perform operations that help keep the shell working correctly. The Refresh function causes the DOS shell to rescan the disk to find out what directories and files are on the disk. The DOS shell performs this operation when you first start it. But you have to perform this function again if you return to the shell after you have temporarily exited to the command prompt to enter a DOS command. That's because the shell can't keep track of the results of commands that are performed outside of it. You also use the Refresh function if you switch diskettes in a diskette drive while using the shell. The shell then rescans the new diskette in the drive so it can display a list of files and directories on that diskette.

The Repaint function redraws the DOS shell screen in the event that the screen is corrupted by unwanted characters. Since this should happen rarely, you won't have to use this function as often as you use the Refresh function.

Some perspective on the DOS 5.0 shell

If you compare the capabilities that are provided by the DOS shell for managing directories and files with the DOS commands that are available at the command prompt, you'll realize that the shell can make it easier for you to manage your directories and files. The directory-tree area makes it easy for you to see, modify, and use the structure of your directories. The selection techniques make it easy for you to select the files for a function. And the pull-down menus make it easy for you to start functions after you've selected the files. As a result, it's easy to create, delete, and rename directories when you use the DOS shell. It's also easy to copy, move, delete, and rename files.

In practice, though, you'll probably use some combination of shell functions and DOS commands for managing directories and files. If, for example, you want to delete all of the files in a directory, you can do so by entering just one Delete command at the DOS prompt. And if you want to copy all of the files in a directory to a diskette, you can do so by entering just one Copy command at the DOS prompt.

Terms

file icon
dragging a mouse
hex code
text mode
graphics mode
view

Chapter 12

How to use the DOS 5.0 shell for switching from one program to another

If you frequently switch from one program to another, the DOS 5.0 shell provides a feature called the Task Swapper that can help you switch between programs more quickly. The capability this feature provides is commonly referred to as *task switching* or *task swapping*. This feature isn't available with earlier versions of DOS, and you can only use this feature through the DOS shell. Also, this feature may not work with older versions of some application programs, so there's a chance that you won't be able to use it with all of your application programs.

In this chapter, you'll learn how to use the Task Swapper. To start off, I'll explain how the Task Swapper works. Next, you'll learn how to activate the Task Swapper and switch between application programs. Then, you'll learn how to set up and use the Task Swapper to switch between programs more efficiently. Because you've already learned the basic techniques for using the DOS shell, you should be able to move quickly through this chapter.

An introduction to the Task Swapper

When you use the Task Swapper, you can load two or more application programs and switch between them without having to exit one program before you switch to the next. Each program that's running under the Task Swapper is called an *active task*. You can, for example, start *WordPerfect* and begin work on a report. Then, you can start *Lotus 1-2-3* and load a spreadsheet file to review some data. When you use the Task Swapper to switch back to *WordPerfect*, it returns you to the place where you were last working on the report. As a result, you don't have to start *WordPerfect*, load the report, and find your place again.

Figure 12-1 illustrates how this process works. When the first task is active, *WordPerfect* and a working document are loaded and are running in internal memory, while the second task, *Lotus 1-2-3* and a spreadsheet file, are stored on disk. When you perform the task swap, *WordPerfect* and the working document are transferred to disk storage, and *Lotus 1-2-3* and the current spreadsheet file are transferred to internal memory. When you switch back to *WordPerfect*, the process is repeated.

How to use the Task Swapper

To use the Task Swapper, first you enable the Task Swapper. Next, you load your application programs so they become active tasks. Then, after you learn a few keystroke combinations to switch between active tasks, you're ready to use the Task Swapper.

How to enable the Task Swapper   To enable the Task Swapper, you select the Enable-task-swapper function from the Options menu. The DOS shell then displays an *active task list* in the bottom right portion of the screen as shown in figure 12-2. After the Task Swapper is enabled, you can load your application programs into it.

How to load programs and switch between them   In figure 12-3, you can see that two applications programs have been loaded into the active task list. To load a program, you start it from the program list. If you have a mouse, just double-click on the appropriate program in the program list. Or if you're using the keyboard, you highlight the appropriate program and press the Enter key. The DOS shell then starts the program and automatically adds it to the active task list. To load another program, first you use the Ctrl+Esc

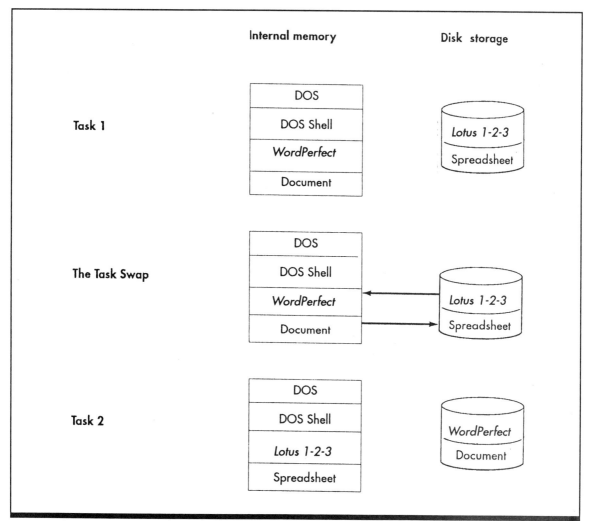

Figure 12-1   How the Task Swapper uses internal memory and disk storage to switch between two programs

keystroke combination to switch back to the DOS shell. Then, you start the next program you want from the program list.

After you've loaded your programs, you can switch between them using the active task list instead of the program list. To switch to the *WordPerfect* task in figure 12-3, for example, you just double-click on the *WordPerfect*

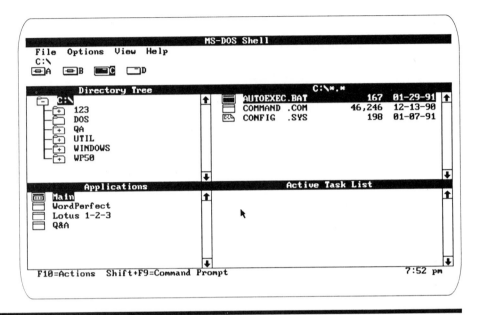

Figure 12-2   The DOS 5.0 shell with the Task Swapper enabled

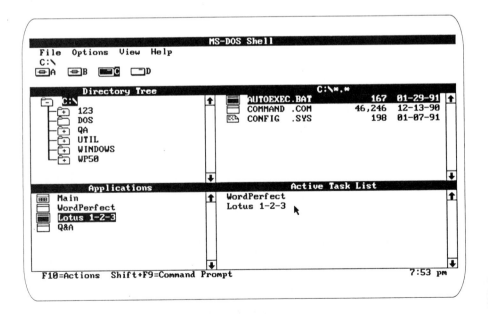

Figure 12-3   Two application programs that have been loaded in the active task list

Keystrokes	Functions
Ctrl+Esc	Switches from the current application program to the DOS 5.0 shell.
Alt+Tab	As you hold down the Alt key and repeatedly press the Tab key, you cycle through the active task list. As the list cycles, the title of each program is displayed at the top of the screen. When you release the Alt key, the Task Swapper switches you to the program you selected.
Alt+Esc	Switches to the next application program on the active task list.
Shift+Alt+Esc	Switches to the previous application program on the active task list.

Figure 12-4   The special keystrokes you can use to switch between programs

entry in the active task list. Then, when you want to switch to the next task, you use the Ctrl+Esc key combination to return to the DOS shell. Now, you can switch to *Lotus 1-2-3* by double clicking on the *Lotus 1-2-3* task entry.

How to switch between programs more efficiently

The Task Swapper also lets you switch between active tasks without using the DOS shell as an intermediate step. To do that, you use special keystroke combinations that DOS 5.0 provides. Or you can assign your own keystroke combinations to each program.

Special keystroke combinations   Figure 12-4 presents the keystroke combinations you can use to switch between programs. You'll probably use the first three most often. The Ctrl+Esc combination always switches you back to the DOS shell. The Alt+Tab key combination switches you back to the most recent task. If you just used the DOS shell, for example, this key combination will return you to the shell. But if you switched from another application program, it will return you to that program. With the Alt+Tab key combination, you can also cycle through the programs on the active task list by holding down the Alt key as you repeatedly press the Tab key. Each time you press the Tab key, it shows the title of the next active task at the top of the

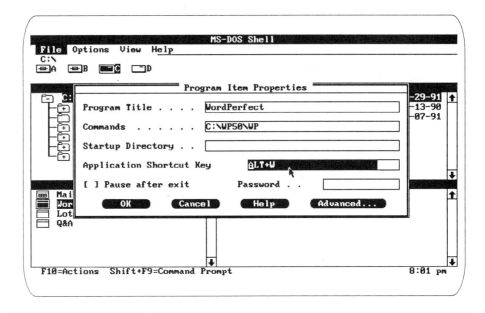

Figure 12-5   The dialog box that you use to assign a keystroke combination to a program

screen. When you release the Alt key, you're switched to the task that's displayed.

The last two key combinations are Alt+Esc and Shift+Alt+Esc. You can use these to switch to the next program on the active task list or to the previous program on the active task list. Most of the time, though, it's easier to switch tasks using the Alt+Tab key combination than using either of these two.

How to assign a keystroke combination to a program   In addition to the keystrokes you've learned so far, you can assign a unique keystroke combination to a program. You can, for example, assign the keystroke combination Alt+W to *WordPerfect*. Then, whenever *WordPerfect* is on the active task list, you can switch directly to it by pressing the Alt+W key combination.

Figure 12-5 shows the dialog box you use to assign a keystroke combination to a program. To get to this box, first you activate the program-list area and select the appropriate program from the list. Then, after you pull down

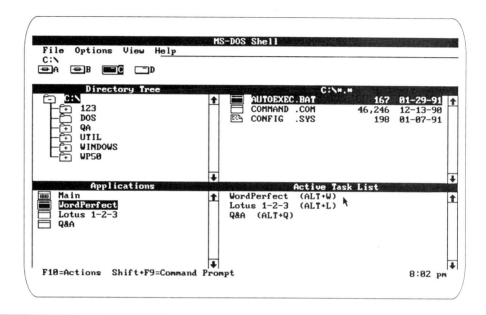

Figure 12-6 Three programs that have had keystroke combinations assigned to them

the File menu, you select the Properties function. In the dialog box, you use the Application-shortcut-key entry to assign a keystroke combination to the program. To do this, you press the actual keystroke combination you want to use. You can use the Alt, Ctrl, or Shift key in combination with another key.

Since you learned how to use the first three entries of this box in chapter 10 to create an option for a program list, most of this procedure should be familiar. In fact, now that you know about assigning key combinations, you'll probably make the assignment when you create the option.

Figure 12-6 shows how programs are displayed on the active task list after you've assigned a keystroke combination to them. This list shows that *WordPerfect* is started by the Alt+W key combination, that *Lotus 1-2-3* is started by the Alt+L key combination, and so on.

Some perspective on the Task Swapper

Without much trouble, you should be able to use the task swapping capabilities of the DOS 5.0 shell. If you occasionally need to switch between two or more programs, the Task Swapper can help you work more efficiently. However, on some PCs the Task Swapper is just too slow to be practical. If, for example, you have an 8088 PC with 512KB of memory and a slow hard disk, it can take more than ten seconds to switch between tasks. In addition, the Task Swapper may not work correctly with some older versions of application programs. As a result, you may find that you're better off running only one program at a time.

If you regularly need to switch between programs, you may want to consider a task switching utility like *Software Carousel* that's more capable than the DOS 5.0 Task Swapper. Commercial task-switching utilities don't require that you run the DOS shell to activate them, and they provide features that aren't provided by the DOS Task Swapper.

If you have a 386 or 486 PC with at least 2MB of memory, you may want to consider a utility that provides true *multi-tasking* capabilities. These utilities actually let two or more application programs run concurrently on your PC. Consequently, you can view and run two or more programs in small windows, each of which is displayed on a portion of the screen. This makes it possible to transfer data between two programs, and it makes it easier to switch between programs quickly. Also, these utilities often let your application programs run more efficiently. Today, the two most popular multi-tasking utilities are *Windows* and *DESQview*.

Terms

task switching
task swapping
active task
active task list
multi-tasking

How to set up your CONFIG.SYS and AUTOEXEC.BAT files so your PC gets started right

If you're like most PC users, you'll rarely need to change your CONFIG.SYS or AUTOEXEC.BAT file. In part, that's because many of the installation programs that come with software and hardware products automatically change the CONFIG.SYS and AUTOEXEC.BAT files if changes are required. So if your PC is working the way you want it to, you may never have to read the two chapters in this section.

Occasionally, though, you do have to make a change to either the CONFIG.SYS or AUTOEXEC.BAT file. Then, the information in this section can help you make the required changes. Before the need arises, though,

I recommend that you read this section so you will understand what these files do and so you'll be better able to recognize the need for a change to one of these files.

Chapter 13

Commands for the CONFIG.SYS file

Each time you start your PC, DOS executes the commands in the CONFIG.SYS file that's stored in the root directory of the C drive. Some of the commands in the CONFIG.SYS file define how DOS will use your PC's internal memory. Other commands provide the support that's required for hardware devices like a mouse, a special graphics monitor, or expanded memory. As a result, the CONFIG.SYS file has an important effect on how your PC starts and operates.

Once your CONFIG.SYS file has been set up properly, you shouldn't have to change it unless you change some of the hardware components of your system or you add a program to your system that requires a special command. If, for example, you add a mouse to your PC, you may have to add a command to your CONFIG.SYS file. Similarly, if you add a utility program to your system, you may have to add a command to the CONFIG.SYS file.

Figure 13-1 shows typical CONFIG.SYS files for two different versions of DOS. In this chapter, you'll learn about the commands in these files and also about other commands that you can use in the CONFIG.SYS file. If your PC is working properly with the current CONFIG.SYS file, of course, you don't have to worry about these commands now. As a result, you only need to read this chapter if your PC isn't working the way you want it to or if you want more perspective on what the CONFIG.SYS file does.

Like a batch file, the CONFIG.SYS file is a text file. As a result, you use the same techniques to create or change a CONFIG.SYS file that you use for

```
A CONFIG.SYS file for DOS 3.3

      files=20
      buffers=20
      device=c:\dos\ansi.sys


A CONFIG.SYS file for DOS 5.0

      files=20
      buffers=20,4
      device=c:\dos\himem.sys
      dos=high
      device=c\dos\smartdrv.sys 320
      install=c:\dos\fastopen.exe c:=50 d:=50
      device=c:\util\mouse.sys /1
```

Figure 13-1   CONFIG.SYS files for two versions of DOS

creating or changing batch files. These techniques were presented in chapter 5.

Two commands you should already have in your CONFIG.SYS file

The CONFIG.SYS file on your hard disk should already have two commands in it: the Buffers command and the Files command. The Buffers command speeds up disk operations so DOS can access data faster. The Files command sets up some internal definitions so your application programs can operate correctly.

The Buffers command   To improve the performance of hard disk operations, DOS sets up and uses small areas in internal memory called *buffers*. By default, it sets up a small number of buffers. But you can often improve the performance of your PC by setting up more buffers than the DOS default. To do that, you can put a Buffers command in the CONFIG.SYS file or change the command that it already contains.

The command format for DOS 2.0 through 3.3

```
BUFFERS=number-of-buffers
```

A typical command for DOS 2.0 through 3.3

```
buffers=20
```

The command format for DOS 4.0

```
BUFFERS=number-of-buffers[,read-ahead-sectors]
```

The command format for DOS 5.0

```
BUFFERS=number-of-buffers[,secondary-buffer-cache]
```

A typical command for DOS 4.0 and 5.0

```
buffers=20,8
```

Figure 13-2   How to use the Buffers command

Figure 13-2 summarizes the format of the Buffers command. No matter what version of DOS you use, you should have a Buffers command that sets up between 16 and 25 buffers. With DOS 4.0 or 5.0, the command accepts a second parameter. Under DOS 4.0, this parameter sets up what DOS calls *read ahead sectors*. Under DOS 5.0, this parameter sets up what DOS calls a *secondary buffer cache*. Either way, this second parameter should use a number from four to eight.

The Files command   This command controls the number of files that DOS will allow an application program to have open at one time. If the CONFIG.SYS file doesn't contain a Files command, DOS automatically sets the files option to eight. But this is inadequate for many application programs. If, for example, you try to start *WordPerfect* when the files option is

---

The format of the Files command for all versions of DOS

```
FILES=number-of-files
```

A typical command

```
files=25
```

Figure 13-3   How to use the Files command

set to eight, you get an error message that says the system doesn't have enough *file handles*. Then, to correct the problem, you must change the Files command in the CONFIG.SYS file so it provides for 20 or more open files.

Figure 13-3 shows the format of the Files command. But you may never need to use it. Today, when you install an application program that requires a certain number of file handles, the installation program that comes with the application program is likely to insert an appropriate Files command in your CONFIG.SYS file automatically. Not all programs take care of this for you, though, so you should know how to add this command to your CONFIG.SYS file when you need it.

Two other commands you may want in your CONFIG.SYS file

In addition to the Buffers and Files commands, you may want to use two other commands that DOS provides: the Device command and the Fastopen command. The Device command is often required to install special programs that provide support for your system's hardware. In contrast, the Fastopen command is an optional command that can help increase the speed of hard disk operations.

The Device command   The Device command lets you load special programs called *device drivers*. These device drivers provide support for hardware components like a mouse, a non-standard disk drive, a custom graphics monitor, EMS memory, and so on. They can also provide support for special

---

The format of a Device command

```
DEVICE=driver-spec [parameters] [switches]
```

Command	Function
`device=c:\dos\smartdrv.sys 384`	Installs the SMARTDRV device driver that comes with DOS to provide for disk caching
`device=c:\dos\ansi.sys`	Installs the ANSI device driver that comes with DOS to provide for enhanced display support
`device=c:\dos\himem.sys`	Installs the HIMEM device driver that comes with DOS to provide extended memory support
`device=c:\util\mouse.sys /1`	Installs a device driver that came with a mouse
`device=c:\util\ems.sys /p=258;268`	Installs a device driver that came with an expanded memory board

---

Figure 13-4   How to use Device commands

hardware and software features like disk caching, which I'll explain in a moment.

Figure 13-4 shows the format of a Device command. Here, you can see that a Device command consists of the keyword followed by an equal sign (=). Then, it lists the drive, path, and complete filename of the driver you want to use. After the driver specification, the command can also include parameters and switches that are specific to the device driver. This figure also shows five typical Device commands.

The first Device command loads a driver called SMARTDRV.SYS. This device driver is a special program called a *disk caching* program. Like the Buffers command, a disk caching program speeds up disk operations. However, the speed improvement is more likely to make a noticeable difference because the disk caching program uses more internal memory. Unlike the

Buffers command, disk caching can use the extended memory that's not needed for your application programs. Here, for example, the 384 parameter causes the SMARTDRV caching program to use 384K of extended memory.

Many disk caching programs are available today. The SMARTDRV.SYS program (often referred to as "SmartDrive") comes with DOS 4.0, 5.0, and *Microsoft Windows*. Similar programs come with utilities like *PC Tools*. Although most of these programs are installed using a Device command in the CONFIG.SYS file, not all are. To learn about the switches, parameters, and other details of the disk caching program that you have, you can refer to the documentation that comes with the program.

The second command in figure 13-4 loads HIMEM.SYS. This is a DOS 5.0 driver that provides extended memory support on 286, 386, and 486 PCs. You'll learn more about the special memory management commands DOS 5.0 provides in a moment.

The third command in figure 13-4 loads ANSI.SYS. This is a display driver that all versions of DOS provide. It must be installed for some of the older application programs to work correctly.

The fourth and fifth examples in figure 13-4 load device drivers that come with hardware components. Both of these drivers are stored in the UTIL directory on the C drive. MOUSE.SYS is a device driver for a mouse, and the /1 switch specifies that the mouse is attached to the first serial port. EMS.SYS is a device driver that provides for expanded memory support, and the switch controls some of the technical options available with the board. When you buy hardware that requires a special device driver, your purchase includes the device driver and instructions on how to load it.

The Fastopen command   The more directories and files you have on your hard disk, the longer it takes DOS to find a file because DOS has to look through more directory entries. However, if you have DOS 3.3 or a later version, you can speed up these searching operations a bit by using the Fastopen command. This command sets up special areas in internal memory for the most recent directory information. Then, if DOS can find the directory information it needs in Fastopen memory, it doesn't have to search for it on the hard disk so the search time is reduced.

Because the format of the FASTOPEN command has changed with each version of DOS, figure 13-5 shows how to use the FASTOPEN command

---

The command format for the Fastopen command

```
FASTOPEN  drive-spec=(number-of-directory-entries,
                      continuous-space-buffers)
```

Typical Fastopen commands

```
fastopen c:=(50,200)

fastopen c:=(50,200) d:=(50,200)
```

An Install command in the CONFIG.SYS file

```
install=c:\dos\fastopen.exe c:=(50,200) d:=(50,200)
```

Figure 13-5   How to install the DOS 4.0 Fastopen command

under DOS 4.0, and figure 13-6 shows how to use this command under DOS 5.0. Fortunately, both of these versions of DOS automatically put an appropriate Fastopen command in your CONFIG.SYS file when you install them so you shouldn't have to. If you're using DOS 3.3, you have to put the Fastopen command in the AUTOEXEC.BAT file, which you'll learn about in the next chapter.

An introduction to the CONFIG.SYS commands and device drivers for optimizing memory usage that are provided by DOS 5.0

Figure 13-7 presents the CONFIG.SYS commands and device drivers that DOS 5.0 provides for optimizing memory usage. These commands and device drivers make it possible to load resident DOS so it uses less conventional memory. They also make it possible to load some utility programs and device drivers into a special area of memory. And they make it possible to convert extended memory into expanded memory. As a result, you can

---

The command format for the Fastopen command

```
FASTOPEN drive-spec=number-of-directory-entries [/X]
```

Typical commands

```
fastopen c:=50

fastopen c:=50 d:=50
```

An Install command in the CONFIG.SYS file that uses conventional memory for Fastopen

```
install=c:\dos\fastopen.exe c:=50 d:=50
```

An Install command in the CONFIG.SYS file that uses EMS memory for Fastopen

```
install=c:\dos\fastopen.exe c:=50 d:=50 /x
```

Figure 13-6   How to install the DOS 5.0 Fastopen command

configure your memory so your application programs can run more efficiently on your PC.

Unfortunately, using these commands requires a high level of technical understanding. In addition, you can only use these commands if you have a 286, 386, or 486 PC. That's why I won't explain all the details of how to use these commands. Instead, I'll introduce you to each command and explain how the commands work together. Then, you can decide if you should be using these commands on your PC. If you decide that you should be, you'll probably want to get technical help instead of trying to put these commands into your CONFIG.SYS file by yourself.

The HIMEM.SYS device driver   Figure 13-8 shows how to use the Device command to install the HIMEM.SYS device driver. This driver provides support for extended memory so it can be used more reliably by application programs and DOS. This driver also lets DOS access a special area of extended

Commands	Function
`Dos`	Lets you specify whether you want the resident portion of DOS loaded into conventional or high memory, and provides special memory support
`Devicehigh`	Lets you load device drivers into a special area of memory to increase the conventional memory that's available to your application programs
Device drivers	
`HIMEM.SYS`	Provides support for extended memory so it can be used more reliably
`EMM386.EXE`	Provides special memory support, and can convert extended memory into expanded memory(EMS)

Figure 13-7   The commands and device drivers that DOS 5.0 provides for managing memory

memory called the *high memory area*, or *HMA*. If you have a PC with a 286, 386, or 486 processor, your CONFIG.SYS file should include this command.

The Dos command   Figure 13-9 shows the format and options for the Dos command. This command lets you specify whether you want to use conventional memory or the high memory area for the resident portion of DOS. Since the HIMEM.SYS driver provides access to this high memory area, the HIMEM.SYS command must precede the Dos command in the CONFIG.-SYS file. On a 386 or 486 PC, this command can also activate support for an area of memory called *upper memory blocks*, or *UMBs* for short. Then, this memory can be put to use by some of the other DOS 5.0 memory management commands.

The EMM386.EXE device driver   Figure 13-10 shows the format of the Device command you use to install the EMM386.EXE device driver. This driver can provide two different types of memory support on a 386 or 486

The format of the HIMEM.SYS device driver

```
DEVICE=driver-spec [switches]
```

A typical command

```
device=c:\dos\himem.sys
```

Figure 13-8 How to use a Device command to activate the HIMEM.SYS driver

---

The format of the Dos command

```
DOS=[high, low,] [umb noumb]
```

Explanation

`high`   Tells DOS to load portions of itself into high memory.

`low`   Tells DOS to load all of itself into conventional memory.

`umb`   Tells DOS to activate support for upper memory blocks.

`noumb`   Tells DOS to deactivate support for upper memory blocks.

Typical commands

```
dos=high
dos=high,umb
```

Figure 13-9 How to use the Dos command

The format of the EMM386.EXE device command

```
DEVICE=driver-spec [memory] [parameters]
```

Explanation

`memory`   Specifies the amount of extended memory in KB that you want EMM386 to convert to expanded memory.

Parameters

`noems`   Tells EMM386 to activate support for upper memory blocks but not expanded memory.

`ram`   Tells EMM386 to activate support for both expanded memory and upper memory blocks.

    Note: If you omit both Ram and Noems, EMM386 will activate support for expanded memory but not upper memory blocks.

Typical commands

```
device=c:\dos\emm386.exe noems

device=c:\dos\emm386.exe 384

device=c:\dos\emm386.exe 2048 ram
```

Figure 13-10   How to use a device command to activate the EMM386.EXE device driver

PC. First, it provides the support, along with the Dos=umb command, for upper memory block access. Second, it lets you convert extended memory into expanded memory (EMS).

The Devicehigh command   Figure 13-11 show the format of the Device-high command. This command provides the same basic function as the Device command. But on a 386 or 486 PC, it loads a device driver into an

---

The format of the Devicehigh command

```
DEVICEHIGH=driver-spec [parameters] [switches]

DEVICEHIGH SIZE=hexsize driver-spec [parameters] [switches]
```

Explanation

`parameters`   Any parameters required by the driver.

`switches`   Any switches required by the driver.

`hexsize`   The amount of upper memory, in hex, that must be available before DOS will attempt to load the driver in upper memory. If the memory is not available, DOS will load the driver into conventional memory.

Typical commands

```
devicehigh=c:\dos\ansi.sys

devicehigh size=39e0 c:\dos\mouse.sys
```

Figure 13-11   How to use the Devicehigh command

upper memory block instead of using conventional memory. As a result, more conventional memory is available for use by your application programs.

Other memory management parameters and switches   If you look back at the last five figures, I think you'll agree that the DOS 5.0 memory management commands are quite complicated. But these commands provide many other parameters and switches that I haven't shown. In addition, these commands are difficult to use because they provide interrelated functions that must be coordinated from one command to another. That's why you'll probably want to get technical help before you try to install these commands in the CONFIG.SYS file for your PC.

How to test a CONFIG.SYS file

After you create or change your CONFIG.SYS file, you have to restart your PC to put the CONFIG.SYS commands into effect. The most efficient way to do that is to hold down the Ctrl and Alt keys while you press the Delete key. This boots DOS, but doesn't force the PC to go through its self test again.

Some perspective on the CONFIG.SYS file

If your CONFIG.SYS file is set up right, you shouldn't have to change it unless you make changes to the hardware or software of your system. Even then, many software and hardware packages have installation programs that make the required changes for you. Once your CONFIG.SYS file is working properly, you shouldn't have to think about it until the next time you add hardware or software to your system.

Terms

buffer
read ahead sector
secondary buffer cache
file handle
device driver
disk caching
high memory area
HMA
upper memory block
UMB

Chapter 14

Commands for the
AUTOEXEC.BAT file

In chapter 5, you learned that the AUTOEXEC.BAT file is a special batch file that DOS executes as part of your system's start-up procedure. You learned how to set up a simple AUTOEXEC.BAT file so your PC gets started right. And you learned four techniques for creating and changing a batch file.

Once your AUTOEXEC.BAT file has been set up properly, you shouldn't have to change it unless you change some of the hardware components of your system, you add a program to your system that requires a special command, or you want to change the way your system starts. If, for example, you add a mouse to your PC, you may have to add a command to the AUTOEXEC.BAT file. Similarly, if you add a shell program to your system that you want the AUTOEXEC.BAT file to start, you may have to add a command to the file.

This chapter starts by reviewing the two commands that you should already have in your AUTOEXEC.BAT file. Then, it presents some of the other commands you may need in your AUTOEXEC.BAT file. These commands install programs that speed disk operations, support hardware, start utility programs, and so on. If your PC is working properly with the current AUTOEXEC.BAT file, of course, you don't have to worry about these commands now. As a result, you only need to read this chapter if your PC isn't

```
echo off
prompt $p$g
path=c:\dos;c:\util
cls
echo Please record your PC time at the computer center when
echo you're done. We're trying to keep track of the usage
echo of each system this month. Thanks for your cooperation.
```

Figure 14-1   An AUTOEXEC.BAT file that contains Prompt and Path commands

working the way you want it to or if you want more perspective on what the AUTOEXEC.BAT file does.

Two commands you should already have in your AUTOEXEC.BAT file

The AUTOEXEC.BAT file in figure 14-1 illustrates the use of the two commands you should already have in your AUTOEXEC.BAT file: the Prompt command and the Path command. The Prompt command sets up the command prompt so it displays the current directory on the default drive. This makes it easier for you to work with commands that you enter at the command prompt.

The Path command establishes a directory list that DOS uses when it searches for a command. This list should always include the DOS directory and the directory that contains your batch files. In addition, this list can include the directories of some of your application and utility programs if it makes them easier to start, but this doesn't work with many programs.

Other commands for your AUTOEXEC.BAT file

In addition to the Prompt and Path commands, you may need other commands in your AUTOEXEC.BAT file. If you're using DOS 3.3, for example, you may want to put a Fastopen command in your AUTOEXEC.BAT file to improve the performance of your hard disk. You may also need commands

```
The format for the DOS 3.3 Fastopen command

    FASTOPEN drive-spec=number-of-directory-entries

Typical commands

    fastopen c:=50

    fastopen c:=50 d:=50
```

Figure 14-2   How to use the DOS 3.3 Fastopen command

that provide support for hardware. And you may need commands that start utility programs.

The Fastopen command   The more directories and files you have on your hard disk, the longer it takes DOS to find a file because DOS has to look through more directory entries. The Fastopen command speeds up this process by keeping track of the most used directory information in internal memory. If you have DOS 4.0 or 5.0, you should install this command in your CONFIG.SYS file. But if you have DOS 3.3, you must put the Fastopen command in your AUTOEXEC.BAT.

Figure 14-2 shows how you use the Fastopen command for DOS 3.3. When you use it, you put it in your AUTOEXEC.BAT file anywhere after the Path command that identifies its directory. If you have more than one drive on your hard disk, you enter one parameter for each of the drives. For each drive, I recommend that you set up space for 50 directory entries. In figure 14-2, both commands set up Fastopen space for the last 50 files accessed on the C drive. The second command also sets up space for the last 50 files accessed on the D drive.

Hardware support commands   Most of the time, you use commands in the CONFIG.SYS file to provide support for hardware components. But some hardware components require support from commands that are put in the AUTOEXEC.BAT file instead. The Msmouse command in figure 14-3,

```
prompt $p$g
path c:\dos;c:\util;c:\pctools
msmouse /a7
pc-cache /sizext=384k
cruise /a /30
pcshell /r
```

Figure 14-3 An AUTOEXEC.BAT file with one command that provides hardware support and three commands that start utility programs

for example, loads a program that supports a mouse. When you buy hardware that requires a command like this, your purchase includes the command and instructions on how to use it.

Commands that start utility programs Many PC users run utility programs that make DOS easier to use or provide functions that DOS doesn't provide. For example, a shell program makes it easier to manage files and directories. Since you may want to use one or more of these utility programs every time you use your PC, you can include the commands that start them in your AUTOEXEC.BAT file.

To illustrate, figure 14-3 shows an AUTOEXEC.BAT file with three commands that start utility programs. The Pc-cache command loads the disk caching program that comes with a commercial utility program called *PC Tools Deluxe*. Although many caching programs, like SMARTDRV, are started by Device commands in the CONFIG.SYS file, *PC Tools Deluxe* requires that you start its caching program from the AUTOEXEC.BAT file.

The Cruise command and its switches start a utility program called *Cruise Control*. This utility controls the speed of the cursor when an application program is operating. Similarly, the Pcshell command loads the shell program that comes with *PC Tools Deluxe*, and the /R switch keeps the program resident when other programs are running. When this command is executed, the opening screen of the shell program is displayed when the start-up procedure for the PC ends.

If you consistently use the same application program, you can end your AUTOEXEC.BAT file with the command that starts this program. If, for example, you only use your PC to do word processing, you can end your AUTOEXEC.BAT file with the command that starts your word processing program.

How to test an AUTOEXEC.BAT file

After you create or change your AUTOEXEC.BAT file, you have to restart your PC to execute this batch file again. The most efficient way to do that is to hold down the Ctrl and Alt keys while you press the Delete key. This boots DOS, but doesn't force the PC to go through its self test again.

Some perspective on the AUTOEXEC.BAT file

Once you have your AUTOEXEC.BAT file set up the way you want it, you shouldn't have to change it unless you make changes to your system. Even if you add new hardware of software to your system, you may not have to change the AUTOEXEC.BAT file because many installation programs make the required changes for you. As a result, you shouldn't spend much time working with your AUTOEXEC.BAT file.

Terms

Appendix A

A quick summary of the DOS commands presented in this book

This appendix summarizes the formats and functions of all the DOS commands presented in this book. For each command, this appendix gives the MS-DOS version in which the command first became available. If you're not using MS-DOS, you may have to check your PC or your DOS manual to see whether a command is available to you. In case you need more information about a command, this appendix also gives you the figure numbers that present each command.

Functional commands

Command format	MS-DOS	Figures	Function
BACKUP source-spec target-spec [/s] [/m]	2.0	8-2, 8-3, 8-5, 8-7, 9-8	Back up a hard disk.
BACKUP source-spec target-spec [/s] [/m] [/a]	3.3	8-2, 8-3, 8-5, 8-7, 9-8	Back up a hard disk.
CD [directory-spec]	2.0	4-3, 4-7	Change the current directory.
CHKDSK [drive-spec]	1.0	4-10, 4-14	Check a logical drive.
CLS	2.0	4-10, 5-1	Clear the screen.
COPY source-spec [target-spec]	1.0	6-5, 6-6, 6-11, 7-7	Copy one or more files.
COPY CON target-spec	1.0	5-10	Create a text file from keyboard input.
DEL file-spec	1.0	6-5, 6-7, 6-12	Delete one or more files.
DEL file-spec [/p]	4.0	6-5, 6-7	Confirm before each file is deleted.
DIR [file-spec] [/p] [/w]	1.0	4-3, 4-5, 4-6, 6-10	Display a directory.
DIR [file-spec] [/p] [/w] [/s]	5.0	6-1, 6-2	Display a directory, including any of its subdirectories.
DISKCOPY source-drive target-drive	2.0	7-2, 7-5, 7-6	Copy a diskette.
Drive-spec	1.0	4-3, 4-4	Change the current drive.
EDIT file-spec	5.0	5-11, 5-12, 5-13	Create or edit a text file.
EDLIN file-spec	1.0	5-14, 5-15	Create or edit a text file.
FORMAT drive-spec [/4] [/n:sectors] [/t:tracks] [/s]	1.0	7-2, 7-3, 7-4, 9-7	Format a diskette.
FORMAT drive-spec [/f:capacity] [/s]	4.0	7-2, 7-3, 7-4, 9-7	Format a diskette.
FORMAT drive-spec [/f:capacity] [/q] [/s]	5.0	7-2, 7-3, 7-4, 9-7	Format a diskette.
MD directory-spec	2.0	6-1, 6-13, 6-15, 6-16	Make a directory.
PRINT file-spec	2.0	4-10, 4-15	Print a text file.

Command format	MS-DOS	Figures	Function
RD directory-spec	2.0	6-1, 6-14, 6-15, 6-16	Delete a directory.
REN source-spec target-spec	1.0	6-5, 6-8, 6-11	Rename a file.
RESTORE source-spec target-spec [/s]	2.0	8-2, 8-4	Restore a hard disk.
TREE [drive-spec] [/f]	3.2	6-1, 6-3, 6-4	Display a directory structure.
TYPE file-spec	1.0	4-10, 4-15	Display a text file.
VER	2.0	4-10, 4-11	Display the version of DOS being used.

Set-up commands

Command format	MS-DOS	Figures	Function
DATE	1.0	4-10, 4-12	Set the system date.
FASTOPEN drive-spec=directory-entries	3.3	14-2	Set up internal directory areas.
FASTOPEN drive-spec=(dir-entries,cont-space-buffers)	4.0	13-5	Set up internal directory areas and continuous space buffers.
FASTOPEN drive-spec=dir-entries [/x]	5.0	13-6	Set up internal directory areas using EEMS memory.
PATH=directory-list	2.0	4-10, 4-13, 5-6, 5-9, 14-3	Set up a directory search sequence for commands or programs.
PROMPT pg	2.0	4-3, 4-4, 5-6	Set up the format of the command prompt.
TIME	1.0	4-10, 4-12	Set the system time.

Batch file commands

Command format	MS-DOS	Figures	Function
ECHO [on] [off] [message]	2.0	5-1, 5-2, 5-6, 5-7, 14-1	Display or don't display the commands of a batch file.

CONFIG.SYS commands

Command format	MS-DOS	Figures	Function
BUFFERS=number-of-buffers	2.0	13-1, 13-2	Set up internal disk areas called buffers.
BUFFERS=number-of-buffers [,number-of-read-ahead-sectors]	4.0	13-1, 13-2	Set up internal disk areas and read-ahead sector areas.
BUFFERS=number-of-buffers [,secondary-buffer-cache]	5.0	13-1, 13-2	Set up internal disk and secondary buffer-cache areas.
DEVICE=device-driver	2.0	13-4, 13-8, 13-10	Identify a file that should be used as a device driver.
DEVICEHIGH=driver-spec [parameters] [switches]	5.0	13-7, 13-11	Install device drivers into upper memory.
DEVICEHIGH SIZE=hexsize driver-spec [parameters] [switches]	5.0	13-11	Install device drivers into specified size of upper memory.
DOS=[high, low,] [umb noumb]	5.0	13-7, 13-9	Load a portion of resident DOS into either conventional or high memory.
FILES=number-of-files	2.0	13-1, 13-3	Set up the maximum number of files that can be open at one time.
INSTALL=command	4.0	13-5, 13-6	Execute the command after the equals sign.

Index

Covers DOS 2.0 through 5.0 for hard disk users

The Only DOS Book You'll Ever Need

by Doug Lowe and Patrick Bultema

This book is for anyone who wants...or needs...to know more about DOS than what's covered in *The Least You Need to Know about DOS*. So if you don't have anyone to set your PC up for you or to help you solve more technical problems, this book is for you. It's also the ideal book for people who provide support to less technical PC users. As a result, we recommend it for every corporate "help desk," for every PC support person, and for the lead technical person in every user department.

Everything in the *Least* book is also in this book, though much of it is in expanded form. So there are chapters on hardware and software concepts and terms, managing files and directories, backing up your hard disk, working with diskettes, using the DOS 5.0 shell, and making changes to the CONFIG.SYS and AUTOEXEC.BAT files. In addition, though, this book covers:

- how to prevent, detect, and recover from disk problems and user errors
- how to improve the performance of your PC without buying new hardware

- the commercial utility programs that actually improve upon DOS (why, for example, should you use DOS to do a function like backup when you can use an inexpensive utility to do it far more efficiently?)
- when and how to install a new version of DOS
- how to partition and format a hard disk
- how to use the DOS 4.0 shell (it isn't nearly as helpful as the DOS 5.0 shell)
- more commands for CONFIG.SYS and AUTOEXEC.BAT
- how to use some of the advanced capabilities of DOS that you'll seldom (if ever) need

So if you want to expand your DOS knowledge still further...or if you're looking for a resource for PC support...get a copy of *The Only DOS Book You'll Ever Need* TODAY!

27 chapters, 550 pages, $24.95
ISBN 0-911625-58-5

To order by phone, call toll-free 1-**800**-221-5528 (Weekdays, 8:30 to 5, Pacific Standard Time)

If you're using *Word* without style sheets, you're working too hard...
and you're not getting the word processor you paid for

Get More from *Word* by Using Style Sheets

by Tim Schaldach

When you use style sheets with *Microsoft Word*, you can format long blocks of copy with just a few keystrokes. That's a marked contrast to the way you have to format your documents without style sheets. In fact, *Word* becomes a whole different word processor—a more powerful, flexible one—when you use style sheets.

Unfortunately, at first glance, style sheets can seem to be more trouble than they're worth. And even if you want to know how to use them, the *Word* manuals don't make them easy for you to master.

That's why you need a copy of *Get More from Word by Using Style Sheets*. It explains what you have to gain by using a style sheet with every document you write. Then, it shows you how to use style sheets to quickly format the words, paragraphs, and pages in all your documents.

But that's not all. Some *Word* features are clumsy and almost too difficult to use by themselves. But they're no problem at all when you use them with style sheets. So this book also shows you how to use style sheets with these *Word* features:

- desktop publishing
- the outline feature
- the running head feature
- the footnote feature
- the table of contents generator
- the index generator

So stop working so hard. Get more from *Word* by using style sheets TODAY!

12 chapters, 245 pages, $19.95
ISBN 0-911625-55-0

Note: This book assumes you know the basics of using *Word 4* or *Word 5* on an IBM PC or compatible. Then, in case you ever switch to *Word 5.5*, the last chapter of the book shows you how to use style sheets with *Word 5.5* (the concepts are all the same, so your existing style sheets will still work; it's just the user interface that's different).

To order by phone, call toll-free 1-800-221-5528 (Weekdays, 8:30 to 5, Pacific Standard Time)

You'll never again dread a writing project of any size
with this handbook on technical and business writing

Write Better with a PC

A publisher's guide to business and technical writing

by Mike Murach

No matter what you write at work—memos, letters, proposals, feasibility studies, procedure manuals, training materials—our writing book will help you break the project down into manageable parts that are easy for you to research and write.

The book is called *Write Better with a PC: A Publisher's Guide to Business and Technical Writing*. In it, you'll learn a step-by-step method for writing any business or technical document. You'll learn the specifics of writing solid, readable paragraphs and sentences (these skills are taught from the top down so you can make the most dramatic improvements in your writing right away). And you'll learn how to use 12 types of PC software to make writing easier and faster for you than ever before.

To be specific, you'll learn:

- how to write the documents that people will read...and act upon

- why word processing alone won't make you a better writer

- how to avoid endless rewrites by planning what you're going to write *before* you start writing

- how to get started on any writing project...no matter how big...and how to keep going without getting frustrated

- how to edit your work to make it stronger... and how to know when to *stop* editing

- when and how to create visual aids that help you get your message across

- how to use spelling checkers, writing analyzers, and outline processors to improve your writing

- when and how to make your documents look better using desktop publishing and other graphics programs

- and much, much more!

So don't wait any longer to improve your business writing skills. Get your copy of *Write Better with a PC* TODAY!

15 chapters, 406 pages, $19.95
ISBN 0-911625-51-8

To order by phone, call toll-free 1-800-221-5528 (Weekdays, 8:30 to 5, Pacific Standard Time)

Want to keep a mailing list on your PC?
Here's the book that will help you out

The PC Mailing List Book

by Patrick Bultema

If you use a PC at home or at work, I'll bet you've at least thought about putting a mailing list on it. After all, it seems like such a simple application. You just enter the names and addresses using whatever software you already have (probably your spreadsheet or word processing program). Then, you can easily print out labels, letters, or envelopes whenever you need them.

But if you've ever tried this, you know it's not as simple as it seems. Spreadsheet, and even word processing, programs have some real limitations when it comes to mailing lists. But how do you know what to try instead? And, if you've already got your mailing list entered on your PC, how do you avoid re-doing it from scratch?

That's where *The PC Mailing List Book* comes in. It helps you:

- analyze your mailing list needs so you know what features to look for in an application program (this is the key to having a PC mailing list that's easy to use and maintain)

- evaluate different programs so you can choose one that meets your needs (screen-by-screen examples of 8 popular programs let you compare their mailing-list features and see which programs are easy to use for

lists like yours...all without spending a penny on software!)

- create labels, personalized letters, envelopes, address directories and reports using the program you choose

- set up your mailing lists so they work best, no matter what software you choose

- transfer an existing PC mailing list to another program if you decide to switch software

- avoid mistakes that seem trivial, but that waste time and money...like getting labels jammed in your printer

In short, this book will give you the perspective you need to set up, use, and maintain trouble-free mailing lists on your PC.

7 chapters, 276 pages, $24.95
ISBN 0-911625-53-4

Shows examples using: WordPerfect, Microsoft Word, Professional Write, Q&A, dBase III Plus, Microsoft Works, Address Book Plus, Lotus 1-2-3

To order by phone, call toll-free 1-**800**-221-5528 (Weekdays, 8:30 to 5, Pacific Standard Time)

Comment Form

Your opinions count

If you have any comments, criticisms, or suggestions for us, I'm eager to get them. Your opinions today will affect our products of tomorrow. And if you find any errors in this book, typographical or otherwise, please point them out so we can correct them in the next printing.

Thanks for your help.

Mike Murach

Book title: The Least You Need to Know about DOS

Dear Mike: _____

_____

_____

_____

_____

_____

_____

_____

_____

_____

_____

_____

_____

Name _____

Company (if company address)_____

Address _____

City, State, Zip_____

Fold where indicated and tape closed.
No postage necessary if mailed in the U.S.

fold

fold

BUSINESS REPLY MAIL

FIRST-CLASS MAIL   PERMIT NO. 3063   FRESNO, CA

POSTAGE WILL BE PAID BY ADDRESSEE

Mike Murach & Associates, Inc.

4697 W JACQUELYN AVE
FRESNO CA 93722-9888

IIIɪ.....IIIɪ.ɪIɪ..Iɪ.ɪIɪ.ɪIIIɪIɪ.IɪɪIɪ.IɪɪIɪIɪIɪIIɪII

fold

fold

Order Form

Our Unlimited Guarantee

To our customers who order directly from us: You must be satisfied. Our books must work for you, or you can send them back for a full refund...no matter how many you buy, no matter how long you've had them.

Name _____

Company (if company address) _____

Street address _____

City, State, Zip _____

Daytime telephone number (including area code) _____

BK/LD

Quantity	Code	Title	Price
_____	LDOS	The Least You Need to Know about DOS	$17.95
_____	DOSB	The Only DOS Book You'll Ever Need	24.95
_____	MWSS	Get More from *Word* by Using Style Sheets	19.95
_____	WBPC	Write Better with a PC	19.95
_____	PCML	The PC Mailing List Book	24.95

☐ Bill the appropriate book prices plus UPS shipping and handling charges (and sales tax in California) to my ____ Visa _____ MasterCard:
Card number _____
Valid thru (month/year) _____
Signature _____

☐ Bill me.

☐ Bill my company. P.O.# _____

☐ I want to **SAVE** shipping and handling charges. Here's my check or money order for $_____. California residents, please add sales tax to your total. (Offer valid in the U.S. only.)

To order more quickly,

Call **toll-free** 1-800-221-5528
(Weekdays, 8:30 to 5 Pacific Std. Time)

Fax: 1-209-275-9035

Mike Murach & Associates, Inc.
4697 West Jacquelyn Avenue
Fresno, California 93722-6427
(209) 275-3335

fold

fold

NO POSTAGE
NECESSARY
IF MAILED
IN THE
UNITED STATES

BUSINESS REPLY MAIL
FIRST-CLASS MAIL   PERMIT NO. 3063   FRESNO, CA

POSTAGE WILL BE PAID BY ADDRESSEE

Mike Murach & Associates, Inc.

4697 W JACQUELYN AVE
FRESNO CA 93722-9888

fold

fold

Order Form

Name _____

Company (if company address) _____

Street address _____

City, State, Zip _____

Daytime telephone number (including area code) _____

BK/LD

Quantity	Code	Title	Price
_____	LDOS	The Least You Need to Know about DOS	$17.95
_____	DOSB	The Only DOS Book You'll Ever Need	24.95
_____	MWSS	Get More from *Word* by Using Style Sheets	19.95
_____	WBPC	Write Better with a PC	19.95
_____	PCML	The PC Mailing List Book	24.95

☐ Bill the appropriate book prices plus UPS shipping and handling charges (and sales tax in California) to my ____ Visa ____ MasterCard:
Card number _____
Valid thru (month/year) _____
Signature _____

☐ Bill me.

☐ Bill my company. P.O.# _____

☐ I want to **SAVE** shipping and handling charges. Here's my check or money order for $_____. California residents, please add sales tax to your total. (Offer valid in the U.S. only.)

To order more quickly,

📞 Call **toll-free** 1-800-221-5528
(Weekdays, 8:30 to 5 Pacific Std. Time)

Fax: 1-209-275-9035

Mike Murach & Associates, Inc.
4697 West Jacquelyn Avenue
Fresno, California 93722-6427
(209) 275-3335

fold

fold

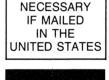

BUSINESS REPLY MAIL
FIRST-CLASS MAIL   PERMIT NO. 3063   FRESNO, CA

POSTAGE WILL BE PAID BY ADDRESSEE

Mike Murach & Associates, Inc.

4697 W JACQUELYN AVE
FRESNO CA 93722-9888

fold

fold

Order Form

Name _____

Company (if company address) _____

Street address _____

City, State, Zip _____

Daytime telephone number (including area code) _____

BK/LD

Quantity	Code	Title	Price
_____	LDOS	The Least You Need to Know about DOS	$17.95
_____	DOSB	The Only DOS Book You'll Ever Need	24.95
_____	MWSS	Get More from *Word* by Using Style Sheets	19.95
_____	WBPC	Write Better with a PC	19.95
_____	PCML	The PC Mailing List Book	24.95

☐ Bill the appropriate book prices plus UPS shipping and handling charges (and sales tax in California) to my _____ Visa _____ MasterCard:
Card number _____
Valid thru (month/year) _____
Signature _____

☐ Bill me.

☐ Bill my company. P.O.# _____

☐ I want to **SAVE** shipping and handling charges. Here's my check or money order for $_____. California residents, please add sales tax to your total. (Offer valid in the U.S. only.)

To order more quickly,

Call **toll-free** 1-800-221-5528
(Weekdays, 8:30 to 5 Pacific Std. Time)

Fax: 1-209-275-9035

Mike Murach & Associates, Inc.
4697 West Jacquelyn Avenue
Fresno, California 93722-6427
(209) 275-3335

fold

fold

BUSINESS REPLY MAIL

FIRST-CLASS MAIL   PERMIT NO. 3063   FRESNO, CA

POSTAGE WILL BE PAID BY ADDRESSEE

Mike Murach & Associates, Inc.

4697 W JACQUELYN AVE
FRESNO CA 93722-9888

fold

fold

Order Form

Name _____

Company (if company address)_____

Street address _____

City, State, Zip_____

Daytime telephone number (including area code) _____

BK/LD

Quantity	Code	Title	Price
_____	LDOS	The Least You Need to Know about DOS	$17.95
_____	DOSB	The Only DOS Book You'll Ever Need	24.95
_____	MWSS	Get More from *Word* by Using Style Sheets	19.95
_____	WBPC	Write Better with a PC	19.95
_____	PCML	The PC Mailing List Book	24.95

☐ Bill the appropriate book prices plus UPS shipping and handling charges (and sales tax in California) to my ____ Visa _____ MasterCard:
Card number _____
Valid thru (month/year) _____
Signature _____

☐ Bill me.

☐ Bill my company. P.O.# _____

☐ I want to **SAVE** shipping and handling charges. Here's my check or money order for $_____. California residents, please add sales tax to your total. (Offer valid in the U.S. only.)

To order more quickly,

Call **toll-free** 1-800-221-5528
(Weekdays, 8:30 to 5 Pacific Std. Time)

Fax: 1-209-275-9035

Mike Murach & Associates, Inc.
4697 West Jacquelyn Avenue
Fresno, California 93722-6427
(209) 275-3335

fold

fold

BUSINESS REPLY MAIL

FIRST-CLASS MAIL   PERMIT NO. 3063   FRESNO, CA

POSTAGE WILL BE PAID BY ADDRESSEE

Mike Murach & Associates, Inc.

4697 W JACQUELYN AVE
FRESNO CA 93722-9888

I||I||I||I||I||I||I||I||I||I||I||I||I||I||I||I||I||I||II

fold

fold